Do
You
Dream
in
Color?

Do You Dream in Color?

Insights from a Girl without Sight

Laurie Rubin

SEVEN STORIES PRESS
New York

Consulting editor to Laurie Rubin: David Tabatsky

A Triangle Square *Books for young readers* first edition,
published by Seven Stories Press.

Seven Stories Press
140 Watts Street
New York, NY 10013
www.sevenstories.com

College professors may order examination copies of Seven Stories Press titles for a free
six-month trial period. To order, visit http://www.sevenstories.com/textbook or send a
fax on school letterhead to (212) 226-1411.

Book design by Elizabeth DeLong

Library of Congress Cataloging-in-Publication Data
Rubin, Laurie.
 Do you dream in color? : insights from a girl without sight / Laurie Rubin. -- 1st ed.
   p. cm.
 ISBN-13: 978-1-60980-424-4 (pbk.)
 ISBN-10: 1-60980-424-4 (pbk.)
 1. Rubin, Laurie. 2. Mezzo-sopranos--United States--Biography. 3. Blind musi-
cians--United States--Biography. I. Title.
 ML420.R8876A3 2012
 782.0092--dc23
 [B]
                                        2012016420

Printed in the United States

9 8 7 6 5 4 3 2 1

To Jenny, my life partner, who saw the girl I was when we first met and who has greatly contributed to the woman I am now and will become.

To my mom who has always gone out of her way to support all of my dreams, my dad who always takes that deep breath with me when I'm about to sing a phrase, and my brother who is one of my closest friends and best mentors.

Contents

Acknowledgments

There are so many people who have enriched my life so much and who were responsible for my successes and how I see the world. I know there are many more than I can mention here, but I would be remiss if I didn't thank the following people.

My entire extended family for their enthusiasm throughout my entire process of writing the book, finding an agent and publisher, and then seeing it come to fruition: Auntie Suzi and Uncle Steve with cousins Eric and Amy, Aunt Debbie and Uncle Tony with cousin Jeremy, and Uncle Ronnie and Aunt Andrea and cousin Rachel.

Cousins Steve, Marla, Molly, and Jordan Kort for your wonderful words of support and encouragement, and for always coming to my jewelry shows and concerts. Laura for going out of your way to plan jewelry parties for me to show my pieces, and for your wonderful support in general. Joyce Lukas for inspiring me to learn how to make jewelry and for hosting my very first jewelry show. And Marcia, my first teacher in the subject of fashion, whose funky bracelets inspired my love of jewelry when I was three years old.

Grandma for instilling my love of reading and storytelling and for being there when I came home from school every Friday afternoon. And Grandpa who always told everyone I could do anything I set my mind to from the time everyone found out I was blind.

Ralph Kohn who sponsored my first CD, *Faith in Spring*, and who was in great part responsible for my concert at Wigmore Hall.

My incredible in-laws Richard and Gail for their unwavering support and excitement about this book. Your positive motivation and outlook greatly contributed to how it was written. Kathy and Cari for cheering me on, and Kyle and Chase for saying again and again that I should be on TV.

A very special thanks to Ted Huffman for getting me to perform my best and for believing I could perform a lead operatic role on stage; to Gordon Beeferman for writing such an amazing opera role and for putting in a good word at the companies who want to perform it; to Beth Greenberg who believes in my artistry onstage and who always champions my work; to Noam Sivan who wrote one of the best song cycles for my voice; and to Bruce Adolphe and Marija Stroke for being so unbelievable as friends and for writing/playing one of the pieces I know I will sing for years to come.

Keeril Makan for introducing my voice to new music and also for reading my book proposal.

Lenore and Steve Fischman for being responsible for introducing me to the best publisher ever!

Dan, Phoebe, Ruth, Gabe, and the rest of the Seven Stories Press family for being so wonderful and for believing in this story so much.

Nelson Yomtov and Francesca Sacasa for wanting to give this book a chance to see the world.

David Tabatsky, my consulting editor who helped form this book concept prior to its finding a home with a publisher.

Steve Harris, my incredible agent who pitched this book so enthusiastically to so many publishers.

Bruce Kluger who inspired the way I write and who spearheaded this whole process by writing that great story about finding a camera in a cab.

Jonathan Kravetz and the entire storywriting class for influencing the direction of this book.

Richard Goodman and the memoirwriting class for your very helpful critique of my work.

Geralyn Ruane for becoming such a great pen pal and friend. Your writing is so fantastic, and you were one of my muses.

Valerie Sorel, my incredible voice teacher who has helped me find so many vocal shades, colors, and other ways to express myself effectively.

David Wilkinson for being with me through so many musical adventures.

Julia, Jennifer, and the entire Cadenza Artists team, my incredible managers who are helping to build my dream career.

Frederica von Stade for the most amazing weekend of music-making and for being a fabulous person and role model.

Dawn Upshaw and John Harbison for bringing me into new music, and to Graham Johnson for making Lieder come alive for me.

John Williams for being such a wonderful, nurturing, and magical conductor and for giving me the opportunity to sing one of the best pieces for soprano and orchestra with you.

Kenny Loggins for being my first music teacher.

Katharine Dain who said, "I totally want to buy your book for all my friends," which gave me confidence going forward.

All my incredible friends, some of whom are mentioned in the book. All of your support, love, laughter, and amazing life experiences we've shared have meant more to me than I can express in words.

All my teachers from preschool through grad school. Your influence on my life is such a significant part of who I am.

Lastly, thank you to Scooby and to Mark, my first guide dog and beloved pet who loved me unconditionally, even when your walks were postponed an hour or two when I was on a roll writing. I know you can't read or write, but you understand my thoughts, so please know how much I love you guys.

The Glass Slipper

It was 10:15 on Sunday morning, and I was making good time. I had forty-five minutes to get from my apartment at 75th Street and West End Avenue to Merkin Concert Hall at 67th Street and Amsterdam. My bag, with makeup for touch-ups, a snack to eat between the dress rehearsal and the concert, and two bottles of water, was already packed. I stopped at the front door, allowing myself to take a breather before slipping on my glass-slipper-like clear sandals.

"Bye, Sweetie," I called to Jenny, who was still in the kitchen finishing her coffee.

"Bye," she said, with a light clunk of her mug on the table before coming over to see me off.

"See you in a couple hours," I said, kissing her goodbye.

My guide dog, Mark, heard me pick up my bag, the signal that usually meant it was time for us to leave together. He came running to the door, snorting happily, wagging his tail and stopping on my left side, ready to work. His tail was like a feather duster, brushing and fanning my legs.

"Oh no, Mark you're not coming with me today," I said, sad to disappoint him. "Bruce's daughter is allergic, remember?"

His demeanor changed as he saw me unfold a bundle of sticks from the umbrella stand until it became a long, red and white cane. The feathery tail slowed and took its melancholy place between Mark's legs.

I walked into the hall and pressed the button for the elevator. Max, the morning doorman, was waiting on the ground floor.

"Hi Laurie."

"Hey Max," I smiled. "Mind getting me a cab?"

His chair squeaked as he rose with a grunt. The air outside felt fresh, as if the intense cold the day before had cleansed it of all the usual olfactory New York refuse. Though the Upper West Side of Manhattan is sleepy on Sunday mornings, there is always the sound of chattering kids, happy to be spending time with their usually working parents instead of their nannies, and the din of people leaving church. As Max whistled and cried, "Taxi," I stood waiting, thankful for the ability to enjoy a rare peace in New York City.

"Got one, Laurie," Max said happily, as if he had caught a particularly large fish.

"Thanks," I smiled at him.

"Where are you going, Miss?" the driver asked.

"67th and Amsterdam. Merkin Hall."

With that, we were off. Another one of the novelties of Sunday mornings is the ability to travel with little to no traffic, and as I leaned back in my seat, I enjoyed the quick twists and turns and the frequent echo of building awnings as we sped past them.

14

It was hard to say exactly why I was particularly carefree this morning. Being on edge was usually my default state before most rehearsals and performances. It always seemed as though I entered situations with just a little more baggage than my sighted colleagues. Walking into a room with a big black dog, a talking laptop computer, and a plethora of braille books makes me aware of how conspicuous I am compared to the person who noise-lessly waltzes into a room, slipping into the seat next to me with very little ceremony. I've been aware of this dissonance since high school. The unpleasant memories of my cheeks growing hot as a teacher singled me out, fretting over how I was going to tackle a seemingly visual assignment, and my heart sinking as I realized I had brought the wrong volume of a braille book to class were permanently burned into me. As I moved from school to the real world, I realized that if anyone else didn't have it together, they were just having a bad day, but if it were me, my blindness was blamed for slowing me down. One day in college, I walked into a voice lesson shortly after being rejected from a summer opera program and my teacher closed the door of his office and said in a hushed voice, "It wasn't because of your voice."

"What?" I gasped, startled.

"I know the director," my teacher continued. "He told me off the record that they were scared, scared you wouldn't be able to learn the music as fast as they would need you to, scared that you would hold the others back." His voice trembled and he gritted his teeth as he finished the sentence.

"Laurie, in order for someone to hire you, you've got to be better than the others. You've got to have something so compelling about your singing that they would justify going out of their way and working past their own fears to hire you over another singer."

It was a lecture I was used to in life, being told I had to be one step ahead of the game at all times. I couldn't be normal, or good, or great. I had to be superwoman. I had to make it my business to know a piece backwards and forwards when I knew my colleagues would be sight-reading it the first time. I spent many tearful hours digging inside myself for profound emotions that made my interpretation of every aria more heartrending than the next singer's. I had to dress better, smell better, and sound better so that the package that was Laurie Rubin was complete, despite the fact that it lacked one basic feature that everyone else took for granted: sight. For this gig that my cab was trundling me closer to by the second, I felt I had done everything right. I was playing with some of the best chamber musicians in New York City, and to them, I was their equal; I deserved to be there. What could possibly go wrong?

"Merkin Hall, you said?"

"Yes."

"It's here on your right," the driver said as the car came to a halt.

"How much?"

"$5.90."

I reached into my wallet, pulling out a five-dollar bill from one of the leather slots and two singles from another.

"Keep the change," I said.

"How did you know?" he exclaimed.

"Know what?"

"That you gave me $7.00."

"Oh," I laughed. "I keep all the different bills separated in my wallet." I held it out to him, indicating the slot for the fives, the tens, and the twenties.

"You're a smart girl," he said.

I smiled. "Just a little trick I picked up along the way." I grabbed my bag, my cane, and the bottom of my gown and slid out of the cab.

"Just go straight," the driver shouted as he sped away.

I turned my back to the spot where the cab had recently disappeared, stepped onto the curb, and heard the echo of my heels' delicate clatter crescendo as I neared the door to Merkin Hall.

"Can I help you?" asked a security guard.

"Yes, I'm singing in the concert this afternoon. Can you direct me to the stage door?"

"The elevator is this way," he said, grabbing my shoulder and unceremoniously pushing me in what I hoped was the right direction. He continued to hold my arm until I was inside the elevator and hit a button before quickly exiting and leaving me alone before the door closed again. I felt the elevator reluctantly take me down one floor.

When the door opened, I stepped gingerly, my cane out in front of me, detecting the carpeting of the hallway. My right foot joined my cane on firm ground, but as my left foot exited the elevator, its heel sank as though into quicksand. I tried to lift my heel from the gap between the elevator and the floor of the hallway, but the wayward shoe would not budge. Carefully, I got down on my hands and knees to wrench it out by hand, my gown's train falling in a puddle around me. In that split second, I heard the elevator door start to shut, and I leaped forward, one shoe on, one shoe off, deciding hastily to relinquish the sandal to the elevator's clutches.

"Oh no," I thought, breathing fast.

The elevator door creaked and crunched terribly before falling ominously silent.

"Oh my God! My shoe jammed the elevator!"

I thought of the concert approaching in two hours and the crowd of families with young children who would be waiting to be let inside.

"I'm sorry," someone would say into a megaphone, silencing the crowd. "There has been an accident, and our elevator is no longer working. We have to cancel the concert." Angry parents and crying children would be ushered somewhere to have their tickets refunded, and Bruce, the director of family concerts at the Chamber Music Society of Lincoln Center and the person who had asked me to do the concert, would be wringing his hands while talking to a maintenance person about removing the offending shoe. The renowned flutist, cellist, pianist, banjo player, and percussionist I had been rehearsing with, and whose musical respect I had been lucky enough to earn, would all change their minds about me. The Chamber Music Society would not hire me, or any other blind singer, ever again.

"Laurie," said a man's voice in the distance, startling me out of my thoughts. "Hey, you look great!" It was Bruce. I was thankful that my gown covered my shoeless foot so that his first impression of me in full regalia wasn't of a half-barefoot fuddy-duddy.

"What's wrong?" he asked, evidently reading something about my predicament in my expression.

"Well," I began, trying to adopt a calm and amused tone, "The elevator seems to have absconded with one of my shoes."

"What?" he laughed.

I told him how the heel had sunk into the gap and how it had refused to move.

"No worries. We'll have someone get it back for you in no time."

He led me to a seat in the green room and I heard footsteps hurry past in both directions. For a few minutes, it was almost silent backstage. None of the other performers had arrived yet for our brief dress rehearsal, so I was left with the green room clock for company. Considering how fast life normally seemed to fly by, it was extraordinary how much space there seemed to be between each second the clock ticked away, and I began indulging in the most dangerous activity. I began to think.

How is it possible to lose a shoe in something as innocuous as an elevator gap? It's not as though some monster with huge jaws had latched onto my shoe and the only means of survival would have been for me to let it go and run away. How could I expect anyone to think me competent enough to navigate an entire career where there are many things much more treacherous than elevators? Everyone acknowledged that I was a good enough musician to learn the very difficult piece I was hired to sing in this concert, but I had the feeling that all anyone would remember would be the fact that I was the first person in the history of the world to lose a shoe in an elevator.

I began to think back to the time I had been on a field trip to an amusement park with my high school choir and orchestra, and I was enjoying a rare moment of laughing and feeling just like one of the group. In fact, this was one of very few occasions when my blindness actually made me popular because we had been told by one of the ride operators that I could use the handicap entrances, thereby allowing my friends to avoid the long wait for each roller coaster. Suddenly, as we were walking back to the bus, laughing about how we had almost lost our lunch on the last loop-de-loop, I tripped. You would have thought that I nearly fell off a cliff by the way my pack of friends gasped and rushed to provide a sea of hands to prevent me from falling completely. The rest of the day, it was not the amusing things I had said to make them laugh, nor the way we had rushed to the front of each line that they relayed to their friends who had stayed behind; it was the fact I had tripped—not even fallen mind you, just tripped.

My nerve-wracking conversation with the noisy clock was interrupted by an argument in the hallway.

"We'd have to stop the elevator to retrieve it, Bill," a man with a deep husky voice and a thick New York accent was saying.

"How could it have completely disappeared?" asked a higher-pitched nervous man. "She said she lost it in the elevator."

"Must have fallen down the shaft," Bill replied.

"What the hell?" the second man exclaimed in exasperation.

The two men's voices continued to grab at some solution to my one-shoed status, but what they were saying was no longer discernible as they rushed off, probably to tell Bruce they'd have to stop the elevator and cancel the concert. Bruce came in a few tense minutes later to tell me the bad news about my shoe.

"Oh God," I said putting my hand over my face. "Did I just put the elevator out of order?"

"Of course not!" Bruce laughed. "But we may not be able to rescue your shoe as I had hoped."

I let out a big, relieved sigh. "That's all right. I can handle losing a shoe."

Luckily for me, Jenny was just a phone call away. She was already planning to come to the concert, and I happened to have a pair of silver shoes that would also match this particular gown. I sprung into action, pulling my cell phone out of my jacket pocket. It was nice to be able to do something about this fix I had gotten myself into, to prevent this blind Cinderella from hopping onstage with one glass slipper.

There were still ten minutes before the start of our dress rehearsal, and other performers were starting to trickle in. After doing some warm-ups, I ventured in the direction of the stage, guided by the sound of stagehands setting up music stands and percussion instruments.

"Hey Laurie," said the cellist. "Heard about your shoe."

I felt my face redden. Word had already spread. "Yeah," I laughed. "Isn't that the most ridiculous thing you've ever heard?"

"Are you kidding? That's nothing," he said. "I bet you there are tons of cell phones and keys all waiting for their respective owners at the bottom of that elevator shaft."

"Hi, Laurie, sorry I'm late," said Tara, the flutist, catching her breath and dropping her bag and coat down on a chair. "I heard about your shoe. What a trip!"

"Sounds like it'll be the new legend of Merkin Hall," Bruce joked.

"At least it's not as bad as the opera singer who jumped to her death in character only to find that the stage manager had replaced the foam mat with a trampoline," I said. Everyone laughed, and I felt myself relax as we began our rehearsal.

"Night of the Four Moons" by George Crumb is a piece in four movements that requires both instrumentalists and singer to create a ghostly, eerie atmosphere. You might hear something resembling the mournful hoot of an owl, frightened high-pitched shrieks, and otherworldly chanting. The piece ends with the instrumentalists, one by one, making their way offstage so that the only music that hasn't faded away is the single high A played by the cello. The piece was the composer's response to the US placing a man on the moon, thereby killing the beautiful mystery the moon provided for us for thousands of years.

The embarrassment and panic from moments before melted away as I felt my voice spin on high lilting passages and then scream with fear and pain in the next measure. Then my hands moved to the apparatus in front of me with several percussion instruments I needed to strike with mallets or pluck from time to time. One thing I didn't know when I first started singing is that I would get to wear many hats, and yet that is the thing I enjoy most about this career I've found myself in. Not only do I get to make my voice sound like an instrument, taking on the silvery qualities of a glockenspiel or the chocolaty timbre of a viola, but sometimes I get to venture into uncharted territory and play other instruments. The high from singing was enough to sweep my mind from the Merkin Hall elevator shaft, bringing it to the same cloud of exhilaration one feels when skiing or riding a roller coaster.

"That was amazing, Laurie!" Bruce said, putting his arm around my shoulders.

"Thanks," I said, taking a steadying breath, hoping against hope that the rehearsal had been successful in making Bruce forget about the shoe incident.

We finished the rest of the program and Bruce led me through the maze of lighting and sound equipment back to the green room where Jenny was waiting with my replacement shoes, along with Bruce's ten-year-old daughter, Katja, a thoughtful, well-read child that I found wise beyond her years. Katja had written a poem about the moon for the concert, which Bruce had set to music and I had just rehearsed.

"So Katja, what did you think?" I asked. "Am I doing your poem justice?"

"Yeah!" she said enthusiastically.

"Do you write lots of poetry?"

"From time to time I do. Now I'm writing a poem about dreams."

"What kind of dreams?"

"You know, the kind you have that seem magical when you're asleep, but that don't make any sense once you're awake."

"Oh I know those kinds of dreams all too well. They're my favorite ones."

"Mine too!"

We continued chatting about dreams until Bruce came back into the room.

"Okay, we're about to start," he announced.

As everyone hurried to their places backstage, Katja asked me a question I didn't have time to answer but that continued to echo in my mind for a long time afterward.

"Laurie, do you dream in color?"

It suddenly occurred to me that I wasn't sure how to answer.

White

White is a fluffy pillow of marshmallows
or a refreshing scoop of vanilla ice cream.
White is the cold, smooth grandeur of marble
I have felt in the palazzos of Italy.
White is the luscious carpet of snow,
quieting a town with its gentle soundproofing.

It is one of the few colors I see.
Bright, piercing, present.

White is the satisfying sound of shaving cream,
gushing out of its can, its thick foam frothing
    through my fingers.
White is the smooth feel of a blank piece of paper,
untouched by a crayon's wax or the ink of a pen.
White is the color of my childhood blanket,
My silky, soothing, sweet white blankie.

The $200 Diagnosis

"Mom, she's not looking at me," Brian said, peering at me, a three-month-old babbling baby girl in the crib. "Why won't she look at me?"

"I don't know, honey," Mom sighed, swallowing away the lump in her throat and turning away to keep him from seeing her face.

"She knows who I am, doesn't she?" Brian asked, a little bewildered.

"Of course she does," Mom said, feigning more certainty than she felt. "She smiles at you when she hears your voice. See, she's smiling right now. Say hi to her."

"Hi, Laurie," Brian said in his high-pitched voice. I reacted with the beginnings of a laugh. Five-year-old Brian seemed satisfied, but Mom was worried.

In search of answers, Mom and Dad flew with me to Houston, Texas, where a well-known eye specialist was supposed to provide them with some hope, but instead he said flatly, "There's nothing I can do for her."

When we returned home, we were confronted with one misdiagnosis after another.

"She has no pigment in her iris."

"She will always have to wear very thick glasses."

"She won't be able to drive, but she should be able to see a little."

Finally, several weeks later at Jules Stein Hospital, I was carried into a doctor's office and bright lights were flashed directly into my eyes. I screamed.

"Her ERG is flat," said the doctor, over the sounds of my wailing.

"What does that mean?" Mom asked.

"As you can see, she is not responding to this." The doctor made an adjustment on one of the many odd machines in his office and pressed a button. "Nor this," he said, showing my parents that visual cues I should be reacting to were causing no response.

"Are you telling me," my mother said, her voice shaking slightly, "that my daughter is blind?"

Without so much as a pause or any sign of bedside manner, the doctor gave his answer: "Yes."

I whimpered and rubbed my still-dilated eyes as my parents sat in stunned silence in the cold, sterile office. The doctor dialed his phone.

"Hi Roger? Rob. How are you?" the doctor was saying, his voice sounding human for the first time since Mom and Dad had stepped into his office. "Listen, I've got the Rubins here. Thanks for the referral by the way. Turns out it's not what you thought.

The baby's got Leber's Amaurosis. L-e-b-e-r-s. Means her retinas never developed. She can't see anything more than light. I've got to go now, but we should have dinner some time."

As a sobbing father and a stoic mother made their way out of the office, pushing their baby in a stroller, not knowing what would come next, the receptionist behind the counter stopped them.

"That'll be $200," she said, as though announcing the price of groceries at a supermarket.

The diagnosis was followed by visits from friends and relatives who sat in our living room with Mom, crying and sympathizing with her, unable to see anything but a labyrinth of unknowns and unending darkness ahead for me. But Mom refused to give up hope, and her research eventually led her and Dad to the Blind Children's Center, a nursery school for the blind in LA, which also had support groups for new parents of blind children. They were taken under the wing of the two social workers, Nancy and Marilyn, who ran the school.

"Remember, all she can't do is see," Marilyn said calmly in their first meeting.

"But how will she go to college?" Mom asked.

"Let's just get her to crawl first," Nancy chuckled reassuringly. "One thing at a time."

I Can Read, Too

I sat amongst my pile of discarded toys, waiting for some sort of inspiration to take hold. Brian sat on the couch, reading quietly. Every now and then, I heard a page turn.

The playroom was the place in the house where Brian and I spent most of our time. Slightly down the hall from our neighboring bedrooms, it had the welcoming aura of a more communal space and was home to all of Brian's and my toys. Dad, who was a partner CEO of a toy company, often brought home blaster balls coated in gun powder, animals made of soft plastic, and a variety of toys that sat neglected on shelves while Brian and I coveted the toys from other companies we saw advertised in commercials.

"What are you reading?" I asked.

"A book called *Watership Down*," Brian mumbled.

"What's it about?"

"Laurie, it's a long story."

My four-year-old mind could not wrap itself around the fact

that my nine-year-old brother considered reading to be more important than answering my questions.

"Can I read, too?"

"Not now," he said firmly.

"Why not?"

"Because I don't want to start reading to you from the beginning."

My heart sank. "But Brian, you always read to me. How come you won't read to me this time?"

"Can't I just read to myself for a little while?" he asked, exasperated.

"Brian?" I asked more timidly, as though treading on thin ice. "Let me read the book."

"Laurie, you can't."

"Why not?"

"Well for one thing, you're not even old enough to read."

"Not old enough? Let me see it!"

After a long pause, Brian let out a sigh. "Here," he said, handing me the book. "Just don't move the bookmark or else I'll lose my place."

I held the book in my hand. It had a hard cover that felt the tiniest bit rough. Other than that, there seemed to be nothing interesting about it. I began to turn the pages, marveling at the fact that I was making the same sound as my brother just before I had interrupted him. I felt each page. I was bewildered. There appeared to be nothing on the pages. My hands could only discern smooth, blank paper.

"Brian, there's nothing here to read," I said, thinking I had just discovered he was playing a joke on me.

"Yes there is, Laurie, you just can't see it."

"No, Brian, I'm looking at the pages. There's nothing there."

"That's because you're touching the pages, not seeing them."

"What do you mean, seeing them?"

"Laurie, it's hard to explain. Can I have my book back now?"

I handed it back and he resumed reading. It didn't seem fair that the book should be revealing secrets to him that its pages wouldn't share with me. What was Brian getting out of this book that I couldn't find by touching it? The pages had been much thinner and much less interesting than the pages of my favorite scratch-and-sniff books that smelled like strawberry, or chocolate, or skunk. Nor was it as fun to touch as the books with cutouts of animals with button eyes and coats of a material that emulated fur. This was something my brother could do that I couldn't, not only because he was older, but because I couldn't see. I had no idea what "seeing" really meant, but I was determined to find out.

❁ ❁ ❁

Though Brian's books never revealed their hidden mysteries to my fingers, there was a vast array of books waiting for me that did. It was those books that taught me to see that the richly per-fumed roses with satin-textured petals in our backyard were deep red, that the smiling light from the sun I could see with my lim-ited vision was lighting up a vivid blue sky filled with birds of all shapes and sizes. Even though these books described gardens far away from where I lived, I knew my favorite characters and I were experiencing the same virtues of nature. It didn't stop there. Princesses dressed in pale pink silk fabric encrusted in sparkling crystals, who sat in chairs clad in rich brocade, became real to me whenever I dressed for family parties or whenever Mom peeked into an antique shop to admire the furniture.

At first, Mom, Grandma, or Brian read these books to me, for I was still too young for the books I would later read with my fingers in what they called "braille." In the meantime, Mom drove me forty-five minutes away to the Blind Children's Center in downtown Los Angeles where my teachers helped me discern different textures as a way of giving my fingers practice for the six-dot braille system I would learn in kindergarten. Instead of being given pictures of animals or different shapes, they would hand me a ball, a toy horse, or a set of keys, and this method taught me to interact with the world with my hands, my ears, and my nose.

I entered kindergarten at Francis Blend Elementary School for the Blind, while Brian continued to go to a Hebrew day school in our neighborhood. I was now being picked up by a bus with other blind kids and driven all the way into downtown Los Angeles to my new school. At last, it was my turn to read. At first, my teacher, Mrs. Schindler, gave me thick pieces of paper, durable enough to withstand dots being punched into them, and showed me that different letters were created by using various combinations of dots.

Letter A was dot #1 on the upper left-hand corner, letter B was made with dots #1 and #2, creating a tiny vertical line, letter C was the combination of dots #1 and #4, which made a tiny horizontal line, and dots #1, #3, and #4 formed a cute little triangle and the letter D. After the alphabet, I learned that if letters were preceded by dot #6, which was the lower-most dot on the right side of the six-dot cell, the letter would then be capitalized. And then came the braille contractions. Because braille was already thicker and much more cumbersome than print (causing one innocent looking print volume to turn into large braille books the size of two *Encyclopedia Britannica* volumes), a system to help limit the amount of braille characters was devised. Dots #1 and #6 created the ch sign, dot #2 by itself either represented a comma when following a word, or the combination of letters E and A when in the middle of a word, and so on.

Even though I was finally starting to read books on my own just like Brian, I became aware of the many other differences between us. Brian was picked up by a carpool of kids who came over on weekends to play with him, while I went on a bus with kids who lived far away. When Brian would do his homework, his writing made quiet, rhythmic scratching noises as his pens and pencils moved across the page, while I wrote braille on a small, mutant typewriter with seven keys whose pounding noise filled the house.

As my years at Francis Blend passed, I became increasingly aware that I was as different from my classmates as I was from Brian. Though all of us attended a school for the blind, some of us were totally blind while others had a limited amount of sight. None of the other kids lived in Encino, whereas most of my brother's schoolmates did. As I walked down the hall to my class-room, I'd hear the squeaking of the wheels on wheelchairs and the loud, creaking scratches of walkers alongside me. Teachers' lectures were punctuated by the high whistling of hearing aids, or a child my own age who suddenly burst into a tantrum worthy of a three year old. We were all at different reading and math levels, which meant teachers had to compromise when pacing the class, forcing some to fall behind and others to move on more swiftly than the curriculum allowed.

"Mrs. Steinman, I finished my worksheet!" I said to my second grade teacher happily one morning. "Can I get a book to read now?"

"Laurie," she said in a low voice bordering on stern, "that was awfully quick to get through it."

"No honest, I did," I assured her, eagerly holding it out to her with my brailled answers in proud majesty.

"If I find that you didn't check it carefully and if you have even one wrong answer, you are going to be benched during recess today, understand?"

Ten minutes later, she approached my desk beaming with pride, apparently finding that my ability to achieve full marks in record time was something to be celebrated.

Again and again, I finished my reading comprehension work-sheets in only half of the generous amount of time she allowed for us, and Mrs. Steinman pulled braille books off her shelf and handed them to me as my reward and to stimulate my curious mind for the remainder of the class period. The books got thicker and thicker, and they all contained the simple adventures of Pam,

Tim, and their friend Meg, written in three- and four-letter words. When I had finished with the books on the shelf in her classroom, she urged me to borrow all the books I could get my hands on from the Braille Institute, an ideal back-to-school shopping haven for the blind. There were shelves of Perkins braille typewriters, thick braille paper, braille and talking watches, and a library with hundreds of books. I delved hungrily into the Ramona Quimby series, becoming kindred spirits with the precocious eight-year-old who made birthday cakes out of toothpaste when bored and who indulged in her vivid imagination whenever school became too mundane. I plunged into the *Anne of Green Gables* series about the misunderstood, but well loved orphan who loved to read.

❂   ❂   ❂

Alicia Jimenez was my best friend at Francis Blend. She was a shy, bright girl who loved to read as much as I did. She was as quiet and earnest as I was outgoing and silly, but once recess came, Alicia's imagination awakened and she would light up as we created fantastical scenarios for our dolls.

"Let's say that the princess gets lost in the forest," I'd exclaim, holding up my Cabbage Patch doll.

"Okay!" Alicia would say, the meekness of her voice when answering teachers suddenly replaced by a glow of enthusiasm. "And then the princess will be saved by the magic horse who will take her to the castle made out of rubies," she would continue, handing me her My Little Pony.

On and on we'd dream, and yet our play dates had not yet extended beyond the playground at recess.

"Mom," I said one Saturday afternoon, hearing laughter from Brian's room. His friend Greg was over for the third weekend in a row.

"Can I ask Alicia to come over to play?"

Mom hesitated. "I don't know, sweetheart," she said, "I think she lives far away from here."

"But Brian gets to have friends over all the time."

Mom finally relented and called Alicia's mother, who let us pick Alicia up and bring her to our house two weeks later.

My heart beat with excitement as I sat in the backseat on the way to Alicia's house. The drive seemed endless, until finally we were in East Los Angeles.

We were greeted by Alicia, her four sisters, and her father who gave me a bear hug.

"It's nice to meet you," Mom said, and I heard Alicia translate into Spanish.

We were invited into the tiny studio apartment where Alicia's family lived. Her mom greeted us warmly from the couch where she was burping a baby.

It was up to Mom to drive the long distance to pick up and drop off Alicia as both of her parents worked, and thus our play dates outside of school were few and far between. Despite the few times we met outside of school, Alicia always took my hand, leading us to music class with her limited vision, ignoring teacher admonishments to let me use my cane. We continued to make up a myriad of fantasies during recess and lunch, and we relayed the tales from our favorite books to one another until I left Francis Blend just before fourth grade.

❋ ❋ ❋

Though there was no getting around the fact that I was different and that my childhood routine of going to an unusual school by bus was vastly different than the one Brian knew at his neighborhood school, we both settled ourselves on the playroom couch in the evenings after we had finished our homework and curled up with our favorite books. After a while, I was unaware of the sounds of both of our pages turning and the soothing terrain of the braille under my fingers. The clock's ticking and the sound of Mom and Dad's TV dissolved as we traveled far away into mysteries with Nancy Drew or into Renaissance England with Shakespeare. Brian continued to read books with his eyes, and I read mine with my fingers, but we were both able to see just fine.

Cane & Able

Mrs. Cooke was an O&M, or Orientation and Mobility teacher, at Francis Blend. From the time I was in kindergarten, she would come to my classroom and call each of our names, pulling us out of class for a one-on-one lesson with her on something nobody in my family had to learn in school. When it was my turn, she took me to the mobility room where several teachers like her were working with students.

"Well, Laurie, do you know why you're here?" Mrs. Cooke said, sounding friendly, but underneath lurked the voice of someone who could be strict and stern.

"I'm here for mobility," I said, matter-of-factly.

"Yes you are," Mrs. Cooke chuckled genially. "But do you know what that means?"

My heart sank. I didn't know the answer, and I hated getting the answer to a teacher's question wrong.

"It means that you're going to learn how to get around by yourself," Mrs. Cooke answered for me.

"Without my mom?" I asked, hoping I hadn't understood her correctly.

"Mom's not always going to be around to take you places," Mrs. Cooke said shortly and continued without pause. "Now, do you have any brothers and sisters?"

"One brother," I said, still nursing the shock of Mrs. Cooke's statement that one day I'd have to go it alone without Mom.

"Is he sighted or is he blind?"

"He can see."

"Okay, then he can get around by seeing where he's going, by looking at street signs, building addresses, and so forth. You, my dear, are going to have to learn several skills that your brother probably won't ever have to think about. Now just give me one second. I'll be right back."

I heard the metal drawer of a file cabinet opening and Mrs. Cooke rummaging inside of it. In a moment, she was sitting next to me again, opening a package.

"Your first, brand-spanking-new cane," she said cheerfully, handing me the strangest object I had ever held in my hands. It felt like a bunch of small metal tubes held together by an elastic loop. One of the tubes had rubber covering it.

"Okay, take the loop off," she said. When I let the elastic go, the tubes began to unfold, and with several little clicks they became one long aluminum stick. Mrs. Cook showed me a small round tip at the bottom of the cane and told me that the rubber covering was the grip I would hold onto when using this new stick, which she called a cane.

"Canes come in all sizes," Mrs. Cooke said. "See this one?" She handed me a large cane that was several heads taller than me. "Canes are supposed to reach the middle of your chest. When it starts to get shorter than that, you'll need a new size."

"I'll never need one of those," I said, indicating the large cane. "I'll never be that tall."

"Oh, yes you will," Mrs. Cooke laughed. "You just wait. The cane is designed to protect you, to act as your eyes. It will hit obstacles to your left and right, and you will have to learn to decide how to get around them. If you use the cane correctly, you shouldn't bump into anything or fall into dangerous places."

She led me outside where she showed me how to tap my new cane back and forth: to the right when I stepped down with my left foot, and to the left when I stepped down with my right foot. It made a hollow, tinny sound as it hit the ground. Then she showed me a technique called "touch and drag," which meant that I would follow the building line on one side to help me detect pathways and doorways.

"You'll need touch and drag to find things like your classroom," she said. "See, Room 1 is the first doorway on your left. Room 17 is the mobility room, and Mrs. Schindler's room is eight doors down on your left after you round the corner."

She had me practice finding the mobility room, counting the doors from my kindergarten class. Then, she taught me a technique called "squaring off," which meant I would put my back against a wall and walk straight from a certain point to another destination. I would square off with the wall two doorways past my classroom and walk straight across to the computer room.

I met with Mrs. Cooke once a week during my first two years at Blend, first learning my way around the building, then branching out and counting the building support posts on my left side, 1, 2, 3, until I hit Irma who sold me my hot lunch. One day, Mrs. Cooke had me sit at the table where she placed a foam board in front of me with four cardboard squares glued onto it, which she told me represented four blocks, and the blank spaces between them represented the streets.

"This is a map of an intersection," she explained. She proceeded to describe stop signs and traffic lights, as well as to show me what parallel and perpendicular mean. She indicated the north, east, south, and west, and northeast, northwest, southeast, and southwest corners of intersections. She explained that the sun rises in the east and sets in the west. These concepts were easy enough to understand on a map, but when it was just me navigating the real thing, it was hard to remember where I was, even if I had seen the whole scope of it in miniature just minutes before.

"Laurie," Mrs. Cooke said in a stern voice when I had guessed that I was facing north when I in fact was facing south. "What are the clues again?"

"The sun, I forgot the sun," I said hastily. "Mrs. Cooke, it's hard for me to remember where everything is when I'm not looking at it."

"I know," she said. "Sighted people can see the whole picture, just like the one I showed you in the classroom. You, however, don't have anything for reference but the place your feet are planted on, and your memory of what I just showed you."

After Mrs. Cooke came Mr. Kleinschtukker, Mrs. Hix, Mr. Takaguchi, and many others who continued to show me how to use the sun, familiar posts, changes in the ground's texture, and the grass line on either side as guides to help me get from point a to point b.

As I grew taller, I was given new canes, along with more daunting and advanced tasks to tackle. As I walked from the place where my bus dropped me off in front of the school to class, I heard the sound of many canes tapping their way to their respective owner's classes. Many canes sounded purposeful, confident, even enthusiastic about the independence they represented. I looked forward to the day that the cane made me feel just as able as my peers.

Perfect Pitch

Kenny Loggins was more than just that '70s and '80s rock-star heartthrob Mom used to play in the car on our drives to school, the market, and the bank—he was my unknowing teacher of Music 101 and an imaginary friend who came with me to nursery school every day.

"Kenny Loggins was in the nap room today," Joanie, my teacher, would chuckle when Mom picked me up from the Blind Children's Center.

One particularly rainy Saturday, Mom decided not to take me on one of her exciting market excursions during which she would let me ride in the shopping cart and hand me tomatoes, green and red peppers, onions, avocados, and all sorts of other fruits and vegetables, while pointing out their distinctive shapes, textures, and smells.

"Don't eat them yet," Mom would tell me. "We need to pay the nice lady first."

Of all the Saturdays I had to be left home, this was the one I wished I had been sitting in the shopping cart the most. Mom came home that day laden with grocery bags as usual, but with an air she had whenever she was about to divulge a particularly exciting piece of news, like the cat who swallowed the canary.

"You'll never guess who I met in the butcher section," Mom said, her voice glowing with mystery.

I guessed Pearl Schneider, my mom's best friend, since the Schneiders lived nearby. Then I guessed several of Brian's schoolteachers, since it was not unusual for us to run into them at Gelson's.

"No, try again!" she would say chuckling, her voice growing more excited and impatient with every one of my guesses.

"I give up!" I said finally, jumping up and down, unable to stand the suspense any longer.

"Kenny Loggins!" Mom said.

My heart did a cartwheel in my chest. "Kenny Loggins? In the market?" I shrieked.

"Yes, and I told him all about you, and how you and I listen to his music together all the time."

Mom could not continue for several minutes as I bombarded her with questions. "Was he nice? What did his voice sound like when he talked?"

"Yes, he was very nice," Mom said quickly. "He wants to give us tickets to his concert in a few weeks at the Universal Amphitheater!"

"We're going to see Kenny?" I exclaimed, making sure my ears were not playing tricks on me.

"Yes, and there's one more surprise. He wants all of us to come backstage afterwards."

❉ ❉ ❉

The minutes between the opening act provided by a comedian and Kenny's appearance on stage felt like hours as we sat in our seats in the crowded amphitheater, and when the moment came, my five-year-old body felt as though it was being swallowed by a gigantic monster as the audience roared the most deafening, enthusiastic applause I had ever heard. The hundreds of speakers around us filled with the first dramatic notes of a synthesizer, which mingled with the continuous screams of appreciation and excitement from the audience, and then layers of sound from the guitars, bass, and drums added themselves to the texture.

"How're you all doing tonight?" cried Kenny's voice, and the applause grew still more uproarious in reply.

The excitement of a concert was almost more than I could bear. Kenny and his large band played all the songs I had heard almost every day, yet they were much louder, ringing with a spontaneous energy I had never experienced before. The crowd around me rose up out of their seats during all the fast songs, and people I had never met before grabbed my hands, urging me to dance to Kenny's beats. In the middle of the show, we all settled back into our seats, and suddenly the large hall felt as though it had shrunk to the size of Kenny's living room as he sat down with his acoustic twelve-string guitar and began to tell us stories about other concerts he had given, and the reasons he had written many of his songs. I finally got to hear his speaking voice, which was several octaves deeper than the high range he was completely at home singing in. He laughed easily too, and I was glad that he seemed nice.

The concert ended with an extended version of the song "Foot-loose." The more people clapped, the more liberties the guitarist, drummer, and keyboard player took in their solos, and Kenny scatted vocal lines, urging them on.

"Let's bring it home!" Kenny shouted, but after the final notes, the audience would not let him go, and Kenny obliged with two encores.

My ears rang as we made our way out of the theater to the stage door to find Arlene, Kenny's assistant.

"Are you the Rubins?" asked a friendly voice, and a woman who smelled like vanilla perfume scooped me up into her arms.

"You must be Laurie!" she said as she led the way, still carrying me, to Kenny's dressing room. I felt Arlene make several turns this way and that, leading us through many corridors, holding doors open with her one free arm for the rest of my family. The sound of people laughing, instrument cases snapping shut, and men asking, "Hey, you wanna grab a bite to eat? I'm starved," emanated from various different rooms nearby.

Arlene stopped at a door and whispered, "This is it," before knocking.

"Yeah, come on in," said Kenny's voice.

Arlene allowed Mom, Dad, and Brian to head in before us. All three of them introduced themselves and told him what a great concert it was.

"And this is Laurie," Arlene said, placing me on Kenny's lap. All the questions I had been dying to ask him melted on my lips. I had wanted to know how he could sing in harmony with himself if there was only one of him, and how he could sing in that high voice mom told me was called falsetto when he had such a deep voice.

"You can ask Kenny all those things when you meet him," Mom had told me over the past several days. Yet words seemed to fail me.

"Laurie's your biggest fan," Mom said, breaking the silence in which I was supposed to address Kenny.

"Was this your first concert?" Kenny asked, smiling down at me.

"Yes," I said, not ever having heard my own voice sound so small.

"What did you think? Loud, huh?" Kenny laughed.

"Yeah," was all I could say.

❀ ❀ ❀

Kenny was in the company of many composers who contributed to my music education. My dad's love of gadgets often resulted in new stereos with impressive speakers that would boom through the house, and the recordings that seemed to do the speakers justice were orchestral recordings of Beethoven's 5th Symphony, Mozart's greatest hits, and a compilation of Chopin waltzes played on the piano. As the speakers boomed in my chest during Dad's demonstration of his latest purchase, I'd sit on the living room couch, the music pulling me into a trance with its timbres of the different strings, winds, and brass sections, the ebbing and flowing movements through different keys and dynamics. Then there was the one instrument that could sound like an entire orchestra, and Mom explained that just two hands playing the piano at a time could make all that sound pour out.

"Soon enough, you will be starting piano lessons," Mom said as she buckled up my car seat for our daily journey to the Blind Children's Center. The thought of me being able to make the same ringing, loud and boomy, or soft and fluttering sounds that so mesmerized me excited me to no end.

One Monday, instead of being picked up from nursery school by Mom, I was led into the music room.

"You must be Laurie," said a lady with a bright, excited voice. "I'm Robin." Tapping a wooden piano bench, she said, "Come sit next to me."

Robin let me explore the large keyboard in front of me. I played all the notes I could reach and began sliding my fingers over the keys, laughing at the sound they made.

"These keys," Robin said, placing my hands on the wider, flatter keys, "are the white keys. And these," Robin placed my fingers on the narrow, taller keys, of which I noticed there were fewer, "are the black keys."

She placed my thumb on a note she called "middle C," and continued to position my fingers on D, E, F, G, and so on. As she had me play each note and taught me its name, I memorized the sound the way one would remember the shape of each letter in the alphabet. It wasn't until years after my first piano lesson that I learned the ability to place the sound of each note with its name was somewhat unusual.

Several weeks after hearing Kenny Loggins singing his song "Meet Me Half Way" in concert a half step lower than when he sang it on the album, I said to Robin, "It was in E-flat last night. Not in E natural."

"How did she know that?" Mom asked Robin.

"What do you mean how do I know that?" I asked incredulously. "Doesn't everyone know that?" Each note on the piano sounded like a different set of colors to me and reminded me of flowers and birds singing. The flats and sharps sounded darker, and reminded me of nighttime.

"Laurie, not everyone can hear the difference in the notes," Robin explained. "It's called having perfect pitch."

❀　❀　❀

Though I went to Francis Blend from kindergarten through third grade to learn to read and write in braille, I got the benefit of a musical education that Mom and Dad could not have predicted. Mrs. Tavis was a soft-spoken, middle-aged woman who lived, breathed, and ate music. Room 16 might have been a regular classroom in its appearance, but the recordings she played while we were inside, such as Prokofiev's *Peter and the Wolf,* where the various animals are played by different instruments to represent their unique sounds and personalities, transported me into a concert hall.

Her classroom was filled with every orchestral instrument in a symphony, and she made us hold each one in our hand, giving us a chance to learn how it's played. She assigned an instrument to each of us, and though we were the most tone-deaf orchestra known to man, she treated us like professionals. Because I had never seen what an orchestra looked like on TV or in concert, I had only had the experience one would have listening to a record or a tape. When Mrs. Tavis showed us how to hold a violin, and how to blow into a flute, a clarinet, or a tuba, I began to understand what it must be like to see a real live orchestra performing, and I fell in love with music all over again.

❂   ❂   ❂

The excitement of meeting Kenny Loggins did not subside, and his concerts became an integral part of our adventures. Many of our trips to Lake Tahoe were motivated by concerts Kenny was giving at Caesar's Palace, and the spacious green room backstage with several fluffy couches became as familiar to us as a second home. The members of his band were becoming old friends, and we grew accustomed to seeing several of the same groupie families who had also taken to building their vacations around Kenny's concerts. Dad's love of gadgets led him to cameras, and he became Kenny's unofficial photographer. He also donated toys from his company to Kenny's "Toys for Tots" Christmas telethons, which we attended every year in Santa Barbara. During school breaks, the families of all the band members would accompany them on tours, and Mom, Dad, and Brian would tell me, when I was still too young to start skiing, that they had an exciting afternoon skiing several slopes in Lake Tahoe with Kenny and the gang.

During one of Kenny's summer tours there, we were invited on a waterskiing excursion with Kenny, all the band members, and many of their wives and kids. As our speedboat loaded up, I heard Kenny's voice, and realized that he and his oldest son were in the boat with my family and me.

"I want to ski, too," I announced as Mom, Dad, and Brian were getting sized for skis.

"But Laurie, you've never gone waterskiing before. We'll have to get you an instructor some time, but not today," Mom said.

"There's a first time for everything," Kenny chimed in, and with that, I heard him step out of the boat, followed by his brisk, purposeful footsteps scraping on the gravel. Moments later, he was back.

"Laurie, this is Scott," Kenny said. "He's an expert water-skier, and he teaches people how to get started."

Shocked at how Kenny had seemingly pulled this man out of thin air, Mom and Dad shook his hand in introduction.

"Nice to meet you, Laurie," said Scott's young voice.

Brian had the first turn, and from the boat came the enthusiastic cries that were my running commentary of what was going on. The "whoas" told me that he had wobbled or fallen into the water, and the exclamations of "Way to go!" told me he had gotten steady on his feet and was sailing flawlessly on the water as the boat pulled him along, its motor revving up and going faster and faster.

"Your turn, Laurie!" Kenny shouted over the engine as Brian climbed back into the boat.

Scott helped ease me into the water and handed me a plastic handle, which connected me to the boat. At first, the boat moved slowly, and Scott held me around the waist, allowing me to experience the rush of the water pressing against my legs.

"Now try to stand up," he said.

"In the water?" I laughed.

"Yes, you can do it."

I made several attempts to move my legs into a standing position, but the water was fighting me violently. My legs first turned into jelly, and then felt as though they had become as light as twigs that moved this way and that so that they were forced out from under me, and I tumbled onto my back. I began to laugh as I spluttered and blew water out of my nose.

Several more clumsy attempts followed, but then my legs seemed to take control of the situation, and Scott's hands were loosening their grip on me just the way a parent's would on a child starting to get the hang of riding a bike.

"You're doing it, Laurie!" I heard Brian shout in the distance as the whooshing sound of the water crescendoed and the boat quickened its pace. My body relaxed and I noticed it slowly elongating and growing lighter as though I were walking on air. The water was carrying me on its surface like a glider, and all I had to do was enjoy the ride. Then, as quickly as it had started, it ended, and some invisible force threw me into the water, and I was panting and snorting water again. For one brief shining moment, I had done it! I had skied on the water!

"I know I didn't stand my first time," Kenny was saying breathlessly as Scott and Dad helped hoist me back into the speedboat.

"How did you do that!" Brian asked.

"It's not about seeing," I explained. "It's all about feeling the water." "And waterskiing," I thought to myself, "is like the fast movement of that Mozart piano sonata I want Robin to teach me."

❋　❋　❋

I was eager to play Bach inventions and Mozart sonatas on the piano, but I found learning the detailed fingerings to be tedious. I preferred serenading Robin with my own vocal renditions as she played the pieces she was about to teach me.

"I think Laurie would much prefer voice lessons," Robin told Mom after several years of me not practicing. "Maybe she'd practice singing more than she practices piano."

Mom met Liz Howard when she was having a manicure. The back room of the salon with its three manicure/pedicure stations also served as a weekly social hour for its regular customers. As Mom waited her turn, she was able to glean enough conversation between Elba, the manicurist she had been going to for years, and the client Elba was finishing up with to deduce that Liz was a voice teacher.

"My daughter has been told that she should take voice lessons!" Mom said. And that next week, I had my first voice lesson in Liz's home studio.

As Mom and I waited in the living room, we could hear the results of Liz's work, an impressive teenager singing "All I Ask of You" from *The Phantom of the Opera* in a pure, silvery soprano.

"Oh, I want to sound like her!" I breathed with excitement.

"Hi, sorry to keep you waiting," said a woman emerging from the studio. Her voice was friendly and thick with a New York accent, and something in her tone sounded painfully honest, more than a little dramatic, and like the kind of person who would say, "Dahling, let's do lunch," the way they do in the movies.

"This is Jenny Kwan," Liz said, introducing us to the student before me. "Jenny's going to do big things, aren't you, Jenny?" Liz said proudly. "You just wait; she'll be Kim in *Ms. Saigon* in the near future, I can feel it."

"You sounded wonderful," Mom said.

"Thanks," said the girl, gathering up her car keys.

"Come on in," Liz said enthusiastically, ushering us into her studio. The room echoed with the benefit of wood flooring and high ceilings. It felt twice as large as our living room with lots of empty floor space, a baby grand piano, and a fancy tape machine called The Singing Magician, which allowed you to record yourself while playing a karaoke track to a song. There were folding chairs lining the wall, which could be set up in rows for studio recitals or classes. The place had the strong smell of lemon-scented cleaning solution, and the floor was slick as though it had been recently waxed.

"Okay, Laurie, tell me a little bit about yourself. What do you like to sing?" Liz asked as she closed the door with an echoey boom.

"I don't know," I said shyly. "I like *Cats*, you know that song 'Memory'?"

"Oh sure, a lot of my kids like to sing that," Liz said. "Well, let's see what you sound like. Have you done much singing before? You know, in a choir, or solo in a talent show?"

"Not really," I said. "Just at home."

"She likes to imitate the opera singers my parents listen to on PBS," Mom said. "It sounds like it comes naturally to her."

"Wow, you like opera?" Liz said, sounding as if her whole face had just lit up. "Opera is my thing. That's what I sing. Most of my kids like pop and musical theater. Do you think you might want to sing opera?"

"I don't know," I said, giggling nervously.

"That's okay, let's start with the songs you know you like first. But we won't do any singing for a while until we vocalize you."

She led me through a series of scales, making me sing on a nasal "aaaaaaaa" and then a peculiar "ow ow ow ow," which was supposed to get my sound to be resonant. I felt my voice stretching like a rubber band as she warmed me up higher and higher, the sound getting harder and harder to produce, making my face grow red.

"Why does it feel so hard?" I asked, feeling out of breath.

"Because you're not used to this," Liz explained. "It's like doing exercises for your body. Sit-ups and push-ups are never fun in the beginning, but they make you stronger."

❁ ❁ ❁

Mom got us tickets to see *The Phantom of the Opera* downtown at the LA Music Center. To see *Phantom* live is to be brought into a whole new realm, a whole different time. As the auctioneer recounts the story of the Phantom and leads us into two hours of flashback with the magic word, "Gentlemen!," the theater erupts with sound as the organ plays the first chromatic notes of the overture, which fills the entire theater with the enormity of the music's force. The sound system and the orchestra penetrate the soul, and take you on a journey via Andrew Lloyd Webber's music into the 1800s as the curtain opens. You watch Christine, the little chorus girl, whose voice blossoms into the unexpected ringing opera, and you see her struggle to stay part of the real world while being pulled down into the fantastical, seductive, and yet lonely world of the Phantom. You feel the Phantom's pain as he grapples with his monstrous appearance and the way the world looks upon him with horror, hate, and revulsion. He holds love in his fingertips, but it is hanging by a delicate thread. And then he dissolves into nothingness with grief when he loses Christine to a seemingly brighter world and the handsome Raoul. As you listen to the Phantom's music box at the end of the show playing the theme of "Masquerade" and you hear him crying with the despair of losing his last bid for happiness, your heart breaks.

"It's not fair," I sobbed in my seat, as we applauded the cast during their bows. "If I were Christine, I wouldn't have left him alone like that."

"Laurie, it's just a play," Brian said. "That sadness is what makes the drama of the story."

"He was still beautiful on the inside. Isn't that what should count?" I continued through my tears.

The next day, I wrote to Michael Crawford, who played the Phantom, and told him he had a new fan. I sent the letter fearing the worst, that it would get lost in a vast black hole full of fan mail that never would get responded to. My nights were filled with dreams, in which I was seeing *Phantom*, and they made an announcement that the actress who played Christine was unable to go on, and they needed someone from the audience to sing her role. I came forward to volunteer and went on as her understudy.

"Liz, I think I want to sing opera now," I said at my next lesson.

"Really? Why the change of heart?"

"Because I want to play Christine one day," I announced.

I learned "Think of Me," Christine's debut aria, which changes her from chorus girl to leading diva, and I sang it anywhere people would listen.

❀   ❀   ❀

"Laurie!" Mom said excitedly, two weeks after I had sent my letter to the Phantom. "I have something to read to you." She began, "Dear Laurie, I received your very sweet letter, and am so delighted you enjoyed the show. I am touched that you feel so deeply for the Phantom's trials and tribulations, and that you are inspired to sing Christine's songs. I know you have already seen the show, but I have arranged for my secretary to leave you and your family four tickets to see the show again, and I would be honored if you would come to say hello to me backstage afterwards."

Before Mom could finish reading, I began to scream, and the countdown began for the thirty days until I would meet Michael Crawford.

❀　❀　❀

Backstage of the Ahmanson was a series of doorways that led left and right to different wings. Michael's secretary showed us past the costume room, a series of dressing rooms, and the orchestra rehearsal room where musicians were nosily putting their instruments away. We met Michael in the makeup room where a woman named Tiffany was peeling layers and layers of makeup off as if his face were the center of an onion.

"Laurie!" Michael said. "Give the Phantom a kiss!"

I stood in the doorway with Mom beside me, shaking like a leaf. Mom took my arm and ushered me forward to stand beside his chair. Before I knew it, he had thrown his arms around me in a bear hug.

"Did you like the show this time, dear?" he asked.

"It was good," I squeaked. "*Good!*" I thought. "*It was wonderful. What's wrong with me!*"

"Would you like to feel his scars?" asked Tiffany. She handed me what felt like a stencil made out of sponge.

"That thing is glued to my face," Michael said with a sigh.

I stood there dumbfounded, as Mom, Dad, and Brian voiced

all the things I wanted to say to him. Tiffany handed me the wig he wore and told me that it took almost an hour to remove the makeup he had to wear for the show every day. My mouth remained agape with amazement during our entire visit.

"Come back and see us again," Michael called to us as we left the room.

And we did just that, thirteen more times before he had his last performance as the Phantom. In the meantime, Liz began teaching me not only songs from *Phantom*, but arias from real operas, and that was the beginning of a long journey into classical music.

❋ ❋ ❋

Further involvement in school and work forged a distance between Kenny and my family, but the last month with him contained the best adventure yet. Arlene announced that Kenny needed a children's choir for two of the tracks on his soon-to-be-released album, *Leap of Faith*. Both Brian and I joined the choir. A few rehearsals in the basement of a church to learn the part were followed by a trip to the studios of Capitol Records. Several takes of the chorus were recorded, and we sang the four-part harmonies that emulated a gospel choir in a song called "Conviction of the Heart" about saving the environment. When Kenny and the producers were satisfied, an announcement was made.

"We need five of you to record little scat solos for another song, 'If You Believe.' Would any of you kids like to audition?" Excited whispers broke out around me. We were called, one by one, into a smaller studio and were given headphones in which we were able to hear the band playing and the backup choir singing.

"Just improvise," Kenny told us.

"Believe! Yeah, yeah!" I sang at the top of my voice, thinking of Whitney Houston.

After all of us had scatted our fill, Kenny announced that I and four other kids had been selected to have our voices heard on the album. Now I finally understood how Kenny Loggins, Michael Jackson, Madonna, and all the other singers of the time were able to produce several tracks of harmony. As Kenny had me start and stop, recording engineers were turning knobs and raising levels on fancy mixing boards. Never in my wildest dreams as a four-year-old dying to ask Kenny so many questions did I envision receiving a brand new CD, tearing off the shrink wrap, and listening very carefully for the sound of my own voice in harmony with that of Kenny Loggins.

The Van Takes Us Skiing

Shortly after receiving the jarring news of my blindness, my parents decided to buy a large, 1979 Chevy van. This may have seemed a strange way to be proactive, but what my parents had in mind was a series of road trips, designed to provide adventures for me to experience the world to the utmost with the four senses I did possess. Our van took us camping all over California, and from the time I was nine months old, long before I was able to remember the trips they put so much effort into planning, we were setting up tents or sleeping in cabins in Sequoia, the El Capitan Beach in Santa Barbara, and Lake Arrowhead.

The van was like a small moving home where you could stretch out and sleep on long journeys. The front seat, which I almost never sat in, felt like it was in a different room from my favorite spot in the very back, a long bench where I would spread out with my dolls and games. Brian and I had to shout over the middle seats, which I called monkey seats, in order to be heard by Mom and Dad all the way up front over the van's low rumbling engine.

Our family friends, the Schneiders, joined us for many of our adventures. Herb and Pearl and their two kids, Eric and Carrie, who were several years older than me, would always liven up the van with games and regular bouts of laughter. Drives on our frequent Lake Tahoe ski trips were party marathons for the four of us kids, munching on Hostess Donettes and other snacks we'd pick up on pit stops at gas stations. Carrie was like my big sister, eight years older than me, but always playing with my hair, showing me her wild jewelry, and imparting big sisterly wisdom during our many girl-talk sessions. She taught me the camp songs she knew from being a counselor, and we would sing them loudly over the adult conversations and Eric and Brian's card games.

The van seemed to possess an optimism of its own that kept it going against all odds. Because its starter would crank noisily, sometimes for five or ten minutes with no results, we often thought our trips would be canceled or postponed. But the van knew better. Eventually, after the starter's voice rose higher and higher until it reached a fever pitch, the engine would turn over and we were on our way.

❋ ❋ ❋

Our loyal yet unreliable van miraculously got my family from LA to Disneyland, to Santa Barbara, to San Francisco, and most often, to Lake Tahoe. It was an eight-hour trip from Encino to Lake Tahoe, and Abba and Kenny Loggins would keep us company, playing on the van's tinny stereo. As the van pulled into its parking space on the Nevada side of the lake, the shock of cold air, thinned by high altitude, always felt foreign to the little girl living in Los Angeles where the temperature got down to no less than fifty degrees, and where the morning frost on our cars would be the closest thing to snow we'd ever see.

The three-story condo owned by my dad's company was cozy and rustic, and yet it was large and mysterious to me. Because I grew up in a one-story house, houses with staircases were enchanting, and I imagined secret passageways like the ones I read about in books. I would climb up and down the stairs and feel my way through the hallways, trying to find the secrets of the place, perhaps ones that had never revealed themselves to anyone else. There were bedrooms on each level, and on the bottom floor, a welcoming living room furnished in a deep rose and dark turquoise opened onto a small kitchen and dining room. A large fireplace crackled loudly, keeping us all warm. We looked out onto a vast expanse of quiet and peaceful forest that smelled like nature, pure and unpolluted.

Mom, Dad, and Brian spent the winter days in Lake Tahoe skiing, while I spent most of my early days with Grandma and Grandpa, who accompanied us on our trips. They showed me how to make snowmen and would push me down hills in a small sled as I cried, "Again, Grandpa!"

When I turned seven, Mom and Dad felt that I was ready for bigger and better sports than snowball-making and sledding. After a series of phone calls, Mom found a school for blind skiers in Kirkwood, about an hour drive away from our place on the lake.

One morning bright and early, Brian and I were roused from the warmth of our beds, and with the help of our parents, we were stuffed into long underwear, bulky wool sweaters, and thick ski pants and parkas of the same material. After the van was coaxed into starting, I climbed in for the first time to join my family at Kirkwood Ski Resort.

Once there, Mom led me into a room that smelled like metal and rubber, and I heard the sounds of heavy objects being taken down with much difficulty from shelves.

"Today will be my daughter's first day skiing," Mom told a friendly man who had me sit on a bench while he fitted me for ski boots.

I was bewildered to find that my ski boots were made of a heavy metal, and clanked loudly on the metal grill-like floor of the ski rental shop, which vibrated every time a person walked by. Soon, the man was lifting my left boot onto something that felt slippery, and I gasped as I started to lose my balance. After a ski was snapped onto my left boot, the man reached for my right foot. "These will work fine. Now you enjoy your first day of skiing, young lady." He removed the skis and set them down by my feet.

"Here, Laurie, try these gloves on," Mom said. She handed me a pair of thick, leather gloves lined with a soft, warm material. Then a fluffy hat was being placed onto my head. With my hands and ears covered and my feet in strange, heavy boots, all my senses were obscured by thick winter gear, rendering me completely vulnerable.

After what seemed like hours later, we made our way into the warm, rustic lodge, which smelled of coffee and hot chocolate.

"Hi, are you Julie?" Mom said to a lady with a sign on her jacket that indicated she was from the ski school.

"Yep," the woman said sharply, her voice sounding robust and athletic. "You must be Laurie."

"Hi," I said reluctantly.

"Are you ready to try out those skis?"

"I think so."

"Don't worry. We'll take it nice and slow."

We followed Julie out of the lodge, down the metal steps of the building onto the carpet of dense snow.

"Give me your hands," Julie said, as she handed me the ends of what felt like two metal poles. "These are ski poles," she explained. "These will allow us to stick together when I'm leading you on narrow cat walks, through ski traffic, through the chairlift line, and so forth."

After walking for several minutes, she stopped and I heard a wet "splat" as she slapped her skis down on the snow.

"Okay," Julie grunted as she pulled herself up after adjusting her skis. "Let me help you with yours." Within seconds, she had snapped both of my skis into place, and my feet were several times longer than I was used to. I tried lifting my foot up off the ground, but it was so heavy, and suddenly, I was waddling danger- ously, like a newly hatched duckling finding his legs.

Julie laughed a deep, harsh-sounding laugh, which did not do anything to reassure me at all.

"If you do that, you're going to get your skis crossed, which is exactly what you just managed to do," she said, helping me untangle my left ski from my right. "Just slide your left foot forward without lifting it up. Then your right. That's it. This is how you will walk in your skis. Now, I'm going to slide your skis into a different position."

As she said this, she moved the front ends of my skis towards each other, and the heels far apart.

"That is what we call the pie position. It will cause you to put the breaks on. Now, I want you to try to move your skis parallel again," Julie instructed. I performed this task quite easily. "And back to the pie position. Good!"

After half an hour of practicing, Julie said, "Time to grab the poles." I held them at one end, she held the other, and we were off.

The snow hissed gently under my skis, and the sound and the sensation of it rippling under my feet relaxed me.

"Okay, Laurie, we're at the top of a very shallow little hill that we call a bunny slope," Julie said. "I want you to keep holding on to these poles, and I'm going to show you how to turn left and right." With that, she helped me glide gently down the hill. It felt like being on a roller-coaster ride, except that I was the ride, and there was no car protecting me.

"Now, try to press your left foot into the snow." I hesitated. Suddenly, I felt like a baby animal learning how to use its gigantic hooves for the first time. When I finally managed to press my left foot down into the hill, I was following Julie into a right turn.

"Now the right foot," she said. "That's good, Laurie, that's the ticket," she said as I pressed my right foot into the hill, leading me into a left turn.

"Wow, Laurie, you're skiing!" Mom was cheering fifty feet behind me.

"I am?" I breathed. I couldn't believe I was gliding and turning down the hill. I was feeling more and more graceful as I relaxed with Julie into a comfortable rhythm.

"These are what we call green runs for beginners like you," Julie explained. "The blue runs are intermediate, so they're much steeper. Then there are black runs, which we sometimes call diamonds for the experts. There are double diamonds for experts with a death wish, and some of these have large bumps called moguls."

"Mom, what do you, Dad, and Brian ski?"

"We ski the blue runs."

"Julie, when will I ski the blue runs?"

"We'll see," she said. "You've got plenty of time to catch up to your family."

"But I want to ski with everyone else," I said.

"You will," Julie said. "Just not today, and probably not this week," she chuckled.

❋ ❋ ❋

"Good morning, Laurie," Julie's voice echoed as she walked towards Mom and me the following day. "Think you might be ready to try skiing without holding onto me today?" At the nervous look on my face she said, "Don't worry, we'll start slow."

Julie guided me on a narrow path, which led us to the slope we had practiced turns on the day before.

"Stand nice and tall. Don't hunker down into those skis." She gently straightened me up from my slouching position. "You're going to slide forward, and you'll pick up a little momentum."

I held onto my ski poles for dear life as we gathered speed, hoping that Julie wasn't suddenly going to let go.

"That's it, Laurie, you're doing it!" she said. Seconds later, I felt my ski poles grow lighter, and I realized with horror that she was no longer on the other end.

"Aaaahhhh," I gasped.

"Laurie, you're just fine. You don't even need me to hold you." She was right. My skis were gently gliding without any sign of me losing balance or control.

"Stop," she said calmly, and I managed to arrange my skis into the pie position. My skis slowed until I was still again. "Now, you're ready for the big stuff."

"You mean the blue runs?" I asked hopefully.

"Not quite yet," she chuckled. "But how 'bout making some turns while you ski by yourself? When you're ready, turn your skis right and press down into that left foot. That will get you going again."

Suddenly, I was plunging into the unknown below me. I turned slowly and cautiously, but I was doing it alone.

"Now left," Julie called. "Right. Left again. Right. And stop.

Well, you got your turns now. I think you're ready for a little more excitement."

She took the ends of my ski poles again and we were meandering this way and that across a narrow catwalk. Within minutes, I heard something that sounded like a gigantic street cleaner in the distance.

"What is that?" I asked Julie.

"That's the chairlift," she said. "It takes you to the top of the runs."

As we drew ever nearer, the sound seemed to envelop us, covering the swooshing of our skis.

"Hey, Julie," shouted a man over the chairlift's engine. "Who have you got there?"

"Jim, this is Laurie," she shouted back. "It's her first time on a lift."

"Hi, Laurie," said Jim's friendly voice. "You're going to love this, but you might be startled the first time a chairlift smacks you in the butt."

He was right. As Julie and Jim maneuvered me into position, they counted to three, and a hard something hit me from behind, knocking the wind out of me and whisking Julie and me off our feet, into the air, and away from the racket below.

"Kind of a weird feeling, isn't it?" Julie said, sounding slightly out of breath.

"Yeah," I said, finding my voice again. It was like being on a large swing that was going in one direction. The air was so peaceful and still, and there was no sound of the skiers below. The chair itself hummed and vibrated gently. In about five minutes, that street cleaner sound was back, and as it grew louder and louder, Julie warned me about the snow I'd soon be feeling under my feet, and at her count of three, I was to stand up again.

The chair beneath me disappeared as suddenly as it had appeared, and I was once again in the snow, gliding at super speed.

"Stop," Julie called. "Okay, let's head over to another run and try your new skills out on something a little more fun."

Julie had the other end of my poles as we began skiing down a significantly steeper hill. Within seconds, she had let go, and I was on my own again. As she called out "right" and "left," I found the skis more difficult to control, and I felt the side of my ski hit a bump, causing me to teeter. Suddenly, there was nothing for me to do but submit to the soft cushion of snow underneath me, and I fell, screaming as I continued to slide with momentum on my back.

"You're okay," Julie said, as I tried to catch my breath. "The steeper incline is just a bit shocking to you, that's all. And that fresh snow caused some bumps in the road. You didn't get hurt though. The snow is nice and soft, isn't it?"

"Yeah, but that was scary," I said, fighting a lump of fear in my throat.

"Oh, don't cry," Julie said, her voice softening. "You've just got to get back on your feet and do it again."

Slowly and with Julie's help, I stood up.

Again, I turned down into the hill below. As I gathered speed, I began to feel weightless. Both elated and terrified as I turned right and left, I went faster and faster until I felt the ground beneath me level off and my skis stopped automatically.

"That's it! You did an entire ski run by yourself!" Julie said with excitement. "How do you feel?"

"Can we do it again?" I asked, a bit out of breath, feeling as if I had just taken a trip on Thunder Mountain at Disneyland.

"Told you this one was more fun," Julie said laughing.

Off to the chairlift we skied, and Jim greeted us happily over the noise once again.

❋ ❋ ❋

Julie skied with me through many more trips to Tahoe, but she did not get to witness my maiden voyage on a blue run two winters later. Brad, a man more than six feet tall with a deep voice, had been telling me about a green run called "Success" my whole first ski day in Dear Valley, Utah, promising me that if I was good, that would be our second to last run that day. The last would be "Home," a short course, but nevertheless my very first blue run.

The bright winter sun was smiling on us, promising to be my companion, cheering me on for my last two runs of the day.

"Here we are," Brad said as we stopped at the top of Success. "Are you ready?"

"Yeah!" I said.

"Okay, on your mark, get set, go!"

I was off. The snow was a lush, rich blanket of gentle powder beneath me, rippling with tiny peaks and valleys. The air was almost balmy, promising an early spring. My skis whistled and hissed through the fluffy snow. Then, with no warning, the roller coaster began in full force. The run was now steeper than anything I had skied before. I was falling in slow motion, and yet I was still standing. Brad began calling "Left! Right! Left!" to me over the cries of our skis. My heart raced with the effort of keeping up.

"There are a few bumps in the snow coming up!" I heard Brad yell to me.

"AAAAAHHH," I screamed. I began to teeter dangerously as moguls began to appear from underneath my feet. Up and down, up and down I went over tiny mountains of snow. But I was still upright, and upon that realization I began to relax, even as the moguls continued to taunt my skis. My screams turned into "Weeeeee!" and once again, I was that little girl on Grandpa's sled.

"Okay, you're hitting smooth ground again," Brad shouted.

Suddenly, there were no skis and no snow, just pure sensation: I was flying. I turned effortlessly with Brad's directions, and the breeze seemed to be carrying me.

"Okay, you're in the home stretch, but it's going to get steeper."

The breeze that had carried me let me go with no warning, and I was falling again. Down, down, down I went, still upright, and in slow motion like a dream. And then, it was over. The ground inclined slightly before leveling off.

"And stop," Brad said, a smile apparent in his voice. "All I can say, kid, is that we should be heading home, or should I say, for a home run."

As we rode the chairlift to Home, Brad said, "In my opinion, whoever labeled Success a green run had a nasty sense of humor."

"What do you mean?" I asked.

"Well, Success is technically much harder than many intermediate runs you'll ski, Home being one of them. Home is kinda steep, but it's a piece of cake after Success."

The sun was still beaming down as we approached Home.

"We're here," Brad said as we got into position. "But before we start, I've got a little surprise for ya."

"Great skiing, Laurie!" said Brian's voice in the distance.

"My family's here?" I gasped.

"Yup," Brad said. "They've been watching you all afternoon. You're skiing the intermediate runs now," he reminded me. "That means you'll be skiing with your family from now on. That's how a family vacation should be, don't you think? I'll just be here to call turns and to keep you out of trouble."

And so I skied my first intermediate run with my family. It was smooth and easy. My body felt loose and graceful. I heard Brian, Mom, and Dad skiing up ahead. It was perfect.

"Ah, there's no place like Home," I heard Brad chuckle as he skied behind me.

Don't Touch!

I have been an avid reader from the time I was three years old. Whether Grandma would read to me or I'd listen to the Disney fairy tales on those tapes that came with the picture books, I was always engrossed in a story. Authors make magic with their pens, creating images and descriptions of places, people, and things so vivid that you can practically see them. Even I, who have never actually seen lace pantaloons and organza dresses placed over unyielding hoop skirts, nineteenth century tapestries in grand drawing rooms, gardens made colorful by an abundance of flowers, or people's faces and physiques, have had my mind's eyes opened by these rich details, so it's like I see them with physical sight. It's as if my fingers have actually touched the places Jane Austen has been, the people Charles Dickens describes in fastidious detail, and the town in which Lucy Maud Montgomery sets all her books about Anne Shirley, my literary soul mate. The words of my favorite authors are worth an infinite amount of pictures, and beginning at a very young age, these pictures turned me into a visual person who wanted to see everything for myself.

Mom, Brian, and I accompanied Dad on a business trip to the East Coast in the summer when I was seven. Going to Washington, DC meant spending our days in the overwhelming Smithsonian and making our way through museum after museum.

I eagerly entered the space museum holding Mom's arm. Space had fascinated and excited me from the time we studied it in science class, and from this one book on tape I had about a kid in the twenty-first century who lived on Mars with his parents. I couldn't wait to touch the parts of old rockets, the specimens from meteorites on display, and the astronaut space suits that lined the museum walls.

"Oooo, Laurie, come feel this moon rock!" Brian said excitedly, placing my hand upon a flat, almost rectangular-shaped object secured to a glass display. The rock felt like one you'd find on any beach but had tiny holes on its surface.

We signed ourselves up for a museum tour, and a man who had been obviously instructed to be enthusiastic and energetic guided us into the first room. He began explaining the first rockets and space capsules, pointing to their parts, which were displayed all around us.

"Mom, can I feel them, please?" I whispered excitedly.

"They're all behind ropes, Honey," Mom said.

"But Mom, I have to feel them!"

"Sir," Mom interrupted the tour guide. "My daughter is blind. She would like to touch the space capsule."

"I'm sorry, Ma'am, I can't allow her to do that."

"The only way she can experience what we're seeing is by touching," Mom said, her voice sounding annoyed.

"We have a special braille exhibit in the natural history museum," our guide suggested, his voice still unnaturally peppy, as if the smile he wore was plastered there forever. "Perhaps your daughter would enjoy that."

"She touches braille all the time," Dad said angrily. "She'd like to touch something she can only touch in a museum."

"Yeah, you try walking through here with a blindfold," I said.

"Laurie!" Mom said sharply. "You let your father and me handle this."

"That's okay," said the tour guide. "She's quite a firecracker, so cute."

With that, he continued shepherding us to room after room with mysterious objects that were roped off. I listened to the people around me ooooing and aaahhhing about what they were seeing.

"Why does everyone else get to see everything, and I have to just stand here?"

"I think they are afraid of the oil on anyone's hands destroying anything. They're trying to preserve history," Mom said.

"Lilly, I don't think the steel of a space shuttle would be destroyed by one kid's hands," my dad responded. "I'm going to let the manager have it."

It was the same stumbling block at every museum. I stood just inches away from sculptures at the art museum, fossils that were thousands of years old at the natural history museum, Presidential furniture at the White House, and I was physically banned from connecting with any of it. It was as if everyone else around me had been inducted into a special club that required eyesight, and I was forced to stand by and let everyone else take it in and learn and enjoy.

Finally, we approached an exhibit I could actually experience. The natural history museum had a petting zoo where you could hold unusual insects in your hand.

"And here," said an eccentric woman, placing a large something that scuttled across my hand onto my arm, "is an endangered roach about three times the size of a quarter."

"EEEEK!" I shrieked with amusement as I felt its large papery wings and shell-like body.

"And here is a caterpillar that you won't find on any backyard plant," she said, chuckling, dropping a plump furry creature shaped like a crescent moon on the back of my hand.

"And here's the butterfly he becomes," she said as she placed something that felt like a magical moving flower on the hand that had acted as the roach's jungle gym.

"Laurie, that butterfly is an electric blue!" Brian said.

"Do you have any sight at all?" the woman asked.

"Just light," I said. "I can see light."

"Well, take the next right and visit our gem room. We have bins and bins of every semi-precious stone known to man," she said. "You can touch 'em all."

"Wow, they don't feel like the ones you have in your rings, Mom," I said excitedly, as I picked up some unpolished amethysts that felt like the ones I had collected at Lake Tahoe.

"That's how they start out before they're cut for jewelry," Mom said.

Nature had worn these stones into fascinating misshapen forms, some almost feeling as if they had intentionally been shaped that way, like tiny abstract figurines.

❋   ❋   ❋

I awaited our trip to England three years later with a breathless anticipation. I had read so much about queens, kings, princes, and princesses, castles, jewels, and ornate architecture. The books had been narrated many times by the voices of English actors, and this would be my chance to be in the London that had been inhabited by so many of my beloved protagonists.

As we waited outside the gates of Madame Tussaud's Wax Museum, I prepared myself to be bored, resentful, and detached.

"Your daughter will get in free," said the lady at the information desk. "And she will be allowed behind all the ropes to touch anything she likes."

Some people die and go to heaven. I died and went back in time. I touched wax figures of kings and queens who had once lived and the embroidered velvet of their regal uniforms. I felt the prominent chins and high cheekbones of actors and actresses from the '30s and '40s whose likenesses had been preserved. I felt the shockingly big hairdos with bejeweled baubles on famous people from each century, and I felt the almost eerie skin-like, realistic faces, hands, and bodies of every figure in that museum.

I began to appreciate the benefits of being on equal footing with my family and those around me, of the open-mouthed fascination that only comes from firsthand experience.

I was greeted with the same warm reception at Stratford when visiting Shakespeare's house and Anne Hathaway's cottage, where I felt the Renaissance embellishments on furniture. I was taken behind ropes at Buckingham Palace and Windsor Castle to feel the prized possessions of monarchs past. I heard indignant shouts from lookers-on as Brian and I touched the naturally formed arches in Stonehenge.

"She's blind. Now run along!" the tour guide told the horrified good samaritans.

❀　❀　❀

France proved just as understanding as England. I felt the Winged Victory, and the Venus de Milo, which filled me with joy since I had just studied Greek mythology. I touched relics of the French Revolution. I felt everything I could touch in Versailles.

When I returned to the US and visited a museum in New York, I was greeted by an attendant who might as well have been a robot.

"You have to pay, and no, you can't touch anything that's roped off or behind glass."

That's when my letter-writing campaign began.

"If I can touch Shakespeare's bed, I think your space shuttles can handle the oil from my hands," I wrote to the Smithsonian.

"Do you realize you're prohibiting a percentage of your population from enjoying your art?" I wrote the Met. "Isn't your mission to allow people to experience art so that they can have an appreciation of it, thus keeping the visual arts alive? Isn't what you're doing in direct conflict with what you set out to do?"

The Smithsonian sent me a form letter, reminding me that I was more than welcome to listen to the audio guides, which would allow any of their patrons to have a self-guided tour through the museum.

The Met at least had the decency to send a small typed note with an actual signature on it, which said that preserving art was of the utmost importance and unfortunately meant not allowing it to be touched by anyone but the curators.

"We want generations of people to appreciate what we hold in this museum."

They had failed to address one glaring problem, that I, and others like me, would never, ever see what they were supposedly preserving for the appreciation of mankind.

Yellow

*An afternoon when the birds are singing to their
    friends,
when I can touch the tallest sunflowers,
and when I can smell the lemons that are ready
    to be picked
is an afternoon in yellow to me.
On such afternoons,
the sun appears to be smiling,
and yes, the sunlight is something I can actually
    see.
The light is creamier than white.
Yellow is the color of laughter, of excitement, of
    new adventure.*

Mainstreamed

I spent many yellow afternoons on the kickball field once I was mainstreamed into public school in fourth grade. It felt good to be out of the classroom and to take in the sounds and the perfume of the outdoors while we ran from first to second base and so on. I was surprised to discover that I was pretty good at scoring for my team. I could run to the bases if someone shouted at me from their location, and I could target their voices. Running the bases and feeling free and mobile was a novelty for me that most probably take for granted. For one thing, I was feeling normal, playing a sport with regular kids for the first time. For another, I was finally experiencing what it was like to have school friends who lived much closer to me now. Like Brian, I was starting to have sleep-overs and to be invited to birthday parties. There were no distinctions between kids. Blind or sighted, we were all expected to read the same books, even if mine were in braille and my friends' books were in print. The only difference between me and my new friends was our different levels in math.

It was because I was so far behind my grade level in math that Mom decided I needed to be mainstreamed in the first place. She put her foot down in a phone call to Joy Efron, the principal of Blend my last year there.

"I want Laurie to attend a regular, public school next year," she said.

"Our totally blind students just don't do that," said Mrs. Efron. "We find that they thrive much better here where they can get the special attention they need."

"I don't believe that Laurie is thriving or learning at the rate she needs to," Mom said. "She comes home from school telling me that most of her day was spent having free time. That's not acceptable to me. I want her mainstreamed next year."

Topeka Drive Elementary School was in Northridge, a suburb about twenty minutes away from home in Encino. It was a neighborhood public school that had a resource room with equipment and two teachers who worked specifically with visually handicapped students. The setup was meant for kids to be integrated in regular classroom settings, the resource room providing any supplemental education visually-impaired students needed. For me, the resource room was a place to go to learn long division and multiplication, something—I was embarrassed to find out—that my friends had already learned in third grade. I was still taken to school on a bus with blind kids, but the drive was not nearly as far as the one downtown to Francis Blend.

I had been used to a class of no more than ten at Blend, and now, I was making my way through a maze of thirty student desks to get to my own. There was more noise in the room as thirty-one kids' pencils scribbled notes, turned pages, coughed, and dropped writing utensils on their desks, but our teacher, Mrs. Chrinehetter (who was Grandma's age), was very strict, and she had eyes in the back of her head when it came to catching someone sneaking candy in class, whispering, or passing notes. She had the same expectations of me that she did of her other students.

"Laurie," she said in a stern voice when returning a spelling test to me one day in early October, "an F is not an acceptable grade in my class."

"An F!" I exclaimed in alarm. "But I studied really hard, Mrs. Chrinehetter."

Mom surveyed the graded paper carefully that night.

"You spelled the word 'happen' with an 'in' instead of an 'en,'" she said. "You know better than that."

"That's how Mrs. Green brailled it," I said, showing her my brailled spelling list for the week.

All my class materials, worksheets, handouts, and tests were given to Mrs. Green, one of the resource room teachers, who would then transcribe it into braille on the same Perkins braille typewriter I had been using since my first year at Blend. Sure enough, Mom found that I was right. Mrs. Green had used the IN sign instead of the EN sign when transcribing the word "happen." As Mom looked down my brailled spelling list, she noticed with horror that almost every word had some sort of braille typo.

"Laurie is going to have a hard time learning how to spell if her study list is brailled wrong," Mom said.

"Mrs. Rubin, I am so sorry, my braille skills are a bit rusty these days," said Mrs. Green, who took extra care when brailling for me in the future, and my spelling scores improved dramatically.

❋ ❋ ❋

The resource room was large, and contained several tables with interesting machines I had never seen before. As kids worked on them, they beeped and spoke in monotone, computerized voices.

"Okay, Laurie," Mrs. Green said. "It's time for you to learn the versabraille."

"What's that?"

"Do your parents have a computer at home? The versabraille is a computer for blind people. It does all of the same things."

With a grunt, Mrs. Green placed a large, heavy box-like machine in front of me. It had six keys, which I knew were the braille keys, and a spacebar. Mrs. Green showed me a flat area about two inches wide and about fourteen inches long.

"Try typing something," she said. As I typed, little braille dots began to pop up from somewhere in the machine, and as I kept typing, the first braille words I had written disappeared to make room for the new ones. They felt like tiny little creatures that came to life every time I moved the cursor with a command Mrs. Green showed me. I began to laugh.

"That's how the words move on a screen," she explained.

"I'm not used to braille moving like that," I giggled. "It's weird."

"That's because the only braille you've seen is on a piece of paper."

She showed me a compartment where a cassette tape was placed.

"The tapes contain all the files you're working on," she said.

"Mom, can I have a versabraille for my birthday?" I asked Mom when I came home from school that day.

"What's that?" Mom asked.

"It's a braille computer-thingy. The braille dots on it move."

"What does it do?"

"When I learn how to use it, I can write things on it, or take tests so that Mrs. Green doesn't have to transcribe the braille I write for Mrs. Chrinehetter."

Mom decided to drive me to school the next day. I found out later that her motivation for doing so was to have a face-to-face meeting with Mrs. Green.

"Laurie tells me that you're teaching her how to use some braille computer," she began.

"Yes, Mrs. Rubin. We teach all our blind students to use this," Mrs. Green explained.

"I think it would be better if you could teach Laurie how to type. That would be a wonderful new skill for her to learn here."

"That is not in our curriculum to teach typing."

"But she can't use a pen or a pencil to write like a sighted person, and I want her to at least have one means of writing that a sighted person would use. Besides, if Laurie is going to be a competitive candidate for a job, she'll need typing more than she'll need a versabraille. If she's going to spend her time in this room, I would like you to teach her a skill she'll be more likely to use in high school and beyond when she is completely mainstreamed in a place without a resource room."

So the next day, when I sat down at the table with Mrs. Green, a manual typewriter was put in front of me. She placed my left pinky on the letter a, and had me practice typing it for the entire hour.

"That's it? That's all you learned how to type today?" Mom asked in alarm.

"Yeah, it was really boring, and my pinky hurt," I said.

"Okay that does it," she said. "I'm going to teach you how to type myself."

Mom showed me how to place my fingers on the home keys, using the detectable dots on the j and the f as markers for me to know where to place my fingers, and began to test me on their location. The next day, she would teach me another row on the typewriter keyboard, until I was well acquainted with it.

❀ ❀ ❀

Brian started in the tenth grade at Oakwood School, one of the top private schools in LA, the same year I started fourth grade at Topeka. Mom and Dad were impressed by the liberal arts college-like education he was getting at Oakwood. He brought home rigorous piles of homework in every subject and learned to express himself through well-written poetry. He studied a new book in English class every other week, everything from Dickens to F. Scott Fitzgerald.

"People have told me that college is a breeze compared to Oakwood," Brian sighed late one night, snapping his book shut with finality.

Brian, who had always loved theater, talked excitedly at dinner about his drama class. Oakwood was known for the high quality productions that were put on there, and this year he had the supporting role of Stephen in the George Bernard Shaw play, *Major Barbara*. In early spring, we went to see the performance in the small, modest Oakwood auditorium. Mom suddenly spotted Dan Everet, the school's headmaster, who never lacked for words and who always gave eloquent, profound speeches at open houses and parent meetings.

"Dan, I want you to meet my daughter Laurie," Mom said enthusiastically. "She will be applying to Oakwood in a couple years for seventh grade."

Dan hesitated and then took my hand. For the first time, Mom saw Dan speechless.

The subject of me applying to Oakwood did not come up again until my fifth-grade-year at Topeka. Mom and Dad arranged a meeting with Dan Everet and the assistant headmaster, Jeanne Wilson, to talk about my applying to Oakwood the following year.

"Our main concern for all our kids is to make sure they are able to be successful here. The curriculum, as you know, is very rigorous, and we would want to make sure she could keep up," Dan said. "We've never had a blind student here. How is she going to take tests? How will she get all her materials in braille? How does she relate to other kids?"

"Dan," said Dad, speaking for the first time in the meeting. "Laurie's disability is very obvious, something you can see the moment you meet her, but I'm sure you have kids here who have many other disabilities that you can't see right up front that pose challenges for Oakwood."

"That is very true," Jeanne said thoughtfully. "Well, we are going to have to give this a lot of thought. The first thing I'd like to do is to come see how she functions in her current school environment."

✦ ✦ ✦

Jeanne made her first visit to my fifth grade class in January.

"Wow," she said, just after I had finished a class reading assignment, "you read so fast."

"Of course I do," I said. "I'm in fifth grade already."

She stayed for an hour, watching me take a history test and type my answers on a Perkins Brailler that was hooked up to a printer, which converted the braille words I typed into print. The machine was noisy, clicking and pounding as I typed and screeching and scratching as the printer did its work.

"Jeanne said she was very impressed at the way you worked today," Mom said.

"How come?"

"What do you mean how come?"

"Why is she impressed?"

"She's never seen a blind person work, and she just can't imagine how you do things. She did say that your brailler is very loud and was wondering if there's anything you could use in school that would be less distracting. We're going to get you a computer, now that you know how to type."

Mom had somehow found out about computers with the capability to read everything on the screen for the blind, and several weeks after Jeanne had come to visit me at school, a man arrived at our house, lugging several large boxes into my room. Their contents smelled like machine exhaust and new plastic. He began hooking things up and setting up the large computer on my desk. When turned on, the unit hummed loudly and its innards clicked as it booted up.

"Accent ready," said the machine, letting me know that its speech program was ready to go.

The computer man, named Steve, showed me how to control the cursor with keys instead of a mouse. If I hit the control key in combination with different letters, Word Perfect or a typing practice game would open. If I hit control+P in a document, the printer would make the noise of a launching space ship, and the words in the file would begin to appear on the pages rolling rhythmically out of the machine.

❖ ❖ ❖

Jeanne continued to make sporadic visits to observe me into sixth grade. She became interested in my progress in math and made sure to time her visits with the hours I spent in the resource room as I struggled to get caught up.

"Jeanne said you seemed tired today," Mom said with concern in her voice.

"Everyone gets tired sometimes, Mom. Can you tell her to stop testing me? Why is it so extra hard for me to apply to Oakwood than it is for anyone else?"

I was now fed up with Oakwood. I had let them observe me in school, I had gone there for several interviews with different administrators in addition to the required one that was part of the application process, I had gotten and learned to use a computer to appease them, and they still didn't seem convinced. I began to question if Oakwood was the place I wanted to go after all.

In addition to Oakwood, there was one other school I was thinking about applying to. Harvard-Westlake, Oakwood's competitor, appealed to me for its music program, which was much larger than Oakwood's. When I visited, I also was given a warm reception.

"We are so happy you are considering us," said the director of admissions. "We know you're an Oakwood family, but we think we'll have a lot to offer you."

I went to visit the school several times. I sat on the edge of my seat through a student-written musical played by the impressive school band and performed by actors and singers who sounded nearly as professional as those in the Broadway casts of productions I had seen. I heard their speech and debate team present a compelling argument against censorship, and I talked with many teachers who never once mentioned my blindness being a concern.

"How could you even think of going to my rival school?" Brian asked.

"Maybe Oakwood is the right place for you, and Harvard-Westlake is the right place for me," I said. "I really liked it there."

❀ ❀ ❀

There was an entrance exam to get into both schools. I took it on the Oakwood campus, reading a brailled copy of it that Oakwood had arranged to get from the Educational Testing Service. The verbal and literary section was a piece of cake, but when I got to the math section, there were problems I didn't recognize, some of them with raised drawings of graphs I was supposed to analyze and terms I had never heard before. I was sure I had lost my chance at getting into either school, and that Oakwood was right about me not being able to succeed academically there.

Brian was undergoing a nerve-wracking application process of his own. For him, it was college he was fretting over. His first choice was Occidental in Eagle Rock, California, just a forty-minute drive from home. We both submitted our applications, all our test scores were in, and we played the waiting game.

Three letters came on the same Saturday in April. One was for me from Harvard-Westlake, another was from Oakwood, and the third was from Occidental. We knew that these letters held the answers to our immediate futures inside the envelopes.

It was Mom's scream that had me rushing into the office. I knew this could only mean good news. Brian had gotten into

Occidental. Mom opened up the envelope from Oakwood next. She let out another scream of joy. Strangely enough, Oakwood had let me in, even after all the skepticism I thought I had felt from them, and even though I did horribly on the entrance exam. Then Mom opened the letter from Harvard-Westlake. It was a rejection. I was shocked. Harvard-Westlake had seemed so eager to welcome me with open arms.

"Yes, but they never invested any time in you to see how you would do things at their school," Mom pointed out. "I know you were angry with Oakwood, but at least Jeanne showed a genuine interest by going out of her way to make sure Oakwood would be the right place for you."

Mom had been right, and because Harvard-Westlake didn't ask any questions, they were not aware of my having to catch up in math, the reason for my poor score on the test.

For as long as I could remember, I always wanted to be like Brian, to do everything he did, and except for games of ping-pong and a few other things, I succeeded in following in his footsteps. Soon I would be starting the next chapter of my life at his school and be a normal kid, just like him.

The Day I Became a Woman in My Pink Bat Mitzvah Dress

The synagogue was full of people when my family arrived. The organist was playing songs of welcome, and Cantor Fox was in a jolly mood as always as he sang "Shabbat Shalom" and greeted people as they came in. My parents exchanged hugs and kisses with friends and regular Shabbat service-goers. Some of Brian's classmates gathered around him enthusiastically, gossiping about the goings on at the various bar mitzvah parties, like how neat it was that one of their friends had a hypnotist. I began to daydream about what sort of entertainment I would have at my bat mitzvah, even though it was still five years away.

My parents had decided to attend Shabbat services more frequently to set a good example for my brother and me. It seemed as if every weekend, another friend of the family's had his or her turn to lead a service and to become a Jewish man or woman.

When the sun had gone down and it was time for Shabbat services to start, I heard the familiar creaking of everyone taking their seats.

"Good evening everyone," said Rabbi Schulweis, his booming voice silencing the din of the congregation.

I listened as he explained the significance of that week's Torah portion and how relevant it was to current events. I didn't understand his big words or exactly what he was talking about, but I listened to the sound of his wise voice and to the mutters of agreement from those seated around me, and I felt quite content and safe.

Soon, we were asked to "please rise" and the cantor began to lead us in a prayer. Mom, Dad, and Brian were singing along, and though I knew the melody, I did not know the words.

"Mommy," I whispered. "How come you all know this song, and I don't?"

"Because we have it in front of us in our books, honey," she said.

"You mean the siddur?" I asked.

"Yes," Mom replied.

"Why don't I have mine in braille?" I asked indignantly.

"Don't start whining now," she warned.

"But . . ."

"Shhhhh," she said. "We can talk about this later."

"You may be seated," Rabbi Schulweis said after the music had ended. "Please turn to page 134."

I listened with fascination as the wave of pages turning filled the room like the sound of wind rustling the leaves on a forest of trees in autumn. I wanted to be part of that sound but had no page to turn.

"Please read responsively," the rabbi instructed us. Mom, Dad, and Brian began reading with the rest of the congregation, and I tried to recite the words as well.

"Laurie, be quiet," my brother said.

"Why? Everyone else is reading."

"Yeah, but you're not saying the right words, and you're bothering everyone."

I shifted loudly in my seat and became silent, hoping that everyone would notice my unhappy lack of participation more strongly than the rabbi's voice and the music.

"It's not fair," I thought repeatedly through the remaining hour and a half of the service.

Soon, Rabbi Schulweis introduced Danielle Rosen, whose bat mitzvah was being celebrated. Proud parents, friends, and relatives began to acknowledge her as she began to lead us in prayer.

"*Baruch ata Adonai*," she began, her voice shaking a little with nerves.

Cantor Fox chanted his response, and the choir began to sing.

"How am I supposed to have a bat mitzvah one day if I can't even read the siddur?" I thought.

After an impassioned sermon from Rabbi Schulweis and some concluding prayers, the service ended, and we all began to file into the social hall for a kiddush consisting of wine, challah, and sugar-dusted cookies called chichel that melt in your mouth the second you bite into them. I always looked forward to the refreshments after services, but on that night I wasn't in the mood.

When we got home, we all retired to our separate quarters.

The familiar sounds in the house that normally filled me with a sense of peace and contentment now seemed to make me feel wistful, isolated, and invisible. I could hear my brother laugh every so often, probably gossiping with a friend about something at school, and I noticed footsteps and clicking sounds as Mom turned off all the lights around the house and locked the doors.

"Laurie," she called after a few minutes. "Are you ready for me to tuck you in?"

"I guess," I said.

I heard her approach my bedroom and felt the mattress sink a little as she sat down on my bed.

"Are you okay, honey?" she asked in a soothing voice.

"I'm fine," I lied.

"You didn't seem happy at all during the service, and you refused a piece of chichel, which you never do," she said.

We sat in silence for a moment. Without warning, I felt my eyes burning, and I realized I was trying to hold back tears.

"You can talk to me, sweetie," said Mom.

"Mommy," I said, trying to swallow away the growing lump in my throat, "will I have a bat mitzvah?"

"Of course you will, you know that," Mom sounded surprised. "Don't we talk about that all the time?"

"But how am I supposed to have a bat mitzvah if I can't read the Torah, or the siddur, or any of the supplements?"

Mom repositioned herself on the bed and said, "You know how Neal has worked very hard to make sure you get everything in braille for Hebrew school?" she asked, referring to the principal of Valley

Beth Shalom Day School, a kind man who led the services for our class. "When you started Hebrew school, Neal was the one who made sure you would be able to do your Hebrew school work along with everybody else. Just like your father and I, Neal knows you would be able to do anything your classmates did, as long as you had it in braille. So, when it comes time for your bat mitzvah, you will meet with the same coach as Brian, and you'll be able to follow his instructions because you will have the braille version in front of you."

"But how am I going to learn Hebrew braille?" I asked.

Mom sat thinking for a moment before she said, "We'll find someone who knows Hebrew braille, and he or she will teach it to you."

"Once I learn Hebrew, does that mean I'll be able to follow along in Shabbat services like the one tonight?"

"Yes, of course. Your time will come, don't worry," she said. She kissed me goodnight, tucked me in, and turned out my light as she left the room. I snuggled under the covers, and began to imagine I was Danielle on the Bimah, leading services. Would I be as nervous as she was? After all, there were a lot of prayers to learn and an entire Torah portion to memorize.

I began to think of the celebration we would have afterwards. Every kid whose party I had been to had a theme. "What would my theme be?" I wondered. "I like Disneyland. Maybe each table will be a different ride at Disneyland!" As I began to imagine tables decorated with colorful Disney characters and a dessert table with Mickey Mouse ice-cream bars and Rice Krispies Treats, I drifted into a deep sleep.

❁   ❁   ❁

As promised, Mom found a Hebrew braille teacher for me, a blind lady named Lynn. Once a week, Mom would drive me to Lynn's home for lessons. Her apartment was small and stuffy and smelled strongly of dirty dog. My fingers felt crowded as Lynn's fingers trailed alongside mine as she kept up with my reading progress.

Lynn explained that since braille was made up of six dots, there were only so many combinations of the dots that could be made. Something that might read as a colon or a dash in English braille might be a vowel indicator in the Hebrew version.

I was motivated to learn it as quickly as possible because of an overwhelming desire not to have to return to that stuffy apartment and to never have those short, stubby fingers, growing sticky from sweat, following mine on the page of those braille books.

The following year, I was ready to start learning Hebrew with the rest of my classmates. The only difference was that they learned to read from right to left, and I read my Hebrew braille from left to right.

"Shalom, Laurie!" Neal said happily on the first afternoon of a new school year. "Did you have a nice summer?" Before I could answer, he interrupted. "Guess what we have here for you?"

"What?" I asked excitedly, almost sure I knew the answer.

"Your Hebrew text books, your siddur, and everything else you'll need for this year! They just came from New York!"

"Oh, wow! Can I see?"

"We need an entire bookshelf for these books. They come in several volumes, so they're in the library," Neal said.

My heart sank. I was all too familiar with the fact that braille takes up more room on a page than a normal textbook. When our class was asked to turn to page 50, other students did so with little to no effort, and I would often discover with horror that my volume of braille ended on page 49. But this did not dim my excitement for long, and Neal proceeded to hand me four very large volumes.

"This one," he said, placing my hand on the topmost book, "is the first volume of the siddur."

As each year of Hebrew School brought me closer to my bat mitzvah, my excitement was being matched by a growing sense of nerves. Leading a Friday night Shabbat service, followed by an even longer one on the next morning, seemed like a scarier and harder feat than skiing down the steepest slope in the Rockies. Before I knew it, my time had come to start coaching sessions with Mr. Dresner. I arrived at his office with sweaty palms and butterflies in my stomach.

"Sit down," he said sharply. "You have a lot to learn, so you must practice with this tape every week." He handed me a cassette and several sheets of paper. "These markings tell you when the chant goes up in your voice, and these markings show you when the chant goes down."

I knew that Mr. Dresner was pointing as he spoke. "But Mr. Dresner," I said hesitantly, "I can't see your markings."

He paused for a moment. "Well then, you'll just have to be perfect," he said simply.

Every week, I chanted along with Mr. Dresner's taped voice, memorizing each passage. Mr. Dresner seemed happy with my progress, and he began teaching me the prayers in which I would be leading the congregation on the Friday night service.

But what girl can become a bat mitzvah without first securing the perfect dress?

With just a few weeks until the big day, I found myself in the dressing room at The Candy House, an exclusive women's dress shop, feeling as if I were dressed in flower petals. The satin was soft, and it fell gently around me like a sheath following the curve of my waist and hips. The beading meandered and twisted up my chest and shoulders, suggesting the shape of vines with tiny leaves. The dress was ice pink, and I felt like some ethereal creature as it floated about me when I walked out of the dressing room for everyone to see.

"What do you think?" Mom asked.

"I love it," I said, feeling overcome with emotion. "I think this is the dress."

I knew I wanted something different than the poofy dresses I had felt in store after store. This dress felt strikingly different, as if it had been spun by fairies from the silk of magical silkworms.

And it was pink! For me, pink is tenderness, like the soft skin of a brand new baby. Pink is the sweet perfume of the first blossoms in spring. The princesses in my favorite childhood books were all dressed in pink. It is the delicate state of girlhood.

"You look like Ginger Rogers in that dress," Mom marveled.

"Just a few alterations," said the saleswoman who began adjusting the length with safety pins. "We should have it ready for you in a week."

I was ecstatic.

The Rubin house was filled with bat mitzvah–related chaos. We had appointments with the calligrapher for the invitations, the florist for all the party centerpieces, the photographer, the videographer, and the bandleader. The anticipation was growing as we attended Shabbat services almost every week.

For once in my life, I wished that time would slow down a little for me to get my bearings. I had learned the melodies of the entire service by heart and had practiced reading my speech over and over, but I still didn't feel ready. Time seemed to be on super speed, and the Friday night of my bat mitzvah weekend had arrived. I felt my heart beating fast as I was led onto the Bimah and to the seat of honor.

"Can everyone take their seats?" called Rabbi Schulweis.

I was aware of the familiar voices of my aunts, uncles, and grandparents as they found their seats. A warm feeling enveloped me, making the nerves more manageable.

"Today, we celebrate the bat mitzvah of Laurie Gale Rubin, named in Hebrew by her parents." Cantor Fox, Rabbi Schulweis, the choir, and the congregation seemed to be celebrating with me as they joined my singing.

"*This is not too bad,*" I thought. "*Although tomorrow will be scarier. Tonight, everyone is singing with me, but tomorrow, a lot of it will be just me up there.*"

After the service, we all filed into the social hall for kiddush.

"Wonderful job, Honey," Mom said giving me a hug.

"Yeah, but tomorrow is the hard part," I replied.

"Hey, I did it and survived," Brian said. "You will, too."

I tossed and turned that night, finding it hard not to be thinking about the big day. When sleep finally did claim me, it led me into dream after dream about my bat mitzvah. Each one played in my head like a sequence of films. They were murky versions of the morning service, and I was on the outside, watching myself lead the way.

"Laurie, time to get up," I heard my mother's voice saying.

"What? Oh my gosh."

"It's 7:15, we're leaving in an hour."

The synagogue was full when we arrived. I found this quite curious since the services were so long, and though they started at 8:45 AM, people didn't usually start filling the place until at least 9:30.

"How are you doing this morning?" Cantor Fox asked cheerfully.

"A little nervous," I confessed.

"You'll be great. Don't you worry about a thing. Just sing in that beautiful voice of yours as usual, and you'll knock 'em dead." He chuckled. "Well, don't knock 'em dead exactly, we've got lots of eighty-year-olds in here."

The first hour consisted of the weekly Shabbat prayers, and at 9:30, my work was about to begin.

"Would Arnie and Lilly Rubin please come up to the Bimah to present their daughter Laurie with her prayer shawl?" Rabbi Schulweis asked.

"Laurie," Mom began, her voice beginning to break. She paused and tried to regain her composure. "Your father and I couldn't be more proud of you. You are a loving, caring young woman, and you go after everything you want in life with perseverance, and the unwavering confidence that we all admire and learn from. You jump into every new adventure with a smile on your face, and with unending excitement for what's in store for you each day. The hard work you have done that has earned you the privilege and great responsibility of becoming a Jewish woman represents your ambition and eagerness to achieve all of your goals and dreams. We are so lucky to be your parents, and to have the joy of seeing you grow into the remarkable young woman you are becoming."

"Congratulations, Laurie," Dad began. "The fact that you, our baby, are now thirteen years old is really making me feel old." The congregation chuckled. "I think you probably remember me telling you about the expression 'where there's horse manure, there must be a pony.' I always think of that old saying when I think of your attitude about life because no matter what obstacles have been thrown in your path, you've managed to get around them. You never let anyone tell you that you can't do something. I learned that the hard way, and I shudder to think of what you'll do when your Mom and I say no to you the more you grow into a full-fledged teenager."

The congregation laughed louder and longer this time.

"But your stubbornness and strong will continue to serve you well, and I know your mother and I don't have to worry about anyone beating you down. You will continue to change the world by being a trailblazer, making the road less traveled much smoother for those who follow in your footsteps. We love you."

"*Baruch Ata Adonai*," I began, saying the prayer over the Tallit, fighting to keep my voice steady and blinking away my mom's contagious tears.

"I now call upon Bernard and Berta Gales, Laurie's grandparents, to say the first aliyah," Rabbi Schulweis announced. Grandma and Grandpa took their places on either side of me.

"*Baruch Ata Adonai elohenu Melach Haolom*," they chanted in unison.

My braille book was placed on the Torah, and I began to sing my Torah portion. Before I knew it, I had finished the first verse, relieved at having made no mistakes.

"Amen," I chanted.

"I would now like to call upon Laurie's brother Brian for the second aliyah," said Rabbi Schulweis.

I chanted the second verse, then the third and the fourth, and my aunts and uncles joined me on the Bimah for their blessings. I was nearing the homestretch.

"Now we will hear Laurie's interpretive comments," said the rabbi.

"My Torah portion tells the story of Joseph, and his coat of many colors. This coat symbolized his father's special love for Joseph. Joseph's brothers were jealous because they weren't treated as well as their brother, and this jealousy was the reason why they conspired against him, staged his murder, and sold him into bondage. Even though this story is significant for many different reasons, the part that is most meaningful to me is about being treated equally. In Joseph's case, being treated differently destroyed his relationship with his brothers and caused his father much pain and anguish. In my case, being treated equally to others has been my most important goal. My family has always treated me equally, including yelling at me when I do something wrong, just as they did with my brother. I have always tried to show people I can do most anything anyone else can do. I can go to the movies and the theater, I can swim, I can waterski, I can snow ski the expert slopes, I can go white-water river rafting, I can sing opera, I can get a good education, and most important to me today is that I can become a bat mitzvah.

"My blindness has given me the opportunity to be a pioneer. I am very proud to be the first blind bat mitzvah at Valley Beth Shalom. Becoming a bat mitzvah takes a lot of hard work and courage, and anyone can accomplish it with strength and determination.

"Part of my responsibilities in becoming a member of the adult Jewish community is giving Tzedakah. Therefore, I will be donating a portion of my bat mitzvah money to the Jewish Braille Institute, which will help make it possible for other blind Jewish children to have bar and bat mitzvahs. I look forward to continuing my Jewish education, taking an active part in Shabbat and High Holiday services, and living an adult Jewish life."

I couldn't believe I was finished. It was now time for the rabbi to wrap up. He placed his arm around my shoulders before he said, "When there is unity, a person can taste sweetness with his eyes. You, Laurie, can taste sweetness with your eyes, and you have given us sweetness today. Thank you, Laurie, for sharing your gifts with all of us this morning. For it is ours to share and to rejoice. This is what it is all about, the attributes of divinity, decency, honesty, courage, will, fortitude, and a wonderful spirit of joy."

Rabbi Schulweis had finished. It was over. After what seemed like several moments of silence, the synagogue erupted in laughter as everyone rose and began throwing candy at me in celebration. To me, that was always the most joyous part of the service. I shrieked and ducked as I felt soft jelly candies zoom by my face in their crinkling wrappers. Congregation members I had never met before introduced themselves to me, some saying they had known me since I was a baby. My aunts, uncles, and cousins all congratulated me, followed by Grandma and Grandpa. "We're so proud of you," they all said, and I felt tears on many of their faces as they kissed me.

Once back at home, Dad unloaded a car full of gifts given to me by our invited guests. We sat in the living room, my mom with a pad of paper, keeping track of what I was opening for the sake of writing thank-you cards later. In addition to the standard gifts of money, savings bonds, and jewelry, I found an assortment of unusual objects. One long, skinny package revealed a rain stick, a Native American wooden instrument with pellets inside of it that sounded like rain when you turned the instrument this way and that. Others gave me ornate containers filled with potpourri and I received an overwhelming amount of music boxes.

"How come so many music boxes?" I asked.

"Well, I think people are sometimes at a loss for what to get a blind person. They figure music boxes make music, so you would appreciate that."

I was touched at people's creativity and thoughtfulness and also quite baffled at the idea of being a high maintenance person to get gifts for. I was a teenager, so clothes, gift certificates, and other conventional items were a hit with me, but people thought they were too visual for me to appreciate.

The rest of the afternoon was spent in hair and makeup, and then it was time for me to get into my pink party dress and head back over to the synagogue for pictures.

"Smile," said the photographer's cheerful voice. "Oh, that's a good one. Okay just one more. Perfect! Okay, can I have the grandparents over here please? Terrific! We're ready for the uncles and aunts."

The party I had been envisioning for five years had begun. Everyone was seated at tables decorated and labeled for different musicals. Since *Phantom of the Opera* had initially inspired me to sing, this seemed to be a perfect theme for my party. Every musical, from *West Side Story* to *Phantom*, was represented.

The band, whose leader and director was totally blind, kept everyone dancing the entire night. "Okay, now it's time for the Horah," Wayne Foster, the bandleader, announced. "Everyone onstage!"

The Horah, an Israeli dance of celebration that has everyone joining hands in a circle, features the guests of honor in the middle, seated on chairs that are lifted high into the air by a number of strong people.

"Havah Nagila," the band sang and played as we danced.

Dinner was served, and mouthwatering courses of pastas, meat dishes, and a variety of salads were set on buffet tables, followed by an even more decadent selection of desserts.

We danced until we were ready to collapse, and it was well past one in the morning when the party ended. I was exhausted but brimming with happiness.

O! Say Can You See?

Dad loved to take the opportunity of having me sing at gatherings with family friends. This was not limited to mini-concerts in our living room. Any time the subject of singing came up at a restaurant, if the waiter happened to mention his first career as a singer, or if there happened to be a pianist playing background music, Dad would jump at the chance to have me sing before dessert came. Even though this embarrassed Mom and Brian, who tried to subtly kick him under the table in a silent, "This is inappropriate right now" gesture, Dad would continue, unaware of the hint. So I obliged, half feeling put on the spot and half enjoying having an audience. As a result, many of Mom and Dad's friends knew of my having recently started voice lessons. As several of them were very involved in the Jewish community, on the event-planning committees of the United Jewish Fund, the Anti-Defamation League, and other groups, they began asking me to start off their events with our national anthem, as well as the Hatikva, Israel's national anthem. After one of these events would pass, another event organizer would call Mom, and tell her they needed someone to sing "The Star-Spangled Banner" at their event. These events were held in ballrooms at the Beverly Hills Hotel and others like it, and had honorees like George Burns, former Prime Minister of England Margaret Thatcher, General Norman Schwartzkopf, and the late President and Mrs. Reagan. Mom and Dad seemed more excited by the star-studded crowds than I did. I didn't know who the comedian Alan King was, nor did I watch movies with Walther Matthau at age twelve, but all of them were very nice to me, allowing Dad to take pictures of me with them.

At a memorial for the Holocaust in a huge park, with thousands of people in attendance, mayoral candidate Richard Riordan heard me sing and approached me afterwards.

"If I'm elected," he said, "you will be the one to sing the national anthem at my inauguration—if you're available and willing."

Mom, Dad, and I all thought this was very nice, but didn't really expect him to follow through. Shortly after he was elected, however, we got a phone call from his office, asking me to accept the mayor's request.

"Oh boy," I thought. "I'm going to mess up the words. I just know it. Or I'll crack or hit a sour high note."

I was now fourteen, and though I had sung for celebrities before, singing for the inauguration of the first new mayor we had had in years and years, which was sure to be a momentous occasion in Los Angeles, made me nervous for the first time. Here I would be singing in front of every important politician in Los Angeles, and on top of that, I would be heard on every local television station.

✳ ✳ ✳

The big day was in July. It was quite hot, and the ceremony was to take place outside. There were security guards everywhere we went, watching our every move, checking for our names on lists before we could proceed.

"Oh my gosh, there's Leslie Uggams!" Mom whispered excitedly to me.

"Who is that?" I asked, feeling sick.

"She's a very famous actress and singer," Mom said. "Laurie, your palms are so sweaty, why are you so nervous?"

"What if I forget the words?" I said, the fear apparently showing in my whole face.

"Don't be silly, you could sing the song in your sleep," Mom said. "This must be the hundredth time you'll have performed it. Here, let's go talk to Leslie. Maybe she has some words of wisdom for you."

She took my arm and led me through a group of people.

"Ms. Uggams, my name is Lilly, and this is my daughter Laurie. Laurie will be singing the national anthem today."

"Very nice to meet you," said a deep rich voice.

"She is very nervous," Mom continued. I blushed. "And I was wondering if you might have some words of wisdom for her."

"Mm-mm, honey," Leslie laughed a deep laugh, as if she were enjoying an inside joke. "That song is hard. I wouldn't wish the task of singing that on anyone. Thank God I'm only singing 'God Bless America.'"

"Well, that was helpful," Mom said later. "I don't suppose that helped your nerves."

After what seemed the longest hour of my life in which my heart beat faster and faster, the opening remarks began. Suddenly, a voice announced my name, and I was guided up onto a make-shift stage and handed a microphone, the sound of which I knew would be heard for miles.

"O! say can you see," I began, hearing my voice echo extravagantly. The words were coming to me with each phrase, and soon enough I was nearing the end, where I could have some fun.

"The land of the free," I sang, holding the high note of the "free" for a long time, hearing the crowd cheering. "And the home of the brave," I finished.

❀　❀　❀

I had done it! It went well, and when we got home, a very proud Mom and Dad began going from room to room where they had recorded the coverage of the inauguration on every TV station.

"Now we have a fourteen-year-old opera star singing the national anthem," said the announcer on Channel 2, his voice coming from the den.

"We have just had the sincere pleasure of hearing singing sensation Laurie Rubin sing the national anthem," said the man on Channel 4 in Mom and Dad's bedroom.

"And now let's go to John who is at the Inauguration with an update," said a newscaster on Channel 5 in the playroom. "John, are you there?" "Oh yes, hi, Laura. Sorry, I was distracted by an incredible up-and-coming talent, fourteen-year-old Laurie

Rubin who has just sung the national anthem at the inauguration here today."

I blushed. In every room of our house I was being announced a different way. Opera star? Singing sensation? I had barely made it through without my heart jumping out of my chest, my voice tremulous from nerves as though it was being played on one of those 1920 gramophone recordings. Why was I being paid all these compliments?

I had only started singing in public just a few years earlier, and my gigs were procured through friends of the family, not some fancy manager or record label. Nor did my voice sound anything like any of the seasoned artists like Beverly Sills or Barbra Streisand who had become my idols. As we sat there celebrating, snacking on Hershey's Miniatures and Goldfish crackers, I felt a determination growing inside of me, to one day be truly deserving of all this overwhelming praise.

The Babysitter's Club

I always looked forward to Friday afternoons. Not only were they the beginning of a short respite from school, but they also signified that period of quality time Grandma set aside every week to spend with me.

After a snack of fruit and cookies, Grandma would always ask, "Okay, what shall we do now?" When the weather was nice, we would go outside to pick lemons, oranges, or persimmons from our trees in the backyard, which Grandma would later take to her friends who made them into pie filling. When I was little, I would swing on the swing set while Grandma pushed me, saying "wee!" as I went higher and higher, laughing and feeling as though I were flying.

Later on, when the sun was starting to set, we would adjourn to the playroom and settle ourselves on the couch where Grandma would read me a book. In the earlier days of my childhood, she read me fairy tales. When I got older, I asked her to read me the stories that were popular amongst my friends in school, books about middle-and high-school girls who were much cooler and older than me. My favorite series of books was called "The Baby-sitter's Club" about a group of thirteen-year-old girls who started a little babysitting business. Each book was another adventure in the lives of these friends. The group consisted of the leader and tomboy, Kristy, who started the club, the artistic and funky Claudia, the shy and sensitive Mary Anne, and the sophisticated and pretty Stacey who had many boyfriends. They would either solve a mystery or help each other out of various teenage predicaments.

As Grandma read, I became immediately engrossed in the story of the loyal, close-knit friends. I enveloped myself in the story and Grandma's voice, and I imagined myself as one of the protagonists: running for president of the Student Council, drinking punch and laughing with friends at a school dance, forming a study group to make homework more fun, or sitting at a Babysitter's Club meeting waiting for the phone to ring with a babysitting job from a client.

As seventh grade was fast approaching, I began to imagine how a new school would be the beginning of a whole new and exciting chapter in life. I would be the leader of my very own Babysitter's Club.

The summer grew hotter, the first day at Oakwood drew nearer, and Mom and Dad helped me prepare in earnest. Like most other kids, I was taken on back-to-school shopping errands for the requisite school supplies. We went through aisles filled with note-books of all different shapes and sizes, boxes of pens and pencils, and backpacks of different styles, and I heard enthusiastic kids telling their parents exactly what items they wanted.

"Wow," I thought. "I didn't think school stuff was all that interesting." As my hands trailed the shelves of notebooks, I noticed little ones that felt as if they were made of old parchment, larger ones that felt like my dad's leather briefcase, and oddly shaped ones with raised pictures of suns, flowers, or cartoon characters made of shiny plastic on the covers. "Oh Mom, look at this one!" I exclaimed, happening upon a particularly unusual feeling notebook. "What does this one look like?"

Mom took it from me to examine. "It has a satin finish, and it's rose colored."

"I wish I could use notebooks," I said gloomily, knowing that the only notebook I would be using was my IBM notebook laptop computer, which was not nearly as cool and about ten times as heavy.

On through the aisles we went. School bags were equally as fascinating to examine.

"Ooh, Mom, I really like this one!" I said, placing her hand on a sleek bag made out of something that felt like a thick and shiny patent leather.

"Yeah, but it's not nearly big enough or strong enough for your braille books, honey," she said. "Here, there are some bigger ones on this end." She led me deeper into the jungle of bags and began showing me a heavy-duty backpack that felt as though a tent and other hiking equipment could fit inside. "And just look at how many compartments it has," she said, unzipping pockets here and there. "See, Laurie, you could easily fit your cane in this one, and look, the main pouch is wide enough for at least two volumes of your math book."

"But what does it look like?" I mumbled.

"It's black."

"Black with what?"

"Nothing; there's no print on this one. What do you think?" she asked hopefully.

"Don't they have the one I liked in a bigger size?" I asked.

"I don't see any," she said, her voice changing direction as she looked around. "I guess that material just can't handle large items."

"Why can't braille books be a normal size?" I asked, remembering why I hated back-to-school shopping.

Mom chuckled. "That certainly would be more convenient, wouldn't it? Is this backpack okay then?" she asked, tapping the many-pocketed monstrosity that was still in my arms.

"I guess."

"Good," she sighed. "You have to meet your mobility teacher in half an hour."

❋ ❋ ❋

The buildings of Oakwood School were totally deserted, save for a few administrators whose voices could be heard every so often coming from various offices. The near silence made the place feel lonely. I envied my future classmates and began to imagine how wonderful it would be for them to just show up here for the first time on orientation day, to survey the place with their eyes, and to learn very quickly where each of their classrooms were. They were probably all on vacation in Europe now or at summer camp in the midst of some wonderfully freeing summer activity like swimming or bike riding. I, on the other hand, grudgingly spent my summer break learning the routes to all the classrooms.

"Where did you go wrong that time?" asked Mr. Takaguchi, my mobility instructor, trying to get me to conquer a particularly tricky route to my future math class. I had to cross a courtyard with no buildings on either side, testing my ability to walk a straight line with no tangible guide to keep me in line.

"I veered to the right?" I guessed.

"No, you actually veered to the left," he said patiently.

"Ah, I'm never going to get it!" I said, feeling a lump of frustration in my throat.

"Give yourself time. You've only done this route twice." He guided me back to the end of the courtyard, and, with the main office behind me, I began to walk slowly, carefully placing one foot in front of the other, putting all my concentration into going straight towards my math classroom. The heat of the day was at its peak now, the sun was beating down hard on the back of my neck, and I felt my energy being sapped quickly, like the air out of a faulty balloon. Slowly and deliberately I went, trying to use the position of the sun as my guide. Within seconds, the slight echo of an awning overhead told me that I had gotten it right, that I had not veered.

"See!" Mr. Takaguchi said happily. "You nailed it! You just have to do it slowly a few times, and then it'll just be ingrained in you. Just keep thinking straight, and try to make sure you have an even arc with your cane on either side. That'll also keep you from going astray."

"Great job, Laurie!" clapped Kim Matthews, the dean of the middle school who had evidently been watching for who knows how long. Suddenly I felt like a specimen under a microscope, and I blushed furiously.

"Hi, Kim," I said, trying to sound happy to see her.

"Recognize my voice already?" she asked, sounding impressed. "I was just doing some paperwork in my office and I thought I'd see how you were doing. I better get back to work now. See you at orientation."

Before I could imagine the hole I would have liked to crawl into, Mr. Takaguchi said, "Okay, let's review how to get to the science labs."

✼   ✼   ✼

Oakwood, known for being a small school and a big family, had several events planned for the new seventh graders so as to make us feel at home with each other before classes started. Parents began introducing themselves to one another and distributed the tasks of organizing the orientation pool party, the ice-cream social, and a myriad of other icebreakers. Mom and Dad agreed to host the pool party at our home.

I stood at the front door with Mom as kids and their parents began to arrive.

"Hi, I'm Laurie," I said, extending my hand out to theirs.

A peculiar pause followed before each of my fellow peers would say, "Nice to meet you, I'm . . ."

I stood listening as the others began to shake hands with each other and introduce themselves, and I noticed that the uncomfortable pause was not there during these other exchanges, and that they seemed to slip into casual conversation more easily.

"Why don't you head on out to the pool, Laurie?" Mom said. "I can wait here to greet the rest."

I led the small group of early arrivals through the swinging screen door, out on to the patio. I heard them unloading their bags onto chairs and running out to the pool. I stepped into the water, shivering slightly as each part of my body received a small shock from its temperature. Waist deep, I waded in the water, listening. The number of voices was growing and I knew that more people had arrived. Several of the girls were in conversation now, and the initial unease of not knowing each other seemed to be fading a bit.

Bracing myself for the last shock of cold, I immersed myself completely, hearing the growing crowd over the soothing rippling and bubbling of the water.

I heard some girls in conversation a few feet in front of me and I paddled over to them.

"I still have to finish our summer reading assignment," one of the girls was saying in a bright high voice.

"Can you believe we haven't even started our first year at Oakwood, and they're already giving us homework?"

"I know," said another, more soft-spoken girl.

"I only finished the book last night."

"What did you think?" I asked.

The same awkward pause I had experienced moments earlier filled the air.

"Huh?" the first girl asked, a little taken aback.

"Sorry," I said, feeling my face grow a little hot. "I'm Laurie. I was just curious what you thought of *Of Mice and Men*."

"Oh," said the softer voiced girl. "It was okay."

Silence.

"What are your names?" I asked hesitantly.

"Stacy," said the first girl.

"Taryn," said the second.

"I'm Alison," said another who had been silent until that moment.

"Nice to meet you guys," I said, trying to sound welcoming.

"You, too," they said in a shy unison.

Silence again.

"Sorry to interrupt," I said. "Talk to you guys soon." I smiled and swam away. "*Will the whole afternoon be like this?*" I thought, wondering what sort of strange cloud was following me to cause everyone to be so uncomfortable.

The screen door was slamming less frequently now, and from the more crowded sound of the backyard and the many splashes in the water, I knew that almost everyone was there.

"Hey, Laurie!" I felt a tap on my shoulder.

"Aviva!" I said, relieved to hear the familiar voice of my Hebrew school friend. "I'm so glad you're here! I don't know anyone else."

"Me neither."

"How was your time in Paris?"

"Oh, it was so cool. We went to the Eiffel Tower, and we actually took the elevator all the way up. I thought I'd be scared of heights, but the view was so amazing up there!"

As we continued to relay the events of our summer to each other, the sinking feeling in the pit of my stomach subsided.

"Are you Aviva Kleinman?" another girl had just joined us.

"Yes, I am," Aviva said.

"I'm Jenna Pierson," said the newcomer. "Your brother and my baby sister are classmates."

"Your sister must be Callie, right?" Aviva said.

"Yes!" shrieked Jenna, as if the coincidence was the best discovery she had ever made.

After another moment of conversation between the two, Aviva said, "Oh, and this is Laurie Rubin. She and I go to Hebrew school together."

"Hi," Jenna said, and took my extended hand. "Oh wait, you should meet Michelle. Her sister goes to Fairmont with our baby siblings." With that, Aviva and Jenna swam away.

"Should I follow them?" I wondered with a sinking heart. I tried heading in the direction of their voices, but they had disappeared into the sea of seventh graders. For several minutes, I listened to groups of kids chatting, noticing the level of laughter rising. This wasn't the kind of first meeting I had imagined. I had pictured myself on the inside of a group, not like a lone flower floating aimlessly around my own pool.

Mom had turned on the radio, and "I Want to Sex You up" was barely audible over the din of the crowd.

"Hi," said a cheerful voice next to me. I jumped slightly.

"Sorry, didn't mean to startle you," said the girl.

"Are you talking to me?" I asked, feeling slightly embarrassed.

"Yeah, I'm Dana," she said.

"I'm Laurie," I said, feeling cheered by having been sought out by someone for an introduction and perhaps a conversation.

"Oh, you're the one whose pool we're swimming in!" Dana said. "It's so cool, and so big. How deep is it?"

"Hmm, maybe nine feet deep."

"Wow! I think I'm one of the few people here who doesn't have a pool."

"Nah," I assured her. "I bet you there are others who don't." There was a pause. "So where do you live?"

"Van Nuys, not too far from here," she replied. "I went to public school from K through sixth. I bet I'm the only one who didn't go to some fancy private school since kindergarten."

"I went to public school, too," I said, glad to finally have something in common with one of my classmates.

"Oh, that's cool," Dana sounded relieved. "It's good I'm not the only one. Have you finished the summer reading assignment?"

"Yeah," I said. "Did you?"

"Not yet," she said, and I heard the sound of eyes rolling in her voice.

"You didn't like it, did you?" I chuckled.

"Hell no," she said. "I mean who wants to read about a bunch of hicks and a retarded guy?"

"Yeah, I guess," I agreed, realizing it wouldn't be a good time to admit I had liked the book.

"And what does the title *Of Mice and Men* have to do with anything anyway?" she said.

"It's sort of a metaphor, you know," I said, hesitating.

"Oh wait, there's Courtney, I just met her a few minutes ago," Dana said, turning her head away for a second.

"Courtney, come on over here. This is Laurie."

"Hi," I said.

"Hi," said a girl with a sharp, high voice. I immediately imagined a petite build, pale skin, and dark brown hair. I later learned that I was quite right.

"We were just talking about our summer reading assignment," Dana said.

"Oh yeah," Courtney sighed. "I haven't even gotten halfway through. I'm thinking about getting the CliffsNotes."

Dana laughed.

"Are you the Courtney whose sister graduated last year from Oakwood with my brother?" I asked.

"Yeah, my sister was Andrea. Who was your brother?"

"Brian," I said. "Brian Rubin."

"Hmm, gotta ask Andie if she knows him."

"I'm sure she does. Oakwood is so small."

"Oh my gosh," Dana gasped suddenly. "Did you see that guy swim by? The one with the blue swim trunks and the sandy blond hair?"

"Yeah, he's kind of cute," Courtney said, her voice changing direction as she turned to look.

"He totally is," Dana said dreamily.

"He's got the most crystal blue eyes. I mean, I tried not to stare at them or anything, but they're hard not to notice. Laurie, did you see him?"

"Nope," I said casually.

"Dana totally pointed, and you didn't look in that direction," Courtney said incredulously.

"That's because I'm blind," I said.

"You must be," they laughed.

I laughed, too. "No, I really am blind," I said, hoping against hope that my tone was casual enough to prevent another set of awkward exchanges.

There was a pause.

"Wait," Courtney said, "is that why you haven't been looking us in the eye?"

"Yeah," I said.

"Oh my gosh," Dana said, sounding serious. "I had no idea."

"It's fine, it's really fine," I said.

"I'm really sorry about what I said about that retarded boy, you know, in *Of Mice and Men*," Dana said sheepishly.

I hesitated for a moment, trying to figure out how to respond. "That's okay," I smiled. "I'm not retarded, just blind."

"That's true," she said, sounding more relaxed again.

The rest of the afternoon was spent people-watching, or rather, Dana and Courtney doing the honors and whispering their impressions and findings to me. I found myself laughing with abandon and just feeling like one of the girls.

❀ ❀ ❀

Before I knew it, the first day of school had arrived. My clock radio woke me at 6:30 to the song "More than Words" by Extreme.

I dressed hurriedly and filled my school bag with braille paper, cane, and the first braille volumes of my "Algebra Basics," "Introduction to Life Science," and "Classic Poetry Anthology." Once my bag looked like it was filled with a ton of bricks, I dropped it by the front door and made my way to the kitchen where Mom was making breakfast.

"Hi, sweetie," she said cheerfully. "Scrambled eggs okay?"

"Sounds fine," I said, sinking into a chair in front of the table.

"You excited about your first day?" Mom asked as the eggs sizzled and popped on the stove and the aroma of cheese and green onions began to fill the room.

"Yeah, I guess."

"That doesn't sound very convincing."

"I hope I make friends."

"Of course you will. Didn't I see you having a great time with those two girls in the pool the other day?"

"Yeah, but everyone else was weirded out whenever I talked to them. I don't get it. All I did was try to join the conversation, and they'd get silent as if they had just seen a ghost."

"Give them time," Mom said. "Most of them have probably never seen a blind person before."

"What do you mean? What's so strange about seeing a blind girl?" I demanded.

"They were probably confused by the fact that you weren't making eye contact with them," she explained.

"Dana and Courtney aren't even in my section," I said. During orientation, we were told that all 60 classmates were divided into three sections of 20, and that we would be having all of our classes with those same 20 kids. My name had been called when Section 3 was announced, and Dana and Courtney were both in Section 2.

"Well, you can see Dana and Courtney at lunch," Mom said.

I nibbled on my eggs, trying to ignore the unpleasant butterflies in my stomach.

At 7:15, I heard a car horn beep, and I knew that Debbie, a senior and my carpool driver, had arrived to take me to school. Mom opened the front door and picked up my bulky computer bag.

"Man, this is heavy!" she said with a grunt.

I hoisted my school bag onto my back and made my way to the sound of Debbie's idling Honda Accord.

The sun was exceptionally bright, and its cheerful welcome made me feel more at ease as I greeted Debbie and let her guide me to the passenger side of the car.

The ride to school was pleasant. I liked the Peter Gabriel song she was playing, and I was happy to have a break from the monotony of the Color Me Badd and Boyz II Men hits on the radio.

"Are you sad that you're graduating this year?" I asked, after spending most of the ride in silence.

"Yeah," she said. "I've made some close friends at Oakwood. But I'm really excited about college, too."

"Do you know where you're going to apply?"

"Not exactly. I'm still doing my research."

With that, I felt Debbie turn into the parking lot and find a spot. I could hear the muffled sound of kids through the closed car window.

The locker area that had been silent and deserted when I had seen it during my mobility training was now packed with students. The indistinguishable voices and slamming of locker doors made me realize it would be almost impossible for me to find Dana and Courtney amidst all the noise.

"Okay, meet you here after school," Debbie said, leaving me at the first row of lockers. Because of my ridiculously large braille books and the enormous laptop, I needed more locker space than anyone else. I was given the two lockers on the very end of the row so that they would be easy for me to locate. They stood out like sore thumbs, being the only two with key locks instead of the combination dials everyone else used. I unlocked the door of the bottom locker. Dad had assembled wooden shelves to make it easier for me to organize and locate my books quickly. The top locker was the home for my laptop and lunch bag. After divesting myself of the things I didn't need for my first class, I wandered to where some of my classmates were gathered, including Aviva, who was talking and laughing easily with Jenna.

"Hi, guys," I said. The laughter stopped suddenly.

"Hi, Laurie," Aviva replied with a curious lack of enthusiasm.

"How are you guys doing?"

"Okay," they said together.

"Aviva, I'm so glad you're in my section," I said. "It'll be good to start off the year by taking classes with someone we know, won't it?"

"Yeah," she said in a stilted manner.

"Jenna, where did you go to school, I mean before Oakwood?" I asked.

"You wouldn't have heard of it," she said. "It's this really small school in Sherman Oaks."

"I live in Encino, so I actually may have heard of it," I said.

"Nah, I really don't think so," she said, sounding slightly irritated.

"Well okay. I'm going to head off to English now and find a seat near an outlet, stupid laptop. See you in class."

I couldn't bet my life on this, but I could have sworn that a moment of silence followed as I turned away, followed by whispers and then laughter as easy conversation resumed between them.

❊ ❊ ❊

Dana and Courtney were nowhere to be found at lunch. Once again, the courtyard and locker area were packed, and I found myself wandering from place to place with my insulated lunch bag. I heard Aviva's and Jenna's voices mingled with those of other classmates I had met briefly at the pool party, and I decided to set myself in the patch of sunny courtyard they had claimed for themselves. They said a quick "hello" to me and continued their conversation about our morning classes and the already overwhelming amount of homework. I decided not to join in this time.

History class was with Tasha, a shy-seeming person who I guessed was in her twenties.

"Laurie, are you able to hear me?" she asked, hesitating a little.

"Yep, I'm blind, not deaf," I said, intending to sound cheerful, though the laughter I expected from her and my peers didn't come.

"Oh, I know, Laurie, I just meant that you have your ear piece in."

My laptop, now plugged into an outlet in the very back corner of the classroom, had a synthesized voice telling me what was on the screen. In order to spare the others in my class the sound of its emotionless drone, I plugged a one-sided earphone into it, which allowed me to listen to the teacher and type notes at the same time.

"I'm glad you're able to hear me then," Tasha said with an awkward chuckle. "You just look like a robot all hooked up to your machine like that. I wanted to make sure you're with me."

I blushed, suddenly feeling like the kid with the pocket protector again. It was no wonder the others around me were so uncomfortable in my presence. I was an alien from outer space, a foreigner with some curious customs, and now, Tasha had voiced out loud that I was a robot, unrelatable, inhuman.

❄ ❄ ❄

"So?" Mom said expectantly as I walked through the front door. The aroma of onions browning for dinner in the kitchen was enveloping me and filling the house with warmth.

"So what?" I asked grumpily.

"How was your first day of school?"

"Can we not talk about that right now?"

"Let's have a snack," Mom said. "I bought your favorite Zebra cookies today."

"It kind of sucked," I finally admitted, the pleasant taste of chocolate opening me up a bit. "Well, it didn't completely suck," I said. "I mean, I really like most of my teachers, and it looks like we'll be studying some really interesting stuff."

"That's great!" Mom said.

"It's just that for some reason, whenever I join a conversation, I seem to unintentionally put a stop to it. I don't know what it is about me, but I know I'm not just imagining it."

"It is your first day though, Laurie. You can't expect to make best friends with anyone right away. It takes time."

"I know that. But how do I even begin if they're all afraid to talk to me?"

"Maybe they just don't know what to say. They're not sure what you have in common with them," Mom suggested.

"Then how come they seem more comfortable with everyone else?" I asked.

"It may seem that way to you. Remember, the grass is always greener."

"No, Mom, I'm not imagining this. There really is a difference, I know there is."

❀ ❀ ❀

Bonnie Rothman was a woman in her mid-sixties who had been working for the LA Unified School District for at least thirty years, teaching blind and visually impaired students who were mainstreamed in regular schools. It wasn't very often that a blind kid found herself in uncharted territory like a private school whose grounds had never been touched by a red and white cane before, so I posed a unique challenge. In the end, they provided me with the textbooks I would need in braille and an itinerant teacher who could transcribe my math and French worksheets and tests in braille. In addition, Bonnie was assigned to be my math tutor, as I was still several years behind. Math was my lot in life, the very bane of my existence. Bonnie's job was to get me on the fast track so I would eventually be caught up to my sighted classmates.

When I climbed the stairs to my math class in one of the converted apartments, Bonnie was right behind me. "I'm going to sit in on your class today," she said cheerfully. "I want to see what you all are learning, and where you are. I have a feeling you and I have a lot of catching up to do."

I grimaced. It wasn't enough that I seemed to have the blind cloud following me everywhere, a gigantic backpack full of large braille books, and a big talking laptop, I now had to have a teacher shadowing me as well. I began to wonder if there was any other way I could possibly be different from the other students.

"Good morning, class," said Pat. "I think it's time we get into some basic algebra."

I heard the rasping sound of chalk on the black board where Pat was writing her first problems on the board. She began tapping the board to illustrate her points in the lesson, and I found that I was completely lost.

"Pat," Bonnie chimed in.

"Yes," Pat said, startled by the interruption.

"You're going to have to explain what's on the board because Laurie can't see it."

"Oh, I'm sorry, Laurie," Pat said without hesitation. "I'm explaining basic equations. What I have on the board is x plus 7 equals 14. Then below it, I have 14 minus 7 equals x. In order to figure out what x is, you have to subtract 7 from 14. Do you understand?"

"I think so," I said in a small voice.

"I'll explain it to you later," Bonnie said in what sounded to me like a stage whisper for all the class to hear.

❀   ❀   ❀

My spirits lifted when I heard Dana and Courtney giggling at lunch in the breezeway between a small hallway of classrooms and the auditorium.

"Hi, guys," I said.

"Oh hey Laurie!" Dana said with an enthusiasm that made me smile.

"Is this your favorite lunch spot?" I asked.

"Well yesterday, we sat outside of the music room, but these creepy eighth graders kept staring at us, so we're trying it out here now."

"Ooh, got it," I said. "Mind if I join you?"

Lunch was as pleasant as our time in the pool. Dana and Courtney kept us all in side-splitting fits of laughter as they gave names to each of the eighth-grade boys they were watching from afar.

"Oh, and that one's name is Rufus," Dana said.

"Rufus, how come?" I squealed, clutching my stomach, which was aching from laughing too hard.

"I don't know, he just looks like a Rufus with a bashed in face like a bull dog."

"Ooh, and there goes Bunny," Courtney said in disgust. "Just look at her with her entire midriff showing and her bright purple press on nails."

"No chance of Bunny getting it on with Rufus, huh?" I said. Dana and Courtney giggled.

"Ah, but look at Olivier," Dana said dreamily.

"Who the heck is that?" I asked.

"He's this tall and slender boy with blond hair," Dana cooed. "He just looks French."

The bell ended our lunch break far too soon, and off to French I went.

❈   ❈   ❈

As the school year progressed, I continued to enjoy my classes, all except for math. We studied the Russian Revolution in history while reading *Animal Farm* in English. I was learning basic grammar in French and was struggling my way through algebra. Science was full of labs that my teacher felt were too visual for me to participate in, so she had me write reports on Alexander Flemming who discovered penicillin and Joseph Lister who discovered the antiseptic technique. Dana and Courtney were never in the same spot at lunch, and my heart sank when I realized that they did not make a point of seeking my company. I took to having lunch in Danny's corner, a tree surrounded by a bench outside the music room, named after an Oakwood student who had died.

Bonnie did not come to every math class, but she occasionally made an appearance, often sitting next to me and taking note of the things she'd need to explain to me later, along with the long division and multiplication she was helping me catch up on. We would meet in a tiny room in the back of the library with a desk, a bathroom, and a tiny space heater for the private tutoring sessions. One day as I was packing up, I heard the door to the back room open, and Allison, the high-voiced popular girl in my class whom I had met at the pool party, walked in.

"Laurie?" she said, sounding embarrassed.

"Oh hi, Allison," I said.

"Laurie, let's go, you'll be late for French," Bonnie said, urging me on brusquely.

"See ya," I said to Allison.

"You're not supposed to know about any other kids who get tutored there," Bonnie whispered, as we left the library.

"Why not?" I asked incredulously.

"Your dean told me that we are not to breathe a word about anyone who uses that room. Sometimes, the kids with learning disabilities go in there to take tests so they can have a longer time to finish them. They also get tutored on subjects they're having trouble with. The students and their parents don't want anyone to know about their special needs."

And there it was, the reason students and even some of the

teachers were uncomfortable, why conversations would stop as soon as I approached to join, and why Dana and Courtney, as nice as they were to me, did not seek me out for lunch or for weekends hanging out at the mall. The truth was that my peers were encouraged to hide what made them different. It was something to be ashamed of to be dyslexic or even just to have trouble with a math problem.

I, on the other hand, had the misfortune of having a disability that I could not hide. Allison's reasons for going to the infamous back room could be hidden behind her blond hair, her flirty blue eyes, and her heavily made-up face, while I was forcing everyone to stare my reason in the face every day.

✻ ✻ ✻

The seventh grade had its first dance party on a beautiful night at the end of October. It was held in Stacy Cambridge's huge backyard in Beverly Hills, which was booming with the deep bass of Boyz II Men, Color Me Badd, and Kris Kross. Mom had dropped me off in the midst of kids struggling to be heard over the loud music. It was the pool party all over again, my searching for friendly voices amongst the indistinguishable mess of sound. Dana and Courtney were nowhere to be found.

"Okay ladies and gents," said a cheerful DJ. "Ready for your first ballad? Go find yourselves the cutest dance partner. I'll give you about a minute."

Just like finding a group to work with in English class, finding a dance partner proved difficult as couples began forming around me.

"Yo, David," I called, hearing one of the boys in my section talking to another guy. "Wanna dance?" I asked.

"Well, okay, but don't get the wrong idea," he said.

"Don't flatter yourself," I chuckled. "I actually have taste."

This made David laugh nervously, and I was proud of my quick wit. We danced awkwardly in silence. After a minute, we were growing sweaty and uncomfortable, and the end of "I Can't Let Go" by Mariah Carey couldn't come fast enough.

When Mariah hit her last whistle tones of the song, David squirmed away as if escaping the jaws of a huge whale. Dana's and Courtney's laughter could finally be heard in the break between songs.

"Hey, guys!" I said cheerfully. "Having fun?"

"Yeah," Dana said. "Haven't done as much dancing as you though, Laurie. How was David?"

"A warm body to dance with," I said.

"Ooooh, I think he heard that, he's standing right behind you," Courtney said.

I wheeled around, humiliated, anxiously thinking of things to say to smooth it over.

"Just kidding," Courtney laughed. "You're gullible, aren't you?"

"Don't ever do that again," I said, sighing with relief. "I think you just caused my first gray hair."

"You already have several, didn't you know?" Courtney said, trying to sound innocent.

"Funny," I said. "Very funny."

"I'm going to get punch," Dana said. "Want anything?"

"No thanks," I said. "So, who are you hoping to dance with tonight?" I asked.

There was no answer. I tried again. Still no answer. Dana and Courtney had gone off together, not telling me to follow, not adding me to their evening of whispering about cute guys. I stood there, feeling my heart sink, wondering why they always made a point of finding each other at parties, at lunch, or anywhere else, and would never look for me. As the evening wore on and I danced like an idiot all by myself, my mood worsened. During a short lull when the DJ had evidently taken a bathroom break, I heard Dana and Courtney again. I headed in the direction of their voices.

"Hey again," I said.

"Oh hi, Laurie," they said in unison.

This time, I was ready when their voices began to trail off.

"Wait!" I shouted over the crowd. "I thought we were friends," I said. "I thought we were having a good time at lunch."

Dana and Courtney did not say anything. At first, I thought they had walked away again, but then Dana said, "What's the matter, Laurie?"

"I just don't understand why you keep leaving me behind tonight, and why you never look for me during lunch. I always have to find you."

"Laurie," Courtney said firmly, "it's just that we don't feel like babysitting you all the time."

"Babysitting? Who says you need to babysit me?" Without any warning, my eyes were filling with angry tears.

I hated myself for crying. I was doing what they expected, what they were most afraid of. I was the fragile thing they felt obligated to protect, and they had made me cry. But who wouldn't have cried if they had been told that? What seventh grader wouldn't have been humiliated by Courtney's proclamation?

"Well," Dana began hesitantly. "It's just that we don't always want to have to look out for you all the time, you know what I mean?"

"When have I ever asked you to look out for me, to do anything for me?" I challenged, barely coherent.

"You're asking us to come find you. Don't you think that's making us look out for you?" Courtney helped out Dana.

"Don't you find each other?" I argued. "Isn't that something you do? Is that because you like each other's company, or is it just that you're looking out for each other, and I'd be one too many to be responsible for?"

"It's just different," they said together, as if they had planned it.

As I stood there, crying and shaking with rage now, I realized there was no reasoning with them. Far from forming my own babysitter's club, I had found myself on the outside of one. I was merely an unwanted babysitting client. The middle-school experience I had imagined had turned on me. I let Dana and Courtney walk away, and I counted the minutes until Mom would be there to take me home.

❁　❁　❁

One day in late November, I could tell something was not quite right. Ten minutes after Marty had started her English class, my first period of the day, I heard footsteps entering the room. I found it odd that she didn't introduce her guests, and that she just continued the lesson as if there had been no disturbance. As I walked on to my next class, I had the sneaking suspicion that I was being followed. I was happy to enter the warmth of the kitchen that afternoon when Debbie dropped me off at home. The weather had grown significantly windier, and the sun had decided not to make an appearance lately, which greatly affected my mood. When I sat down at the kitchen table, Mom sat down next to me, serious and concerned.

"Laurie," she said hesitantly.

"What?" I said munching on a piece of apple.

"I got a call from Kim, your dean, about a week ago with some concerns from your teachers."

"What do you mean?" I asked, suddenly alarmed. "My grades on tests and papers are good."

"It's not about your grades," Mom said. "They have a whole list of concerns that have nothing to do with your academic achievements."

My heart fell into my stomach now and was throbbing and pulsing uncomfortably.

"Marty, who loves you by the way and thinks you are the cat's meow, is concerned that kids are not sitting next to you in class. Linda, your history teacher, says you don't seem to be paying attention in class, even though you're doing well on your essays and tests. Madame Tocar is convinced that the reason you're doing so well on your French tests is because you're cheating. And Pat is worried that you're not understanding your math well enough to keep up."

"Is there a single teacher at Oakwood who is not concerned about anything regarding me?" I asked angrily. "For your information, I do not choose to sit alone in class. And of course I'm paying attention in history class. I always get the answers to Linda's questions right. If my French teacher thinks I'm cheating, can she explain how I would look over my shoulder at other people's answers? Pat's the only one who has a valid point. I don't understand algebra worth a damn."

"Laurie, please don't use that language with me. I'm on your side," Mom said firmly. "Anyway, Kim asked if there would be anyone I could recommend, a social worker or someone who knows you, to come in and observe you without you knowing so they can see what it is the teachers are really concerned with. I asked Nancy and Marilyn from the Blind Children's Center to come in. They were there all day today."

My heart was beating loud and fast in my ears now, and my cheeks flushed. I was too paralyzed by hurt and anger to say anything. Mom continued, "Your first class was English today, right? Marty did a group exercise on purpose to show Nancy and Marilyn how you have trouble finding people to work with."

"I don't have any trouble at all," I protested, my voice beginning to shake. "The dumb asses in my class have the problem."

"Then you had your math class, and Bonnie purposely did not come in today so Nancy and Marilyn could see how you follow along with the other kids. They actually said you seemed to be doing just fine, getting answers right, and so forth," Mom said. "Then during science class . . ."

I interrupted, "There was no science class today, at least for me. There was a lab that was too visual for me to be involved in, so Bonnie and I had a math catch-up session."

There was a pause. Mom seemed to be steeling herself for what she was about to say. "There was no lab today, even for the others," she said, faltering a bit. "Nancy and Marilyn used the double period to talk with the kids, to find out what it feels like for them to have you in their class. It was very productive and gave them a good idea of what's going on."

"What did they say about me?" I asked as my eyes began to fill with tears, dreading the worst, but wanting to know once and for all what was actually going on in their heads.

"Some of the girls said that you often try to join their conversations, and it makes them uncomfortable. They say it kind of freaks them out when you just stand there, listening to what they're talking about."

"What am I supposed to do? How else am I supposed to get to know people without doing that? Isn't that what any sighted kid would do?"

"Some of them were saying that you make them uncomfortable because you have to discuss everything, where people are going to sit at lunch, or what they're laughing at. They say that sometimes they don't know where they're going to be every day, every lunch period. They can't always tell you what they're laughing at because the source of it may be within earshot, and your insisting they tell you is just drawing attention to the person."

"All I want to do is find out how to find people since I can't see them, to let them know I want to sit with them. How do I do that without asking since they never bother to look for me? And how can I be part of a conversation if I don't even know what the joke is about?"

"Some of the kids expressed concerns that if they are friendly to you, that you might start to depend on them for your every need."

A sudden rush of horror struck me like a bolt of lightning. I had lunch with Courtney and Dana today. Had Nancy and Marilyn been following me at lunch?

"Then you had lunch," Mom continued, as if she had read my mind. "Nancy and Marilyn were careful to stay out of sight, but they were observing from afar. They said everything seemed to be going fine, and you were all talking and laughing freely. They also planned their visit around a French test, and they of course confirmed that there was absolutely no sign of you cheating."

The meat and tomato sauce simmering on the stove that usually filled me with warmth was now as unpleasant to me as paint fumes, and I was feeling sick.

"Nancy and Marilyn observed some things that they feel might subconsciously be causing some of this discomfort. They notice that you don't dress in the same clothes the other kids wear. At your age, the clothes you wear really matter. Kids are buying their clothes from The Gap these days, and your clothes are looking a little out of date, now that Marilyn and Nancy have drawn my attention to it. That's not your fault. I know you hate clothes shopping, Laurie, but this weekend you and I should take a trip to The

Gap, and get rid of those clothes that are much too young for you. They say perhaps you'd be more relatable if you dressed more like the other kids. They also say that you look down in class while the teachers are talking. They believe this is why Linda feels you're not paying attention. I notice that too, Laurie. When you're deeply engrossed in a story, or in a discussion, your head is down when you're absorbing the information. Sighted people make it a point to visually show the person talking to them that they're paying attention. As for joining a conversation, Nancy and Marilyn are trying to figure out what you could do that would look more visually natural to the other kids. Maybe they feel like you're lurking, when what you're really doing is trying to listen pleasantly. They also noticed that you tend to express yourself more verbally and to come across as more articulate than the other kids. You know, you tend to find words for everything that many kids might use a throw-away bit of body language for. That could be a factor in you unintentionally setting yourself apart. It's not cool for kids to show how smart they are."

"What do you mean?" I said, bewildered and confused.

"Well, Laurie, when you were about a year and a half, I would hand you a stuffed animal, and you would tell me exactly what that stuffed animal was—a dog, a horse, a cat. When Brian picked up a stuffed animal, he often just called it a dog. Every four-legged animal he saw was a dog. When Brian wanted something, he could just point, but you needed to find verbal labels for everything, because you couldn't just show us visually what you wanted. Your verbal development was so quick because of that. You were so cute when you were still in your high chair, speaking to me in full sentences. Even now, kids your age are more comfortable when they don't have to talk as much, when they can just use visual cues, and that's why you're often not on the same wavelength. You shouldn't worry about that so much. You should be proud to be the intelligent, articulate person that you are. Maybe what would help is just spending time listening more, and talking less."

So there it was. I was the big freak of the school, imposing my strange ways upon the innocent teachers and students who did not ask for their harmonious lives to be intruded upon. It wasn't enough that I displayed my blindness in the form of my out-of-date clothes, my tapping cane, and my lack of eye contact, now I was also sending a message to the kids in my class that it was okay to lie, sneak up on me, and talk about me behind my back.

I got up from the kitchen table without saying another word. I knew that if I tried to speak, the tears would come. I walked straight to my room and began emptying the contents of my backpack on the bed, knowing full well that I wouldn't be able to concentrate on homework. Several thoughts in a row came into my head. Did the teachers and my peers at Oakwood feel like it wasn't a good idea to have me there? Even though I was doing well in my classes, was I failing them and my parents who expected me to thrive there? Would Kim or anyone else recommend that I transfer to another school? Was I really that different than the other kids, or were the teachers finding certain things odd about me that they wouldn't even question in a sighted student? It was as if I were sinking, working so hard to keep up, to prove myself, but a stronger current, that of the student's and teacher's discomfort around me was pulling me under, about to cause me to wipe out, to be lost at sea forever.

* * *

Casa Vega is a restaurant that my parents frequented well before Brian and I were born. As of late, it had become the place Brian and I would go on the weekends to catch up on life, with him telling me about his freshman year of college, and with me inevitably bursting into tears whenever Brian would ask, "How are you?"

The Saturday night following the visit from Nancy and Marilyn was no exception.

"Oh no, you're not going to cry on me again, are you?" Brian asked, reaching for my hand.

I laughed through my tears, slightly embarrassed. "Brian," I said. "Nancy and Marilyn say I freak the kids out when I try to join their conversations. What's wrong with me? Am I really that obviously blind or something?"

Brian thought for a minute before saying, "Well, one thing you have never done, because you've never seen other people do it, is nod your head. Sometimes if you're just standing there listening, it can look like you're not participating in the conversation. People will often nod to acknowledge something someone said."

"Why didn't anyone tell me this before?" I moaned, covering my face in horror. "I've been looking like a dork all along, and you and Mom never told me?"

"Laurie, you know we've been totally honest with you, like the times we remind you to face the person you're talking to. It's just that there are so many visual things that are so hard to explain. You also get used to a person's mannerisms, you know what I mean? I'm so used to you not nodding, but I can tell that you're listening to me. I know you so well, but the kids in your class don't, that's all."

"Show me how to nod," I said excitedly, brushing tears away from my eyes, and sitting up straight, ready for the nodding lesson.

"Okay, so a nod is kind of like a head movement back and forth."

I began to slowly move my head all the way forward and all the way back. Brian laughed so hard that it took him a few minutes to catch his breath. I began to laugh equally as hard. Brian's laugh was always contagious, and I'd do anything I could to make him laugh just so I could hear it.

"Okay, first of all," he said, trying to regain composure, "you don't move your head all the way back and all the way forward. You look like you're in a heavy metal concert. You just move it slightly back and forth."

I attempted a nod again.

"Okay, that's much better, but don't do it that slowly. Try it faster. Yeah, that's better. Now do it a few times, as if you're saying 'yeah, yeah, yeah' with your head, not just one 'yyyyyyeeeee-aaaaah.' Yeah! That's it! You're nodding."

"Okay, Bri, try talking to me now, and I'll try nodding, and you can tell me if it looks right."

Brian began to tell me about his very dark roommate who used gargoyles to decorate their room, which clashed with the colorful Disney posters Brian tacked on his side of the room.

"Okay, you're nodding way too much," Brian laughed again. "You're making me feel like you want me to get on with my story already. Just nod when you would normally say, 'Uh-uh' or 'mmhmm?' Yeah, that's better. Another bit of body language that you miss out on is shrugging. That's the same idea as nodding, but it's a casual, nonchalant 'I dunno' that you use only sometimes."

Brian and I continued to laugh through dinner as I butchered the shrug, shaking my entire body too much instead of my shoulders. Shaking my head "no" proved less clownish, as I was starting to catch onto these subtleties.

I was on a mission, well on my way to finding a window display that would let the sighted world around me know who I was. It was as if Brian was finally teaching me a language whose country I had inhabited all along, and I was eager to become fluent in it as soon as I could.

Grey

I love being dressed in grey.
It makes me feel cool, hip, not too girly,
more handsome than beautiful.
I know grey can be a sign of aging,
and I imagine it to be attractive on others
who sport it like a medal for reaching
a certain place of importance in life,
a sign of wisdom and experience.
Grey is the limbo between the black I experience
when there is no light in the sky at night
and the white light I can see with my limited
  retina.
When the sunlight is obscured by heavy rain
  clouds,
I can tell, and it dictates my mood.

Kissing Fate

The blind friends I had were few and far between. Kirstin, my best friend from Topeka Drive Elementary, and Alicia, who I had been so close with at Blend, were the only two, though neither of them were completely blind. I was afraid that having too many blind friends would force me into a box I didn't want to be placed in.

To me, being "too blind" was something to be embarrassed about. My sighted friends somehow made me feel more normal and did not force me to be reminded of all the things that made me different. So when Mom, who was heartbroken by my painful social struggles at Oakwood, suggested I try sleep-away camp for the blind for two weeks in the summer before eighth grade, I protested vehemently.

"I don't want to go to a camp for blind people," I shouted.

"I think there must be other blind kids your age who are going through the same kinds of things, and you might meet people that are like you."

Had the loved ones who once thought I was so different from

other blind kids changed their minds since I failed to make friends at Oakwood? Were they having second thoughts and thinking the only place I could be happy was in some institution with people supposedly like me?

❋ ❋ ❋

"I'm so mad at my mom today," I told Kirstin on the phone that night. "She said I should go to Camp Bloomfield this summer."

"What's so bad about that?" Kirstin asked.

"She thinks that the only way to solve my problems is to hang out with a bunch of blind people."

"You know my friend Maya, the one I told you about in my English class?" Kirstin said. "She went to Camp Bloomfield last summer, and she was trying to convince me to go some time. Maya is really cool, and I actually thought about going."

"If you go, then maybe I'll go too," I said.

❋ ❋ ❋

Camp Bloomfield, set in the mountains of Malibu, is a rustic place with a classic sleep-away camp setting. Hilly dirt paths lead to the campfire pit, wooden cabins, large dining hall, and stables, which housed the horses Kirstin and I couldn't wait to ride. When Mom dropped me off, I noticed that the air was more pure, and the smell of being in the woods brought me back to memories of Lake Tahoe.

Mom had been right. Kirstin and I began making fast and close friends with girls like us, some with a bit of vision like Kirstin and others who had no vision at all like me. There was nothing embarrassing about the way I felt around them. We talked about guys, gossiped about couples forming around us, and laughed heartily about ongoing inside jokes. There was Toni who would talk to me in whispers about her boy problems, Carla who wanted to be an opera singer like me, Anja with the wicked sense of humor who would casually take out her prosthetic eyes to freak out the sighted counselors, and many others whose personalities and awareness about normal teenage life uplifted me about my own identity as a blind person. Though we all hailed from different parts of the country, Toni being from Missouri, and Carla from Vegas, we stayed close during the year through frequent phone calls and taped letters, which allowed us to hear each other's voices.

"See, I told you," Mom said when I announced that I wanted to go back for a second and then a third summer. "I knew you would have a great time."

❋ ❋ ❋

Jessie Smith was an athletic eighteen-year-old who had lived with partial sight for most of his life. He lost his remaining sight completely after a surgery on a detached retina, but he continued to be his school's best shot-putter. Jessie told me all of this at the ice-cream social that was held by the pool on the second night of camp. Kirstin and I had run across Jessie and his friend Brandon briefly, and we had most definitely heard about the romances they had with various girls at camp the previous two summers we were there.

"You're Laurie, right?" said the voice of a guy who, I could tell, had become an expert at charming the ladies.

"Yeah, how did you know?" I asked.

"I always remember the voice of a pretty girl," Jessie said.

Kirstin and I had steered clear of the infamous "players of Camp Bloomfield" the two previous summers, but we were fifteen now, and ready for a little adventure.

"Thank you," I said, smiling at him.

"So how's life been treating you?" Jessie asked.

"It's been going well," I said. "It's good to be back here again."

"I'm a veteran of this place. Been coming here for five years now," Jessie told me.

Brandon was taking a great interest in Kirstin, and the two of them joined us on the ground near the water's edge. There was a gentle summer breeze caressing our faces, and the balmy night made the feeling of being noticed and flirted with exciting.

There's something peculiar about summer camp that cuts the period of small talk short and leads people into conversations about one's deepest emotions and desires. As the night wore on, and UB40's cover of "Can't Help Falling In Love" played on speakers all around us, Jessie and I found ourselves exchanging life stories, and our counselors were rounding us up to take us back to our cabins all too soon.

✿ ✿ ✿

"So?" Kirstin whispered quietly as we huddled in the corner between the cubbies and our bunk beds to exchange details about each other's evening.

"Well, he's really sweet," I told her.

"He is totally into you."

"And Brandon is very into you. Do you like him?"

"I think so," Kirstin said, her voice glowing. "He said he's going to come find me at lunch tomorrow."

"That is so cool. I'm so happy for you!" I said, giving her a hug.

✦ ✦ ✦

Horseback riding, swimming, and other camp activities kept us busy during the day and separated from the groups of boys whose schedules never seemed to coincide with ours. Jessie and Brandon found Kirstin and me every night during the hour break between dinner and the time for us to sing songs in front of a campfire. Jessie had started putting his arm around me and whispering, his lips brushing my ear.

"Don't you just hate that we have no privacy?" Kirstin vented one night. "I mean, there's no time for us to really hang out with Jessie and Brandon."

"I know," I said, secretly thankful that we weren't left alone, fearing what could happen.

"I think Brandon is getting very close to kissing me, but there never seems to be a good time."

"I don't know, he and Jessie seemed to find time with their girlfriends before," I said.

✦ ✦ ✦

Three days before the end of camp, our counselors announced that there would be a dance in the dining hall, and that lights out would be at midnight instead of 10:00. Jessie and Brandon met us at the refreshment table, and after drinking cups of punch, they pulled us into the large empty space where the meal tables had previously been. After several fast songs, a Celine Dion ballad was played, and Jessie pulled me in closer.

"You know I really like you, don't you?" he whispered in a low voice.

Tiny insects seemed to be stirring inside my body. As he held me close in a slow dance, he began kissing my neck softly. My heart began to beat nervously. Something felt strange. Why was I so uneasy? Perhaps romance took a while to grow on a girl, and I just needed a chance to get used to it.

I was relieved when a fast song followed the ballad, and Kirstin and Brandon, who were in very good spirits, came to talk with us.

"We made out!" Kirstin whispered into my ear. I gasped.

"How was it?"

"Totally amazing. Did Jessie kiss you?"

"Kind of," I said.

"Isn't it just great?"

"Yeah," I said, now knowing that I would have to let Jessie kiss me, I mean really kiss me tonight, and I was going to have to like it.

"Okay, last dance of the night, ladies and gents," said the cheerful voice of the DJ. Here's 'Love Is' by Vanessa Williams."

Jessie pulled me into a slow dance position again, and I let my body move with his. My heart was beating fast. He was so much bigger than me, and any other girl would have probably felt safe, protected in those strong, muscular arms. He smelled good, the Ralph Lauren cologne blending sensuously with the scent of the night air that was wafting into the dining hall.

"That's a cologne I would love to wear," I caught myself thinking.

"Come here," he said. A cool breeze and the fragrant summer air was blowing in gently from outside. Jessie was leading me in the direction of the door. Still holding me close, he walked me outside, not stopping until we were several paces away from the din of the dance. He began rubbing my back gently and I felt myself shaking. And then, as if in slow motion, I felt his hands pulling my face towards his. I felt my body tense with the anticipation of one who was about to get a shot, and then he was kissing me.

I had always heard the girls in my class talk about kissing. Conversations about it made me think that kissing was supposed to be the magical peak at the end of a big crescendo of anticipation. The music in my head resembled the kind you hear in a movie just as something scary is about to happen. The kiss itself wasn't bad, but something about being in Jessie's muscular arms didn't feel right. Adults were always warning us not to have sex too early, not only because of the danger of getting pregnant, but because of the emotions behind it they felt kids my age weren't ready for. Was I uneasy because I wasn't ready, or because of inexperience? Jessie and Brandon did not have any time alone with us after the dance, putting our kissing to an end, and I allowed myself to push the nagging feeling of discomfort to the back of my mind.

❋ ❋ ❋

"You kissed a guy?" Dana and Courtney gasped as I relayed the events of my summer to them when we had returned to school for the first day of tenth grade. "Wow, you're so lucky, Laurie. What did it feel like?"

"I think it felt nice," I said.

"You think?" Courtney said. "Hey, Dana and I haven't kissed anyone yet, so at least give us details about how it happened to you."

I secretly enjoyed the feeling of having more experience than Dana and Courtney with guys. I knew they wanted boyfriends more than almost anything else, and yet I who was blind, I who they had felt in some way was too different from them, had kissed a boy before they did.

❋ ❋ ❋

I never saw Jessie again after our two weeks together, but it was nice to know that not all the guys in the world thought I was a freak like the ones at Oakwood who took care to avoid any possibility of being alone with me. I wondered, though, if most girls felt the same feeling of uncertainty and unease whenever they were alone with their boyfriends. Several months later, the beginnings of an answer to my inner mystery presented itself to me.

I was at my junior prom. I was dancing with my date. I wore a black tuxedo, which made me feel sleek and handsome as I held the petite girl closer to me. She wore a silky slip dress that clung tightly to her slight form. Her hair fell long and wavy down her back. I embraced her more tightly still, and remembering how Jessie had pulled my face towards his, I took her porcelain smooth face toward mine and began kissing her lips tenderly. They felt plump and soft, and I didn't want to stop. I just kept pulling her closer, dancing with her, kissing her, feeling the magic I knew I was supposed to feel. I felt her breathing deeply in my arms, and neither of us were aware of the dance floor full of teenagers and chaperones around us. Nobody intruded, and we stayed there in our own little world, frozen in a dance that had just changed my life.

I awoke with a start. I was breathing hard, tangled in a mess of sheets and blankets. What had just happened? Had it really been a dream? She had felt so vivid, and the tingles I had felt in my dream were still coursing through me. But I had never liked girls, not Dana and Courtney, not my friends from Camp Bloomfield. The thought of Dana and Courtney filled me with terror. What would they do if they knew I had a dream about making out with a girl? They would think I liked them in that way and would stop hanging out with me all together. I could never tell them. But the feeling, that wonderful harmonious dream still pulsed inside of me in tandem with my rapidly beating heart, and I closed my eyes, holding onto it, holding onto her, and I let the dream turn into a daydream. Something that had been dormant all this time was awakened inside of me, and though I did not know it at the time, there was another part of my identity I would later have to explore.

Green

Green is the rustling of the wind in the trees,
the pungent smell of freshly cut grass.
It is the sound of a young man or young woman's
voice,
still innocent, full of energy, bursting with life and
ideas.

Green is that feeling when I'm on a camping trip
in the forest,
surrounded by nature alone,
and the evergreens gently brush my arms,
like the fingers of the most nurturing person.

Green is the invigorating, distinctive taste of mint.
It's the color of the summer I spent in Tanglewood,
Massachusetts.

Tanglewood

The Tanglewood Estate in the Berkshires is home to the Boston Symphony Orchestra, as well as classical music training programs for high school and college students. In my quest to find musical ways to spend my summer, I had found Tanglewood, sent in an application tape, and received an acceptance letter two months before the program started during my sophomore year.

There's nothing quite like setting foot on the Tanglewood campus. It is green and bursting with life from the different varieties of trees and the plush green lawn in front of the rustic amphitheater-like shed. Music could be heard from all directions, as though the very trees themselves were exuding it like oxygen. The doors of barns converted into rehearsal rooms stood open, letting the sounds of violins, flutes, clarinets, French horns, and men's and women's voices echo magically through the place. I myself felt green that summer, bursting with newfound emotions triggered by Beethoven's *Egmont Overture* played by the Boston Symphony, Berlioz' *Nuites d'Ete* sung by Jessye Norman, and by hearing Yo-Yo Ma and Itzhak Perlman, not on a recording, but in person.

My heart sank during the first few days when I discovered that the others in my program seemed almost as apprehensive of me as my Oakwood peers. Little cliques were starting to form, and I feared that my six weeks away from home would be spent with me relegated outside of all of them. At the end of that first week, however, something happened to change my destiny that summer. An informal recital was scheduled in which each of us had to sing a song or aria of our choice in front of each other and the faculty. I sang an aria from Mozart's *The Marriage of Figaro*, and suddenly everyone around me began to behave differently, as if the Laurie they had met the first day was totally different from the Laurie who had just sung for them. Perhaps all the things I didn't convey through the body language they were used to surfaced in my voice that day, or perhaps they felt that if I were capable of singing well, then I must likely be a normal person. Friendships, deep as the music we were sharing together, began to form. I was now walking the three-mile stretch of woods from our dorms to the Tanglewood grounds with the groups I had thought formed without me, and together, we'd watch the regular concert-goers spreading out on the grass, eating fancy cheeses and tasting wine before the concert. The friendships grew every time the sun set, and the Boston Symphony would begin to take us through a series of magical moments that brought us closer together. Night after night, we would relive those moments in one of our dorm rooms, well after lights out. And it was then that the real conversations would begin.

"Hey Laurie, I've never told anyone this before, but I think I'm bisexual," Kelly whispered to me.

"Really?" I said, sitting up straighter on Kelly's bed. "How can you tell?"

"I kissed a girl, I mean, really kissed a girl."

Something inside me rose up from a place I never knew existed, a combination of envy and burning desire I did not comprehend.

"What did it feel like?" I asked hungrily.

"Like something only two women can experience together."

I closed my eyes, and I knew instinctively what Kelly must have been talking about. It was something tender, perfectly in sync, a confluence of music and nature just like Tanglewood concerts on the lawn.

"I had a dream once," I said, recounting the dream about the girl I had taken in my arms at the prom. We sat in silence for a moment before I whispered, "And I wished it had been real."

After getting three or four hours of sleep, we'd wake up early for music theory class and voice lessons with recent Juilliard or Boston University graduates with polished beautiful voices who we wanted to become in four or five years. We spent our afternoons in choir rehearsals, at which time a spontaneous afternoon storm would dump buckets of rain over Lenox, Massachusetts, giving us some relief from the intense heat and humidity. The barn's live acoustics would make the powerful sound of our choir of voices ring, and the breeze brought us the smell of fresh rain and New England air. It was summer at its best, full of unbridled adolescent enthusiasm.

After a day of rehearsals, there were chats with Candace—who liked English literature and movies as much as I did—over ginger muffins in a quaint coffee shop, or uncontrollable laughter with Tyler Jones, the blond-haired, blue-eyed tenor with the irresistible, sweet voice, in Bev's Ice Cream, or heart-to-hearts with the sexuality-exploring Kelly in her room before dinner time.

The culminating project for the voice students was to perform a concert of opera scenes. I had been assigned to play the role of Dido in the last scene of *Dido and Aeneas* by Henry Purcell, the love story about Dido, Queen of Carthage, and Aeneas, the Trojan hero. In the last scene, Dido is told that Aneas must leave her and, filled with grief, she kills herself. As she dies, she sings the famous aria known as "Dido's Lament" in which she asks her subjects to remember the strong leader she was when she was alive, not the reason she died. In the staging, I was carried off stage by a small choir of admiring subjects who just happened to be the close friends I made that summer. As they sang the words of grief at losing their beloved queen, the sad four-part harmony pierced me. It wasn't just my friends' acting that I sensed. I also felt their love, and I wondered if the friendships I was missing out on in high school were as deep as the ones I could feel in the arms and voices of my fellow singers.

After our bows and the enthusiastic applause, we gathered in a tearful huddle.

"It really felt like you were Dido," Kelly said. "I'm just so glad you didn't really die."

All too soon, the last day arrived, and the program ended in another recital in which we all sang the pieces our voice teachers had assigned and worked on with us. As all fifty of us gathered for our final bow, we made a spontaneous decision to sing Bernstein's "Make Our Garden Grow" from *Candide*, which we had sung as a choir that summer. It became our anthem. Our pianist and coach began to play the song for us, and we ended the program as one unified voice. I did not make it through the song. My body was overtaken by a fit of tears I could not hold back. Suddenly, I was being pulled into a group hug, and the wet cheeks I felt pressing against mine told me that I was far from being the only one crying.

"This is not good-bye," Kelly said.

"We'll see each other again," Tyler said.

"I promise to write letters," sobbed Candace.

❀ ❀ ❀

It was the hardest thing in the world to go back to reality in the fall and return to school. I was invisible again as the girls in my class around me enthusiastically hugged each other. It was now my junior year. I had been at Oakwood five years, and I had grown no closer to my peers. Yet lifelong friendships seemed to form in just six weeks during my summer at Tanglewood. As the fall set in, the ache for my friends and for the music seemed to weigh on me more and more like an impenetrable fog.

"Laurie, I think I found something that might cheer you up," Mom, who had been worried about my sadness that hadn't lifted, told me one day. "There's a competition called the LA Music Center Spotlight Awards. It's a competition for high school students excelling in one of several categories, classical or modern dance, classical and jazz instrumental, and classical and pop/musical theater voice. The prize is $5,000 and the opportunity to sing in the final round at the Dorothy Chandler Pavilion."

I had seen many LA Opera productions at the Dorothy Chandler with Mom, soon after Liz began giving me arias to sing. It had felt like such a grand place with a stage that could transform into different villages or countries, one that could take you back in time as the orchestra played everything from Mozart to Puccini. It was hard for me to fathom the possibility of performing on that very stage.

"How do I apply?" I asked.

"There's a live audition at the music center in October."

"Okay, I'll do it."

The auditions took place in one of the LA Music Center's rehearsal rooms, a large space conducive to dancing and blocking scenes. For the purpose of auditions, a row of chairs had been set where a panel of judges sat facing each singer as he or she performed.

"My name is Laurie Rubin, and I will be singing 'Juliet's Waltz' by Gounod," I announced, and then I proceeded to sing the florid aria in the opera *Romeo and Juliet* in which Juliet appears for her first time in public. My legs felt shaky and my voice tremulous. I could hear the judges scribbling furiously on paper, no doubt writing about every single vocal flaw.

"I don't think I made it," I said sadly after leaving the audition room.

"Why do you say that?" Mom asked.

"Because I sucked."

Two months went by with no word from the Spotlight Awards. Then, on the first day of winter break, Mom shouted from her office,

"You got the letter!" I ran to meet her as she tore the envelope open.

"Dear Ms. Rubin," read the letter. "Congratulations, you have been selected to be one of our ten semifinalists. We had over two hundred applicants in the category of classical voice from all over Southern California, and we are delighted that you will be continuing into the next round of the competition.

"The second round of auditions includes a master class, which all semifinalists are expected to attend, given by LA Opera pianist and coach, David Anglin, in which he will work with each of you on your audition arias. We will hold auditions on the following day. The audition weekend will take place in February, and you will receive further notice when the dates have been finalized."

My next several voice lessons were spent polishing my performance of "Juliet's Waltz," with Liz trying to get me to finesse every single note.

"You didn't prepare well enough for that high note," she would say. "Remember, those are your money notes, your competition winning notes."

January seemed to drag on with the anticipation of the semifinal round. The prospect of singing on stage at the Dorothy Chandler Pavilion was closer now. It felt as though it were being dangled in front of me, and all I had to do was conquer the fierce dragon to procure the treasure. Each day that brought me closer to the next audition made me grow more nervous.

Finally, the audition weekend had arrived, and I was back in the rehearsal room where the preliminary auditions had taken place. The ten of us sat in the two rows of chairs with our parents, anxiously waiting for our master class teacher for the day.

"This is so nerve-wracking," said the tenor sitting next to me. "Do you do a lot of competitions?"

"No, this is my first one," I said. "You?"

"I've done a few, and it never gets any easier."

"Hello, everyone," said a deep, authoritative voice. "As you know, I am a voice coach, and I have a lot of experience working with professional singers. You all are very talented aspiring professionals, and congratulations to you for making it this far in the competition. How many of you have participated in a master class before?"

I had sung in several master classes at Tanglewood and had been an audience member at many others. Every Friday morning, we were asked to dress up in our audition best and work with successful musicians, singers, conductors, and coaches who were all there to perform or to have some other important role in the Tanglewood Music Festival.

"Ah, I see about three or four of you have done these before. Well, a master class is an opportunity for a group of singers to come together in order to work with someone in the field. Each of you will perform an aria, and then we'll have a few minutes to work on it together. Your time up here will greatly benefit every-one else, and we have enough time for everyone."

When each semifinalist got up to sing, I felt like I was home again. The voices were those of kids who had evidently been studying with voice teachers, and so many of them sang pieces that I associated with my friends who had performed them that past summer at Tanglewood.

"Make sure as soon as you get on stage to be in character," David advised, stopping a soprano before one phrase.

I was the third person to go.

"Did anyone ever tell you that you might be a mezzo?" David asked.

"They say I'm too young to tell," I said.

"Well, from what I'm hearing, your voice may do even better in some of the mezzo roles. You sing this aria well, but I really think you should look into some Rossini and Handel mezzo arias. Even Stefano's aria from this same opera would be better for you."

My heart sank. Did this mean I had no chance of winning the competition? Would the judges think I had not been prudent in my choice of aria?

"You sounded awesome," said Danielle, a girl with a ringing high voice, mature beyond her years.

"You, too!" I said. "How do you get your high notes to sound so full?"

"You have good high notes, too," she put her hand on my shoulder.

"Not like yours."

My pounding heart and nervous stomach woke me early the

next morning. The audition wasn't until that evening, so I had the whole day to stew in my nerves. I had adopted the tradition of warming up in the shower, letting the steam help loosen the cocoon of morning phlegm around my voice. I would turn into a prune under the water, oblivious to time and everything else as I attempted to perfect the high notes I worked on with Liz.

"Laurie, you have to eat something," Mom begged, as I sat down at the kitchen table before putting on my audition clothes.

"But I feel like I'm going to throw up."

"You are not going to throw up. You're just nervous."

After choking down a half a bagel and some grapes, I changed, and Mom drove me through downtown traffic to the music center.

"Hi, Laurie!" said the tenor who had sat next to me at the master class as we entered the waiting area full of quiet, nervous singers. We could hear the voices of those in the room auditioning, and their voices shimmered as they resounded through the echoing hallway.

"I don't think I told you my name," the tenor said, "It's Nova."

Nova's social energy seemed to be contagious, and the waiting area grew louder, with everyone introducing themselves and letting out little shrieks of anxiety when it was their turn to enter the audition room.

"Good luck," we all shouted. And far too soon, it was my turn.

"Good afternoon," I said in a composed voice that I hoped would calm me down. "My name is Laurie Rubin, and I will be singing 'Juliet's Waltz'."

The aria began with a lead-into a high note and a chromatic

scale down, already giving the judge a sense of whether or I could handle some impressive vocal acrobatics or showing painfully that there was room for growth. It went reasonably well. I continued through the aria smoothly for several measures. Then through the exclamations of "ah" "ah" "ah," I found myself running out of air, not a dire emergency but a disappointment nevertheless as I had done that better in the past. Then I hit a series of high G's that came out nicer and more voluptuous than usual, and before I knew it, it was time for me to hit the high C, the climactic note of the aria that, if done well, would cause a chorus of "Brava!" from the audience who had gone to see the opera that night. It could have been better, could have crescendoed in a more exciting way, but it was decent, far from painful.

"Thank you, Ms. Rubin, that was lovely," said one of the women judges.

"Oh my gosh, Laurie, that was soooo awesome," said Christian, the one baritone competing.

"Yeah, that was cool, now I'm nervous," said Nicole, a tall soprano with an impressive, big voice.

"I'm equally nervous after having heard you guys," I said.

It was fun to be in friendly conversation with the people I was competing against, and the easy chatter loosened the tight grip the nerves had on my stomach muscles.

"My gosh, when is the waiting going to be over already?" Nova groaned. "I hate this part."

"Hey, at least you're not last," Nicole said. "Look at poor Danielle over there who has been waiting to sing this whole afternoon."

Another half hour later, Barbara Haig, the competition coordinator, ushered us into a formal-looking room.

"This is probably where all the important people go to schmooze with Domingo," Christian said.

"I know, don't you kind of feel special?" Nicole said, her voice changing direction as she turned to glance at the spread of cheeses and gourmet-looking cookies. The room smelled of expensive perfume, no doubt from its most recent occupants, and the carpet was thick, making our high heels sink an inch or two every time we took a step.

"Too bad we're not old enough to drink," Danielle said. "A glass of wine might make the waiting more bearable." She gasped suddenly. "Here they are."

The room fell silent as the four judges entered the room. We knew the big announcement about who would make it to the final round would be made within minutes.

"Hello, everyone," said Barbara's voice, immediately silencing the group of semifinalists and our parents. "I'd like to start by congratulating all ten of you for making it this far. You must know by now how incredibly talented and accomplished you all are."

She paused and everyone clapped.

"I'd also like to sincerely thank the parents for nurturing the beautiful voices of these incredible young men and women. They couldn't do what they do so well without your support and investment in their hard work."

More applause.

"Before I announce our two finalists, I would like to quickly tell you about the Spotlight Awards Ceremony in April, which our two selected finalists from today will participate in. As you know, the event will take place at the Dorothy Chandler Pavilion, and finalists from several other performing arts categories will participate. The evening is a special celebration for you, and it is extremely well attended. We've had celebrities at the event as audience members and as MCs. We ask all finalists to dress in formal concert attire. This is your night to shine."

An almost imperceptible wave of energy swept through the room, all of us coveting the opportunity, knowing that only two of us would get it.

"After all finalists have performed, our MC will read the results from a new panel of judges and will announce the winner and runner-up in each category."

Nova fidgeted next to me through Barbara's speech, and my heart pounded harder than I knew humanly possible. There was a pause, and we knew the next words out of Barbara's mouth would be the names of two people in the room. My heart obligingly played the anticipatory drum roll.

"Our first finalist is Corinne Vashigian."

A soprano across the room shrieked in disbelief as we applauded for her, wondering which one of us would be called to fill the second spot.

"Our second finalist is Danielle de Niese."

The sinking feeling in my heart was immediate, as though it had physically plummeted several feet. But I continued to clap, partly thrilled for Danielle and Corinne and hoping that cheering for them would mask the hollow feeling inside me.

Corinne sobbed uncontrollably into her mother's shirt. "I don't believe it!" she gasped.

Danielle remained composed, graciously accepting everyone's congratulations.

"You deserve it," I said, giving her a hug.

"So did you," she whispered. I smiled at her and fought a lump in my throat.

"Hey Laurie, we must keep in touch," Nova said.

"Yeah," echoed Christian and Nicole.

Their enthusiasm about exchanging numbers cheered me up considerably, and I turned to leave with three pieces of scrap paper in my hand.

"Laurie," said a woman's voice just as I took my mom's arm to walk out the door of the reception room.

"I'm Patricia, one of the judges. Just wanted to say that you were wonderful, and it was very hard to make that decision today."

"Thank you," I said.

As Mom and I pulled out of the parking lot, tears streamed down my face. Music had been the thing that welcomed me with open arms, pulling me into a world of deep emotions and friendships. It was something I knew I was good at, and I was one of the top high-school singers in the country, according to Tanglewood's acceptance letter. Yet tonight, music had betrayed me, casting me aside after bringing me so close to a dream come true.

"Laurie, you did great tonight," Mom consoled. "That's all that really matters."

"Not good enough to make the finals," I sniffed.

"Wait a second. Everyone has to deal with rejection some time. It's just a part of life. Even the most famous opera singers have not gotten every role they wanted. And there are seven other people who are probably driving home now, feeling as terribly as you do."

"But now I only have one more shot," I said. "What if I don't make it next year either?"

"You can't worry about that. It's out of your control. The only thing you can do is keep studying hard and audition again next year."

❋ ❋ ❋

The Spotlight Awards loomed over me like a black cloud for the next several days. I did not sing around the house the way I usually did when coming home from school. However, past disappointment from being denied the middle and high school social life I had been hoping for showed me resilience, and it had taught me how to look deeper to find happiness. That's how I had found music in the first place. In less than a week, the black cloud began to dissolve, and as always happens after a storm, everything seemed brighter and I was filled with a sense of renewal. Mom had been right, there was always next year, and this time, I could be more prepared.

I began working in earnest on improving my breathing techniques, strengthening the foundation of air that supported my voice. I took the time to do exercises I had previously abandoned because they were tedious, slowing down fast passages of coloratura and gradually picking up speed, which helped me bring out and clarify all the notes. I began removing the consonants in legato parts of arias to make them as smooth as a musical phrase played by a violin, and I slowly added the consonants back in when my muscles began to respond.

Suddenly and miraculously, my school social life began to improve. In March, the annual Oakwood Arts Festival, our fancy word for a talent show, was held in the auditorium. As I waited backstage for my turn to go on and sing an Indigo Girls song while accompanying myself on the piano, I heard an unmistakably good oboist playing scales. Oakwood was small, and I was sure I'd have known if there was someone there who, like me, was interested in classical music. I began to walk toward the sound.

"Hey," I said. "Sorry to interrupt."

"No please, interrupt away," said an enthusiastic male voice that showed all signs of going through puberty.

"So, are you and I the only two classical musicians at Oakwood, or are there even more of us hiding somewhere?"

"Hey, you too? What do you play?"

"I play the voice," I said.

His laugh at my little joke told me immediately that we were instant friends. "As far as I know, we are the only two."

"Only two what," said another younger voice, this time belonging to a girl.

"This is Sarah. I'm Aaron. We're both in eighth grade."

"Oh my gosh, you're Laurie Rubin, aren't you?" Sarah said. "I have to hug you. I love your singing!"

"Thanks," I squeaked, as Sarah pulled me into a nearly rib-crushing hug.

"I heard you in the chorus in the winter concert, and you sang that one solo. I sing, too."

"And then there were three," I said.

"Laurie, you're up," said Larry, my English teacher who also doubled as the enthusiastic Arts Festival chairperson.

"Wow, you play the piano, too?" Sarah said.

"Yeah, and she can belt," Aaron said.

"No, I really can't," I said. "I just like the Indigo Girls, so I fake it sometimes."

Aaron and Sarah took to finding me on the bench in the courtyard at lunchtime every day, and at long last, I was beginning to know the feeling of having friends at school. It didn't matter to me that we were an unconventional bunch, certainly one you wouldn't find in any Babysitter's Club book. I knew it was never cool to befriend people three grades behind you and three years younger, but then again, neither was liking Mozart.

During one particular lunch period when Sarah and I decided to loudly serenade the groups of our classmates around us with an operatic rendition of "It's a Small World," a seventh grader named Sadie approached us, asking if she could join our noisy trio.

"Sure, have a seat," Aaron said.

"Are you that much of a masochist to want to have your ears blown out by our singing?" I asked.

"Anyone who is willing to piss off the popular girls in every grade is my friend," Sadie said. "Besides, you guys just seem much more friendly than anyone in my class."

"I hear it's a cliquey one," I said.

"Yeah," Sadie said, and I immediately recognized the familiar sadness in her voice.

"Hey, welcome to my world. I have no friends in my grade."

"Really?" she said, her voice perking up. "But you seem too cool not to have friends."

My heart swelled. Nobody at Oakwood had ever called me cool before.

I began to identify more and more with Sadie. I witnessed the way she was being overlooked by the other seventh graders and realized that whether blindness was the catalyst for that kind of treatment or simply just marching to the beat of your own drummer, it could happen to anybody. Sadie had an artistic nature and a mind that worked differently than those of the other kids. It was nice to be in good company with her, and to be there for her as someone who had gone through teenage isolation before. It was she who asked me to get together outside of school first.

"My parents are going out tonight, and they said I could have a sleep-over," she said shyly on the phone.

Sadie and her dad, Alan, came to pick me up that Saturday afternoon.

"Laurie, is it true that you're an opera singer?" he asked.

"I'm studying to be one," I said.

"Sadie tells me you're really good."

"Daddy, she's not good. She's amazing," Sadie said, throwing her arms around me.

"Maybe you'd enjoy coming to the party Sadie's mom and I are going to tonight. It's just an informal get-together at our friend Michael's house, but he's a composer, and you might enjoy meeting him."

"Oh, I'd love to," I said, a little embarrassed. "But I'm not dressed for that."

"Don't be silly, you'll blend right in."

Five minutes later, we were walking through his friend's door.

"Hey Alan, you're just in time!" said a man's enthusiastic voice.

"Let's go sit outside," Sadie whispered.

"Okay," I said, eager to get away before they could see my faded old shorts and baggy T-shirt, fit for movie-watching with very close friends only.

It was mid-April now, and the smell of spring flowers complimented the balmy night air. We sat on lawn chairs talking, happy to be by ourselves away from the adult chatter.

"Hello, ladies," said a man coming out of the house to join us. The voice was deep and had a distinctive, almost guttural quality to it. I had heard that voice in movies and had thought it could only belong to one person.

"Oh, hi," Sadie said, in a voice that told me she had met the man before.

"Enjoying the lovely weather, are you?" said the man, his British accent quite evident now.

"Sir, you sound just like one of my favorite actors," I said.

"You don't say," he said, smiling at me. "And who might that actor be?"

"Alan Rickman," I said.

"Laurie, this is Alan Rickman," Sadie laughed.

"Oh my gosh," I said, feeling my cheeks burning. I quickly pulled myself together. "I just saw *Sense and Sensibility*, and I loved you in it."

"That's very kind of you."

Before any of us could say another word, the other Alan, Sadie's father, called out, "Laurie, I told Michael that you are a wonderful singer, and he would like to show you his recording studio."

"Michael wrote the score for *Robin Hood*," Sadie whispered as we began to walk towards the house.

"So that's why Alan Rickman is here."

"Yes, and Mary Elizabeth Mastrantonio is too," she said nonchalantly, as if being in this kind of crowd was a daily occurrence for her.

"But how do you know all these people?"

"My mom works behind the scenes in lots of film, doing computer stuff."

"Hi Laurie, I'm Michael Kamen," said a man, reaching out to take my hand as we entered a large room.

"Come check out this piano," Sadie said. She led me to a grand piano that had something curious and electronic attached to it. I had never seen anything like it before.

"It can record what I play," Michael said. "And it sounds great. Wanna hear it?"

"Yeah, I would," I breathed.

"I'm going to play a piece you might know," he said, the piano bench creaking slightly as he sat down. "This was one of my grandfather's favorites. He played recordings of it over and over when I was a child."

I shuddered in astonishment as he played the first notes. Tears immediately filled my eyes as I was brought back to Tanglewood by the chromatic notes of "Dido's Lament". When the introduction had finished, I began to sing, "When I am laid, am laid in earth, may my wrongs create no troubles in thy breast. Remember me, remember me. But ah, forget my fate!"

"You know this aria?" Michael exclaimed.

"Sorry," I said. "I couldn't help it."

"Would you do me a favor?" he asked, taking one of my hands in both of his. "Would you come sing it again with me, this time for everyone? I have a piano in the living room, and I think we're all ready for a bit of music."

"That was absolutely lovely," Alan Rickman said after our second performance.

"Yes it was," said the familiar voice of Maid Marian. "I'm Mary Elizabeth," she said.

"It's so nice to meet you," I said.

"How was the sleep-over?" Mom asked on the way home from Sadie's house the next morning.

"Pretty cool, actually," I said. "Her dad actually took Sadie and me to a party, and Alan Rickman was there."

"You do realize that April Fool's has passed, right?" Mom chuckled.

"I'm not joking. It was at Michael Kamen's house, the composer of *Robinhood*, and he had several people from the cast there."

At that moment, Mom's cell phone rang. It was Brian, who had moved to New York just that past September and had gotten a job as a publicist with a theater PR firm. "Brian? You're never going to guess what your sister did last night."

"I know," I could hear Brian's voice through the phone. "I heard all about it."

"How is that possible?" I asked as mom handed me the phone.

Mary Elizabeth was a good friend of Brian's boss, Philip, and told him about meeting a blind opera singer last night. Philip, only knowing of one blind opera singer, asked Brian if it were me.

"Word travels fast," Mom said. "What a small world."

❀ ❀ ❀

The Spotlight Awards auditions came again in October, and in December I received notice that I had once again made the semi-finals.

The tension and anticipation I felt the previous year had doubled, and the weeks, days, and hours leading up to my semifinal audition dragged on torturously. Finally, the time had arrived. Nicole and Christian greeted me enthusiastically after I had signed in. Nova had graduated the year before and did not get a second chance to audition as Nicole, Christian, and I did.

"Are you nervous?" Nicole asked, putting a hand on my shoulder.

"Oh yes," I sighed. "You?"

"I already went, so now, it's just about waiting."

"Laurie," Barbara Haig said, as the door to the audition room opened. "You're up now."

I entered the rehearsal room for the last time, knowing that this was my only chance left at becoming a finalist in this competition.

"Nobles Seigneurs, salut!" I sang. For the past several months, I had been working on an aria from a rarely done opera called *Les Huguenots* by the composer Giacomo Meyerbeer. Though portrayed by a mezzo-soprano, the aria is sung by a male character, a page boy who takes ample time in the limelight and oversteps his bounds when introducing nobility. The aria is meant to be tongue-in-cheek, hammed up, full of graceful little bits of impressive coloratura.

"How did it go?" Nicole and Christian asked.

"I gave it everything I've got. I think it went well."

After an hour of nervous waiting, Mom, Nicole, and I followed the small crowd into the reception room. Christian had disappeared. My stomach was too tense to even entertain the possibility of petit fours, fruit, and cheese.

"Hey Laurie, Nicole, you've got to come and see this!" Christian said, running over to us.

"Christian, the judges will be in here any minute now," Nicole said.

"You only get behind the stage of the Dorothy Chandler so many times in a lifetime, you know," he said. "Just come with me. It'll only take a second."

He led Nicole and me through a labyrinth of hallways, holding doors open for us now and then. We made our way past dressing rooms, racks with costumes, and prop tables.

"What opera are these for?" Nicole asked in awe.

"I have no idea. Just keep moving," Christian urged.

The music from a live orchestra was growing closer. We began walking up steps to what I could tell was the very stage of the Dorothy Chandler.

"Even if we don't make the finals this year, at least we can say we've been on stage here."

Just ahead of us was a thick curtain, the only barrier between us and the LA Philharmonic and Emanuel Ax who were finishing up the last notes of Brahms's Second Piano Concerto. Nicole took my right hand and Christian took my left, and we stood there, letting chills go down our spines, feeling the current of the music go through all of us.

"It was worth it to do this competition just to meet you guys," I whispered. They squeezed my hands in reply.

When we returned to the reception room, Barbara Haig was beginning to get everyone's attention. Nicole and Christian continued to hold my hands. I felt our palms grow sweaty through the same speech Barbara had gone through the year before. Then, her pregnant pause arrived, and we all held our breaths.

"Our first finalist is Jeffrey Kim."

A countertenor with a pure voice, as delicate and feminine as some mezzos I had heard, stepped forward. We applauded, and then another split second pause that felt as long as a lifetime followed.

"Our second finalist," she began, "is Laurie Rubin."

I lost myself completely. I jumped. I screamed. Christian was lifting me in the air, and Nicole was kissing my cheek. When Christian put me down, Mom gave me a hug, working hard to keep her composure and fighting back happy tears.

"You guys both deserve this, too," I said to my two friends.

"We're just happy you got it," they said.

As Barbara began to talk to Jeffrey and me about the evening of the finals, I stood there, trying to comprehend the reality of what had just happened. It had not quite sunk in yet. "I made the finals," I kept thinking to myself, each time being taken over by fresh tears.

❀ ❀ ❀

The Spotlight Awards fell on a Wednesday in the first week of April. I was to arrive at 5:00 PM to get ready for a 7:30 PM start time.

"Wow," I said, entering my very own dressing room, where I put on the black strapless gown Mom and I had bought for the occasion. I was then led into the room where LA Opera singers have their hair and makeup done for their respective productions. A hair stylist and makeup artist who had worked on several movies were hired for the occasion, and each of us spent a half hour in his chair, getting beautified.

At 7:30, the voice of an MC could be heard over the monitors backstage, followed by enthusiastic applause. The USC concert band had been hired to play in between each finalist, making the event feel like the Oscars.

"Ms. Rubin," said a frantic voice. "Can you tell us a little bit about yourself and how it feels to be in the Spotlight Awards so I can get it on camera? We're going to run this right before you perform."

After my brief interview, I sat in the green room to wait, as I would be the last to perform. The MC introduced each finalist and before each performance, a short video of the person was played. I gathered that the cameraman must have hastily rounded all of us up before the show. I heard bits and pieces of virtuosic jazz and classical bass, piano, and violin, as well as impressive renditions of show tunes and pop songs. Then two modern dancers and two ballerinas performed. Finally, it was time for the category of classical voice. I waited in the wings as Jeffrey Kim sang an aria usually sung by a mezzo from Mozart's *The Marriage of Figaro*.

Suddenly, I was hearing my own voice loudly echoing through the place, and I knew they were playing my video. The audience applauded loudly; many of them were friends, family, and teachers who had known me my whole life. The pianist guided me onto the stage, which felt enormous, and I couldn't believe I was about to sing on the stage where I saw my first opera. The first nervous notes of "Nobles Seigneurs" came out of me, and then suddenly I was at home, living the moment, enjoying the roller coaster. As I finished, the audience cheered, electrifying me.

When I returned to the wings, all the finalists were lined up by category.

"May I have a drumroll please," said the MC. One by one, he announced the runners-up and winners in each category. Each time, the band played a short tune as the audience cheered.

"In the category of classical voice . . . the runner-up is Jeffrey Kim."

"Oh my gosh," I gasped.

"The winner is Laurie Rubin!"

The happy roar from the audience filled me from head to toe as I was led back on stage to receive an envelope with a check and a large trophy. It felt as though I were watching someone win a Best Actress award on TV, and yet it was me up there as the band played and the audience cheered. Then I was ushered into the crowded lobby where my family and friends were pulling me into hugs this way and that. A man who had made his way through the crowd took my hand.

"Laurie," said Dan Everet, the headmaster of Oakwood School. "I just wanted to thank you. Do you remember how nervous we all were about having you come to school at Oakwood? Well, you opened all of our minds to so much more than we knew was possible. Thank you so much for bearing with us through our learning curve, and for offering more to the school than we could have ever imagined."

Once Upon a Time When Being Blind Was Celebrated

Senior year came and college applications had taken the place of driver's licenses in conversations between my classmates. Mom and I had taken a tour of colleges the year before so that I could start thinking about where I wanted to apply. We began flipping through college guides and making lists of places with strengths in the humanities and excellent music programs.

"Wow, Laurie, listen to this," Mom said. "Oberlin is a liberal arts college with one of the most reputable conservatories in the country. It says here that Oberlin is known for a wonderful accepting environment." She began to laugh.

"What's so funny?" I asked.

"This quote from an Oberlin student says that green hair on campus is as common as a pair of Levi's."

That was it. I was sold. If Oberlin was a place where it was cool to be different, I knew it was the place for me. We visited Princeton, Barnard (which had a cross-registration program with the Manhattan School of Music or Juilliard), and a small college/conservatory called Lawrence University in Wisconsin, and then we made our way to Ohio where Oberlin was nestled in the sun belt a half hour southwest of Cleveland, surrounded by nothing but cornfields. I felt like Goldilocks as I scrutinized colleges. Princeton didn't have enough music, Barnard was too immersed in an overwhelming city, Lawrence University was too isolated, but Oberlin was just right.

I stayed overnight in Dascomb, one of the college dorms, with a student who had volunteered to host me and show me around the school. She took me to dinner in the dining hall with a warm crowd of enthusiastic friends who seemed to be welcoming me to Oberlin as if I were already starting my freshman year. She took me to a concert given by the student-run a cappella groups, and she talked with me through the wee hours of the night about everything.

The next day, I was allowed to sit in on a voice class and listen to every single student singing so perfectly that I turned to Mom and whispered, "I feel small."

Their teacher, Richard Miller, who was world-renowned for the books he wrote on vocal pedagogy, shook my hand and said, "Looking forward to hearing your audition next year."

As Mom pulled the rental car out of the Oberlin Conservatory parking lot, I burst into tears.

"What's wrong?" she asked, alarmed.

"I have to go to Oberlin! What am I going to do?" I sobbed.

❋　❋　❋

I didn't eat for the first two months of my senior year. Teachers called Mom, telling her they noticed I was getting too thin, but I could think of nothing but writing college essays. Math pulled my SAT scores down so that they were not competitive enough for Oberlin's standards. While many of my classmates grappled with the task of narrowing college choices down, I had narrowed it down too much, and I knew that I only wanted to go to one place and one place only.

"Laurie, take some deep breaths," Mom said, trying to get me to eat my favorite meal of roast chicken with rice she had made for me.

"I can't, Mom," I said weakly. "My life will be ruined if I don't get into Oberlin."

"It will not!" she said firmly. "I think you're going to get in. You've been working so hard in your voice lessons and you're sounding great. Your college essays are beautiful. What's not to like about your application?"

"But if I don't get in . . ."

"If you don't get in, you need to find a really good second choice, and I promise you, your life will be just as wonderful, no matter where you go to college."

"But I applied to Oberlin early decision," I said.

"Which gives you several months to apply to other places if you're deferred."

❋ ❋ ❋

The phone call from Oberlin came when I was in court to watch Dad and his toy company seek justice as they had fallen victim to embezzlement committed by a trusted family friend and business partner. Mom had forgotten to turn off her cell phone and was racing outside to answer it. Minutes later, as I sat engrossed in the cross examination, I felt a tap on my shoulder.

"Laurie," Mom's voice whispered.

"Yeah?" I said, startled. There was a pause as she began sniffling through unmistakable tears. "Mom, what is it?"

"You got into Oberlin," she sobbed into my ear.

The courthouse, the stern judge, and the arguing lawyers were forgotten. I rose from my chair and started screaming, turning to hug Mom, tears dripping unabashedly down my face.

"And Mr. Miller wants you to study voice with him!" Mom continued.

It was only when the judge hit his gavel and yelled, "Order in the court!" that I was brought back to my senses.

That night, my appetite returned, and I enjoyed the rest of my senior year, knowing that Oberlin was in my future.

❋ ❋ ❋

College orientation just wouldn't be the same without those ice-breakers that the enthusiastic team leaders come up with. It was like being at summer camp again as I stood in a circle of nervous freshmen, and an older student with a resonant, enthusiastic voice led us in a series of games intended to help us get to know each other.

"Okay," she said. "This game's one of my favorites. It really makes you describe who you are in a nutshell, and it tastes good, too." She began laughing at her little joke. "I'm going to give each of you three M&M's, and for each one, you're going to describe a trait of yours, a fact that people wouldn't know unless they really knew you." She began to walk around, pouring M&M's into each of our hands. "Okay Laurie, let's start with you."

"Hmmm," I said. "Well, let's see. When I laugh, the entire room usually gets suddenly silent because it's so loud and operatic." I put one M&M into my mouth. "I eat cereal without milk." I ate another M&M. "And I love chocolate." I ate the last M&M.

"Awesome, Laurie," our orientation leader said in her bubbly voice. "I love chocolate, too. Okay, let's keep going around."

About five people and fifteen M&M's later, a girl with a husky voice took a deep breath and began without hesitation, "Hi, I go by my middle name, Thayer; I'm a dyke; and I don't shave my legs."

And there it was, right out there on the table. Some people like me talk about loving chocolate, and there were others like Thayer, practically running out of the closet. As Thayer finished her last M&M, the entire group cheered in response to her proud intro-duction, in celebration of who she was. I knew then and there that I was in the right place.

❋　❋　❋

"Hi, I'm Karen!" said the high voice of a girl who sounded like she was constantly laughing.

"I'm Laurie," I said. "Nice to meet you."

"Nice to meet you too, roomie," Karen said, taking my hand and dancing me around the unpacked boxes inside our dorm room. The room had that familiar college dorm smell of old carpet, a mustiness that comes from who knows where, and flimsy wooden furniture. The halls were lively with excited freshmen introducing themselves to one another, and the sound of peeling masking tape could be heard at frequent intervals as people covered their walls with posters.

"I hear you're a voice and English major," Karen said, as she flitted about the room with the light grace of a nymph, her quick manner making her seem like she was aerodynamic enough to fly.

"Yeah, I am."

"That's sooooo cool," she said. "I wish I could sing. I play the cello, but I'm not getting my degree in music."

"I found out at orientation today that you can still audition for the Oberlin Orchestra, even if you're not in the conservatory."

"Really?" she said, sounding delighted.

And just like that, we were having a conversation, no discomfort that needed to melt away, no glaring difference between us simply because I was blind and she could see. I realized that I was experiencing the sheer pleasure of being treated like a human being, something taken for granted by most, but a true gift and novelty for me.

"Let's start moving in, shall we?" Karen suggested.

"I'm up for that," I said.

Mom and Dad had helped me put up posters on my side of

the room the day before. A large *Phantom of the Opera* poster covered a large chunk of my wall. Hanging beside it was a poster from *Rent*, the musical I had recently fallen in love with. On the bulletin board Karen and I shared, I tacked some pictures of Brian and me on our river rafting trip, my Tanglewood friends and me hugging right after our opera scenes, and one of Sadie, Sarah, and Aaron, my three friends from Oakwood. A picture of Diva, the yellow lab who had been with my family since I was in eighth grade, stood in a little frame on my book shelf.

"Come check this out," Karen said, indicating her side of the room. "This is a quilt my friends and I worked on together." She placed my hand on a quilt with each patch made of a different fabric.

"Was each square made by a different person?" I asked.

"That would mean I had a zillion friends," Karen laughed. "Nah, it was four of us, and we all passed it around and alternated. See, these are my patches."

"Wow, they're all different. Some are almost like satin, and this other one feels like it's embroidered."

"That's because I embroidered some leaves on it. And this is my rocking chair," she said, as she placed my hand on something wooden. "I know it's ridiculous to bring something this big all the way from North Carolina, but Oberlin just wouldn't feel like home without it. Here, take a seat in it."

The wooden chair had intricate curlicue patterns on the back, and it creaked as I gently rocked in it. Karen was definitely a homebody, and our room was feeling cozier the more she placed random objects here and there around the room. We spent the remaining afternoon hours unpacking and talking easily, taking turns putting our CDs in the stereo Dad had gotten for me.

❂ ❂ ❂

"Hall meeting!" shouted Katy, the resident coordinator for our hall. Karen and I made our way down to the third floor lounge where people were gathering. Katy began to list the rules about keeping the bathroom clean, not eating other people's food items out of the communal refrigerator, and so on. After the meeting ended, we all milled about, making yet more introductions.

"Hey, I'm Jolene," said a high voice next to me. "I'm a junior here."

"Oh, hi, are you talking to me?" I asked.

"Yeah, who else?" she giggled.

"I'm Laurie. And I'm a freshman."

"Nice to meet you, Laurie. Are you in the college or the conservatory?"

"I'm actually in both," I said.

Jolene laughed, "Well, I'm a creative-writing major."

"Really? That's cool. I love writing."

We continued to chat until the room began to empty out.

"Have you been to the Feve?" Jolene asked.

"No, but I've heard about it. Isn't that Oberlin's greasy spoon, right off-campus?"

"Yeah. I feel like a late night snack. Wanna grab one with me?"

The smell of old, rancid oil inside the Feve had a curious way of making one feel hungry for something unhealthy. Jolene and I ordered buffalo chicken wings and chocolate shakes.

"These shakes are reminding me of a conversation I had with a friend recently."

"What about?" I asked.

"Sex or a milkshake? Which one would you take if you had to choose?"

"Hmmm," I said. "Since I haven't had sex yet, I'd have to go with a milkshake."

"Good choice!" Jolene said, sounding vindicated. "I'm with you. I've had sex, and I'd still go with a milkshake. A chocolate orgasm lasts longer."

"I'll take your word for it," I laughed. "Of course, I'd like to experience both while I'm here at Oberlin."

"Well, you've had your milkshake experience," Jolene said. "By the way, I just have to ask you this because it's been bothering me since I met you."

"Shoot," I said.

"Why don't you look at me? I mean, do I have something in my teeth you can't bear to look at? Is it my hair?"

"Sorry," I said. "My eyes have trouble focusing and making eye contact."

"Why is that?"

"I can't see. I'm blind, but then you already knew that, didn't you?"

"You're blind!" she exclaimed. "Oh, now I feel so much better. I thought it was me, or that you were some sort of snob and you just didn't look people in the eye."

"That's not it at all, and it certainly isn't you!" I said. "Where are you from?"

"Jersey. I'm Jamaican though. What? Why are you looking like that?"

"I was just thinking that I didn't know there were many white people in Jamaica," I said hesitantly.

"There are, but I'm not one of them."

"But you sound as white as I do."

"Okay, I put my foot in my mouth about you not looking at me," Jolene laughed. "I guess it's your turn. Not all black people sound black, whatever that means."

"So you are black?" I asked.

"Black as you are blind."

I began to blush. "Who knew that we both didn't know these things about each other before we went for a snack," I said. "You'd think both would be pretty obvious. I thought you knew I was blind because you took my hand and walked with me all the way to the Feve."

"I just like holding people's hands," Jolene laughed again. "That's one of my quirks."

When we finished our wings and headed back to campus, Jolene took my hand again, this time guiding me on purpose.

✹ ✹ ✹

"Welcome to your first studio class, everybody," Richard Miller said in a resonant tenor, his voice genial and warm.

"As most of you know, we always have our first class during

orientation week so that we can all introduce ourselves, and if parents are still here, we always welcome them. We only have one new freshman in this studio this year, and it is my sincere pleasure to introduce Laurie Rubin."

Everyone clapped loudly.

"Don't worry, Laurie, we seniors don't bite," said a booming baritone voice.

"Oh my God, is he gorgeous!" whispered Mom, who had been staying at the Oberlin Inn to make sure I was settled in.

"Mother!" I whispered back, hoping nobody had heard.

"And Skippy is quite the joker," Mr. Miller said with a smile in his voice. "Anyway, if any of you have an aria prepared, please feel free to come up and sing. I've asked Laurie to sing 'Una Voce Poco Fa.' Ms. Rubin, why don't you go first?"

Mom got up from her seat next to me and led me towards the small stage of the recital hall, which also held all the studio classes. I sang my aria, feeling nervous, thinking I would sound like a baby compared to the other, more experienced students of Mr. Miller's. To my amazement, everyone clapped and hooted when I had finished the last melisma of Rosina's first aria in *The Barber of Seville*.

"Bravo!" Mr. Miller said. "Anyone feel like following that?"

"Not really," said Skippy, "but I'll try."

Skippy's rich and resonant baritone was followed by the luscious tones of a mezzo, and then one soprano with a voice as crystal clear as a bell concluded the class.

It was now 5:00 on the last day of orientation, and a reception for conservatory students and their parents awaited us in the lounge just outside Kulas Recital Hall.

"That was kick-ass singing," said one of Mr. Miller's tenors. "And you're a freshman?"

As people continued to come up to chat with me, Mom made herself scarce and found a discreet place by the lounge's large windows. As she looked out at the beautiful end-of-summer day that had settled upon the park nearby, and at the students who were happily enjoying the weather, she began to ponder her now empty nest. It was hard enough when Brian left for college, but he had chosen a school nearby and had weaned himself from my mother slowly by getting his driver's license and having an active social life. I, on the other hand, had retired Mom as a 24-7 mother quite suddenly. She had driven me to every rehearsal, every voice lesson, and every competition. When my high-school classmates were at parties I wasn't invited to on Saturday nights, she was always my date, taking me to Chili's for dinner, Robin Rose for ice cream, and then a movie. Now, as she watched me making the friends I hadn't made in seventh grade, she realized that a big part of her job was over. Thinking that nobody was looking, she let the tears pour out of her eyes and cried silently by the window.

"Don't worry, we'll take good care of her," Skippy said, putting a gentle hand on her shoulder.

Mom wheeled around to see the tall form with the blond hair standing next to her, his kind eyes smiling down at her. "Thank you," was all she could manage to say.

❃ ❃ ❃

I was surprised by how swiftly the weeks flew by. Classes were hard but riveting. We were learning everything from the Renaissance period through twentieth century music in Music History 101 with a strict, elderly man who turned dry textbooks into fascinating novels through his lectures. I was reading surrealist books about the Civil War in English, and I was being given beautiful and esoteric pieces to sing by Mr. Miller that I had never heard before.

Karen had gotten herself a boyfriend, a sophomore cellist who was head over heels for her. They spent every waking minute together, mostly in our room.

"Now I know for sure that I would take the milkshake over sex," I told Jolene, who spent almost as much time in my room as Karen and her boyfriend. "I heard them last night. Man, that was uncomfortable."

"They had sex in front of you?" Jolene said, sounding appalled. "You should have kicked their asses out of there."

The next evening, I came back from dinner to find them in Karen's bed experiencing the worst hangover known to man.

"Oh Laurie, please don't turn the light on," Karen said.

Seconds later, Jolene knocked on the door.

"Oh, and don't do that either," moaned the boyfriend.

"You guys are disgusting wastes of space," Jolene spat at them.

"Thank you," they mumbled.

"Hey Laurie, can you make us some tea?" Karen asked in a

pleading voice, as if a sip of tea would be the very breath of life that would bring them back from this self-induced sickness.

"Laurie, don't get them anything," Jolene said. "You're not their servant."

"We love Laurie. We know she's not our servant," Karen said.

"Okay, kiddies," I said, putting on the shaky tone of an old woman. "Auntie Laurie will take care of you."

I realized then and there that I had no idea how to make tea. Mom had never let me near anything hot or sharp, which pretty much meant I was banished from the kitchen. I seemed to remember Karen putting water in the hot pot on the dresser, plugging it in, and waiting until it sounded like it was boiling before pouring it into mugs. As I filled her hot pot at the bathroom sink, I realized it was not annoyance I was feeling at the wastes of space in my room. It was a deep and loving feeling that seemed to be emanating from every pore of me. Never had anyone trusted me to take care of them, even to do something as simple as making tea. For weeks, Jolene was coming to me when she needed to talk, people were asking me to be in study groups with them, and now Karen was asking me to do something that would help make her feel better. As Jolene played Sarah McLachlan on my stereo, ignoring the hung-over couple's complaints, and as I made tea for them and raspberry hot chocolate for me and Jolene, I felt a big smile take over my entire face that I knew wouldn't fade for a long time. I was in my little community, my little niche with people I loved who loved me just as much in return.

A Window Opens

I was not the only blind student at the Oberlin Conservatory. I met Josh Pierce, a composer in his junior year, at orientation. Every student and every teacher had been telling me that I should meet Josh. Even before I met him in the resource office for people with disabilities, I knew that I would have some pretty big shoes to fill. To everyone else at Oberlin who knew him, Josh was the epitome of what the ideal blind student should be, dripping with musical talent, almost smarter than all his professors, exuding an air of reverent confidence that made people feel as though he were experiencing the world on a deeper, darker plane than they were.

"Josh is God!" other admiring composers would tell me.

I had been called into the disabilities office to be told about what resources were available to me, and Josh had been asked to meet me there and tell me about his three years experience going through the conservatory as a blind student. As exciting as being a pioneer can be, it was so nice to have that tiresome role removed from my shoulders once Oakwood had ended. Now, someone else who had been blind at a school before me could guide me, be my mentor, and alleviate my concerns.

"So you're a voice major, right?" Josh asked.

"Yes, I am."

He chuckled. "Ah, opera singers, a fun but dramatic bunch of people. So tell me, how did you take tests and do your schoolwork before coming here?"

"Braille books, books on tape, tests on floppy disks, you name it," I said. "My laptop has become my best friend."

"Don't I know it," Josh smiled. "Well, I can tell you that readers have made my life at Oberlin a lot easier."

"Readers? What do you mean?"

"Fellow students who are in our classes with us who basically get paid to do the reading they're assigned to do in the first place, as long as they read it out loud to us. The disabilities office will cover the cost, and sometimes it's the quickest way of getting anything done. Professors can be a bit flaky about getting handouts to the office here to be brailled or put in some other format for us in advance."

"How are professors about the whole blindness thing?" I asked.

"Depends on the person," Josh said. "Some of them are great and are very responsive when I tell them what works best for me. Others are not open-minded at all and won't change a thing about the way they explain things when they teach. One professor, who I think you're having this year for music history, always acted like test-taking would be this huge stumbling block. Even when I explained to him that there were multiple ways I could accomplish this, he just seemed completely overwhelmed. I apologize in advance if I haven't helped make things easier for you after taking that class."

"You're forgiven."

"This office is getting stuffy. Would you like to grab lunch in the cafeteria to continue this conversation?"

Josh walked even faster than any sighted person I knew. I found myself running into people as I attempted to keep up with him. The tapping of his cane grew fainter as we left the building, making our way out into the hot, sunny day.

"Josh, am I still with you?" I shouted over the noisy chatter of students around me, feeling disoriented.

"I'm over here," he yelled from fifty feet ahead.

The more I got to know Josh, the more fascinated I became with him. It seemed like he could do everything perfectly. He could even balance a tray of food in one hand while using his cane with the other. I could barely keep a tray straight with two hands. People seemed to flock toward him, either stopping to say an enthusiastic "hello," or to join his table at meals. Many would ask for his advice about anything from music to their love lives, and he would always give it, his demeanor calm and confident.

Josh began to introduce me to all his professors who seemed to worship him just as much as the students did. "Laurie is a new freshman this year," he would say.

"Oh, it's so wonderful to have you!" they would exclaim. "It was such an inspiring experience having Josh in my class, and I hope I get the honor of having you this year."

Everyone expected me to be special in the same way Josh was, to function and perform in an identical fashion. I knew this would be impossible. We were two different people, and yet I yearned to be as amazing as he was. I began to view him as my mentor, and he thought of me as his little freshman protégé, teaching me the ways of an Oberlin conservatory student. I hoped that by being around him, I would somehow obtain the gifts of one-handed tray balancing, flawless, speedy travel around the Oberlin campus, and confidence by osmosis.

❋ ❋ ❋

Josh lived down the hall from me in Dascomb, and I found myself making frequent visits to his room to pick his brain about this or that.

"Hey, stay for a while," he said smiling, one night in the first week of school. "Come sit here on my bed. I want to play you something."

I heard him fumbling through CDs, and then, the sound of strings playing an eerie, dissonant piece of music filled his stereo speakers.

"'Central Park in the Dark' by Charles Ives," he said, his voice suddenly sounding as though he were in a trance.

The strings took us through a murky atmosphere of sound. The piece began to build, and I noticed that Josh and I were getting closer to each other on his bed. Then, the brass came in, playing fragments of military band music. It was an image of New York in the 1920s, a juxtaposition of ominous darkness and the ghost of something ironically festive. Josh and I moved closer still as the music began to grow quiet again, the sound dissolving into nothingness, and then our lips met. We stayed frozen in that one kiss for several minutes, neither of us moving a muscle. The thrill of transcending the mentor/protégé relationship with Josh, and the idea of this person everyone revered letting me into that deep, secret place of his sent shivers up and down my spine. Uttering a single word would have broken the delicate thread of that moment, and so I left his room that night in silence, not daring to question him about what had just happened.

❋ ❋ ❋

"Oh my God, you kissed?" Jolene screamed. "That's kind of sickeningly beautiful."

"What do you mean?" I asked.

"I don't know, the two blind musicians finding each other . . . it just kind of seems like something out of the movies, don't you think?"

"Laurie has a boyfriend," said Karen.

"Honey, you're drunk," I teased.

"Hello, you made out," Jolene said.

"No, it's not like that with Josh," I said. "It was just something we shared because of the music."

"Not sure he feels the same way about it," Karen said.

"Oh yeah? And what makes you think that?"

"You two have been sitting at the same table at dinner almost every night. He acts as though everything you say is the funniest or the cutest thing he's ever heard."

I didn't see Josh for several days. He had gone to Kentucky for some composers' conference to present a paper. It wasn't until the following week that I heard the tapping of his cane in the distance as I made my way out of a practice room. We met in the stairwell.

"Hey," he said, sounding happy to see me.

"Hi, how was the conference?" I asked, my voice sounding awkward.

"It was really interesting. I can tell you all about it when I'm not rushing off to class. How was your week?"

"Oh, fine. But don't be surprised if you hear a rumor going around campus about us."

"What rumor?" Josh asked, amused.

"Everyone thinks we're dating."

He grew quiet for a moment.

"I'm so sorry. I hope I didn't upset you."

"Frankly, I am a little taken aback," he said, his voice suddenly serious. My heart sank. "I thought we were on the same wavelength about this, and that the other night proved it. I guess I totally read the signs wrong."

He started to walk away.

"Wait," I called. "You mean you want us to be dating?"

"Well, yeah."

"Oh my God, I'm so clueless."

"What did you think that kiss was all about?" he asked.

"I don't know . . . one of those moments that two people share sometimes."

"Is that all you wanted it to be?"

"No, well, um, I think maybe we should give it a try . . . dating I mean."

⁕ ☀ ☀

I spent many nights in the following weeks in Josh's small single room. We made out for hours as music played softly on his stereo. I'd spend Saturday afternoons with him at the out-of-tune piano in the first floor lounge of Dascomb, as he played songs for me that he had written.

The end of 1997 when I started college seemed to be the time that the world exploded into a new era of technology. Words like "email" and "ethernet" had been introduced to our vocabulary. My computer now read the letters I was receiving on it electronically. I came home one day after studio class to find Josh's name in my inbox.

"I had watermelon today," my computer said to me, reading his words without feeling. "As I bit into it, I thought of you. It's refreshing, but there's something else about watermelon that's like you. Perhaps it's the way that every bite is so full of juice, and the way you enter a room is so full of joy for life."

Even after a month of dating Josh, it still surprised me when he complimented me in the same reverent way he talked about certain pieces of music. Because the emails were rare, I was made to feel special, honored that Josh was bestowing the few high compliments he ever gave on me. That seemed to feed me in the relationship.

One evening almost two months after we were together, we were in his room as usual. Our clothes lay beside us on the bed, our hands making us take the step to a new level of intimacy. Suddenly and inexplicably, the connection between us felt as dissonant as the Ives piece that had somehow brought us together. As his body shuddered against mine, I realized I was experiencing Josh at his most vulnerable, stripped of all the music, the admiration, the unique skills he had that I had wanted so badly. After that night, I began to see Josh in a new light. Had I merely been infatuated with an idea of Josh and not Josh himself? I pushed the feelings to the back of my mind, and things continued as normal, until one day a week later, when Katy asked Josh and me to give talks about blindness to the various dorms.

"All the RCs are so curious to know what it's like to be blind," Katy had said. "They really want you to share any insights you can with their residents about how your lives are different because of your blindness."

So we made the circuit through the different dorm lounges of Oberlin where large groups of students sat, listening to Josh, who I realized was monopolizing the floor.

"One thing that is different for me because I'm blind is that I often lack the ability to know who has approached me when they greet me. Most of the time, they don't tell me who they are, so I'm left in the awkward position of trying to figure out who I'm in conversation with. I think people assume I can recognize voices."

"And that goes to show how all of us blind people are different," I chimed in. "I tend to be good at recognizing the voices of people I know reasonably well. I think I feel my blindness the most when I get lost and totally disoriented in places I should really know better."

"I've never had a problem finding my way around," Josh said, resentful that I had been so bold as to say my piece. Yet, we had both been asked to speak, and I felt that everyone should know what both of our experiences were like, no matter how much they differed from each other. There was no one textbook blindness experience. Perhaps our differences were the most important things we could impart to the people we spoke to, in order to show that we were just two people, experiencing a lack of sight in our own, unique ways, just the way two sighted people would experience vision differently.

Josh and I grew more annoyed with each other as we continued speaking our way across campus. I was tired of him trying to make me feel bad about the person I was, and he began to express his displeasure at "being contradicted."

"Well you never let me get a word in edgewise," I said angrily. "It's really not all about you."

"You're just confusing the issue when you insist on making a point that is completely the opposite of one I took the time to make."

"What I have to say is just as valid," I retorted. "And I think you should give people credit for realizing that we just happen to be two different people, blindness or no blindness."

And I grew more and more tired of the comments from my music history professor who kept comparing me to Josh.

"Actually, I would prefer to have my tests in a written format,"

I said in early October before our first exam. "If you have it the day before, you can send it to the disabilities office, and they can arrange to have it brailled for me."

"That's not the system Josh and I worked out," he said indignantly. "I don't have time to send it to that office. I just scheduled a time to read it to him and write down his answers, so what's good enough for your friend Josh should be good enough for you."

Nothing made me more self-conscious than agonizing over an answer to a test question in front of a professor. I knew he was judging me for not studying well enough.

"You know, Josh used to amaze me by how quick he was," he said. "He'd always have the right answer before I even finish asking the question. I guess not everyone can be like him."

"That's right," I thought grudgingly.

❂ ❂ ❂

I had been greatly looking forward to hearing the music Josh composed, and an opportunity presented itself just before Halloween. The concert fell on a particularly busy day for me. There had been no break between my morning classes, and a Jewish Women's Group meeting had taken place during lunchtime. The afternoon had not let up either, and as a result, I entered the larger of the conservatory's two concert halls before Josh's concert with an empty stomach. It was a set of songs he had written for piano and voice, each one being about three seconds long with thirty-second intervals of silence between them. I realized that I must have lacked a certain depth, because the audience was completely riveted by the music, or lack thereof, and I could glean nothing from the sparse music. It would end as quickly as it would begin, and the long period of silence between each one made me forget what I had just heard. Just as the singer and pianist walked on stage, my stomach took the opportunity to grumble its hungry displeasure loudly. You could hear a pin drop in the space between the songs, except for the sound of my stomach, which resounded loudly through the echoing hall. I felt my face begin to grow hot. Josh was sitting next to me, so there would be no hiding where the obnoxious swooshing and swirling of stomach juices was coming from. I tried desperately to silence it, as though trying to calm a crying baby, altering my position, but nothing helped. It merely grew louder and louder, and Josh's planned out periods of silence were far from silent now. Finally, the longest, most humiliating five minutes of my life ended as the audience began to applaud enthusiastically.

A week later, I woke up on my birthday to a crisp November morning, the sounds of people moving about the room and the smell of cinnamon rolls. At first, I thought I was dreaming, but then I felt a gentle tap on my shoulder.

"Happy birthday," Jolene said. "We have breakfast in bed for you."

I sat up as Jolene placed a napkin and a plate of food on my lap.

"Pastries from the Fox Grape, your favorite," Karen said cheerfully.

Jolene filled up the hot pot with hot water and bustled around, making hot chocolate.

"You guys are the best," I said. "I've never had breakfast in bed before."

"Where the hell is Josh?" Jolene asked sounding annoyed. "He was supposed to be here fifteen minutes ago."

The three of us began eating and chatting happily. I hadn't been to the Fox Grape, my favorite place to have breakfast in town, in a long time, and I savored the taste of the moist cinnamon roll with the crunchy top. Both Karen and Jolene had early classes, so our breakfast had to be cut short. There was a knock on my door just five minutes after they had left.

"It's unlocked," I said.

Josh entered.

"You missed a really good breakfast. I don't think we left anything for you."

"That's okay. I ate breakfast early this morning," he said.

"Why in such a somber mood?" I asked.

He didn't answer.

"Okay, you're really starting to freak me out here," I smiled. "Did somebody die or something?"

"I didn't want to do this on your birthday," he began, "but this has to be done sooner or later."

"You're breaking up with me," I guessed, my tone flat.

"I don't think things are working out between us."

I began to cry. I knew that Josh was right, but I had not let that revelation sink in. For the first time, someone was breaking up with me, and on my birthday no less.

"Laurie, I'm sorry."

"No, you're not. Please, just get out of here."

Try as I might, I could not stop my tears from pouring out through Italian class and then into lunch.

"What an asshole," Jolene said, hugging me. "Let's get out of here and do something completely insane."

Jolene, being one of the few people who lived in our dorm with a car, was always asked to go on alcohol runs, to help move furniture, and to get people out of the little town of Oberlin for a few hours. As I sat in the passenger seat, the crying fits subsided. It was a beautiful day. The sun was bright, and I imagined a perfectly blue sky above us. Though it was forty degrees outside, the air felt soothing on my tear-stained face, and it had a pure, autumn smell. We were driving for at least a half hour before parking at a place I was sure I had never been.

"This is an antique store I saw once when I was driving to a doctor's appointment," Jolene said. "It just looked so cozy in there, and I've been dying to take a closer look since."

We walked into a warm, spacious shop that smelled like wood. The floorboards creaked as we made our way through the store to a rocking chair with intricate leaves and flowers carved into its back. The supports that held the arms of the chair were shaped like a harp.

"I love it," I said.

"Knew you would," Jolene beamed.

We took turns rocking in the chair for almost an hour before she said,

"Wanna split it?"

"You mean buy it?" I asked in surprise.

"Yeah, it's only $200. We could take turns having it in each other's room, and that way, we'd always have something with our friendship in it when we need the good energy."

We managed to fit the rocking chair in Jolene's small back seat.

"The chair can start in your room, since you need some positive energy right now, and it's your birthday."

When I returned to the Dascomb lounge, Katy greeted us.

"You're just in time," she said happily. "We're about to have birthday cake for you and Peter, whose birthday is also today."

A crowd of dorm-mates joined the festivities, and we received a loud, enthusiastic chorus of "Happy Birthday." Several of my friends from the Jewish Women's Group and others from the conservatory had stopped by to spend some birthday time with me, all getting a slice of chocolate cake. Suddenly, it hit me that I was extraordinarily happy. Somehow, the worst birthday of my life had turned into the best one, getting the healing process after my first breakup off to a good start.

❀ ❀ ❀

There is nothing like the wonderful enthusiasm you feel when being a freshman. Everything from hearing an organ live, feeling its deep notes resonating in my own chest, to seeing an Oberlin opera was new to me. Now that I was not spending every night in Josh's room, I had time to find myself in the vast array of new college experiences. Oberlin's production of *Carmen* went up the weekend before Thanksgiving, and I went to see it on opening night. When the orchestra began to play the famous overture, its grand sound made me feel as though I were seeing a professional production. As the curtain opened and the singers' voices were revealed one by one, a new level of excitement took me over. Maybe I would have the opportunity to sing in an Oberlin opera when I was a junior or senior. Like the stage of LA Opera, the stage of Hall Auditorium, where Oberlin's operas took place, had turned into another city from a different century, the large sound of the chorus making it come to life. There was so much history in it, so much we could recreate as a way of never letting the past fade from our consciousness.

In my second semester at Oberlin, three of the leads I had seen in *Carmen* who were now seniors asked me to sing a quartet with them.

"But I'm only a freshman," I said in disbelief. "Are you sure you want me to sing with you?"

"It doesn't matter what year you're in," said Martha, the soprano who had had my favorite voice in the entire production. "It only matters how good you are, and you're just what we're looking for."

It was like a celebrity had just initiated me into a small club, and in late spring, we sang the Brahms Liebeslieder Waltzes in the small recital hall in the conservatory. I learned just as much from singing with people more experienced and polished than me as I did from my music history and theory classes. I became more in tune with a deeper level of musicality when I was forced to match the quality of their singing.

Then more seniors began asking me to sing with them, and I

was propelled into a chamber music frenzy. The more repertoire I was introduced to for combinations of more than one voice or for different instruments like oboe, clarinet, violin, cello, and harp, the more I began forming chamber music groups of my own for the music, the friendship, and the fun of it.

❉ ❉ ❉

It was hard to say good-bye to Oberlin at the end of freshman year. So many of my friends were seniors. But as hard as it was to leave, I knew that not only would I be coming back for the next three years, but that there was another experience of great significance that was about to happen for me.

My friend Lindsey, who had been in my voice teacher's studio with me during high school, kept in touch over the phone through our first years of college. She had told me about a new friend who fascinated her.

"Eve's the first lesbian I've ever met!" she had said, as though describing her first time seeing an orca on a whale-watching cruise. "I think you guys should talk since you said you might be bi. Oh, and I already gave her your phone number, so be expecting a call from her."

"Wait, Lindsey, what are we supposed to talk about?" I had asked her, panic-stricken. "Talking about possibly liking girls can only last so long."

Apparently Eve had been having the same reservations, because she did not call me until March, several months after Lindsey had attempted to play Cupid. One conversation turned into several, and then we were on the phone at least two nights a week for hours. We could talk about the most seemingly mundane things and yet lose ourselves in the silly minutiae of it.

"I'm excited for you to come back to LA," Eve said. "We have to get together."

"Totally," I said. "It'll be cool to meet you in person."

Though we kept the conversation casual, we both knew our first meeting in person would be a date.

"Oh my gosh, Lindsey, what if we totally don't hit it off in person, and it's all awkward? And what should I wear?"

Lindsey laughed. "Is this your first date or something?"

"Kind of. Josh and I never really had a date. We just got together."

❀ ❀ ❀

Eve pulled up to my place at 6:00PM sharp the Friday I returned home from Oberlin. "Hey, you look nice," she said in a deep voice. "Are you ready to go?"

As I called out to Mom, letting her know I was leaving, Eve guided me out the door to her car. The conversation was easy, about nothing in particular, but I knew immediately that the evening would go well.

"I'm taking you to my favorite restaurant in my neighborhood," she said. "It's nothing fancy, but the burgers are killer!"

Eve was right. We said "mmmm" in unison with mouths full of

the juiciest burgers we had ever tasted. Then, the fact that we were on a date was confirmed when Eve paid for dinner.

"Have you dated girls before?" Eve asked on the way home.

"No, but I've wanted to for a really long time. What about you?"

Eve sighed. "Just one, but she was my first love, and she really broke my heart. I don't talk about that with many people."

She proceeded to tell me about coming out, how she had hated herself for years for knowing she liked girls, and how she had been sure her parents would kick her out of the house when they found out.

"And yet, it didn't feel wrong to be gay," she said. "It just felt like I was being me."

"I think I know what you mean," I said softly. "What really feels wrong for me is the feeling I get when I reach a certain level of intimacy with guys."

Suddenly, I felt Eve shift the car into park, and she turned off the engine.

"Sorry, we're almost back to your house, and I don't want to end the evening yet, if that's okay with you."

"Yeah, it's fine," I said happily.

We talked long after the light had faded from the sky, and the evening turned into the most perfect summer night I could remember. The balmy, fragrant breeze blew through Eve's open windows, and other than our conversation, it was completely still outside, as though nature was holding its breath for us, awaiting the discovery I had waited many years to make.

"Holy crap, it's already 11:30," Eve said. "I better get you home. Your mom will never let me hang out with you again." She turned on the engine, and we sat idling for a moment. "I had a really good time tonight," she said in a soft voice. "Can we do this again?"

"I'd really like that," I said.

Then, it happened, the moment I needed to confirm the suspicions I had about myself since that memorable dream. Eve took my hand and held it there as time suddenly froze. Everything made sense, the soft, feminine feel of her fingers, the thick, long, black hair that brushed my shoulders as she moved closer, the racing of my heart, the tingles that were making their way through my entire body such as I had never felt, and the striking notion of this being completely and utterly natural. Eve had shared her soul with me in the gentle grip of her hand, and I had let her into mine. We didn't need a pair of eyes to act as windows to our souls now. They were perfectly visible to both of us.

Eve and I shared the perfect summer romance. When we weren't swimming in the pool in my backyard or walking along Santa Monica Pier, we were on the phone talking until we were tired enough to sleep or lying in bed together. When we made love, I was taken over by the same natural feeling that had filled me when she first took my hand.

And just as quickly as it had started, it was over. After a long, tearful good-bye, I took off for my second year at Oberlin, and she for hers at Cal Arts. Though our time together was brief, its impression on my life was profound. College was leading me on an exciting path toward self-discovery, but Eve had led me to a place deeper inside myself than I had known existed. In one year, I had fallen in love with music all over again, and now, for the first time, I had fallen in love with love.

Brown

Brown is a color one can truly taste.
Chocolate, one of my favorite things, tastes of
  many shades.
The darker brown the chocolate, the darker and
  richer the taste.
"It's a delicious shade of brown!" Grandma would
  say,
on one of those rainy days perfect for baking
  cookies or brownies.
I always knew that brown meant ready to come
  out of the oven.
Nothing beats the mouth-watering aroma of
  chocolate chip cookies in the oven,
or onions browning on a stove.
Those delicious, brown smells will warm any
  house.

Brown is nature's signature color.
So many of Mother Earth's gifts in their rawest
  forms are brown,
like rocks washed up on the shore such as the ones
  I used to collect as a child,

the fragrant bark of a tree, animals and insects I
have touched,
and the moist and rich soil I have dug with my
hands, planting flowers.

On my twenty-first birthday, a close friend who
understood my love of nature
gave me a necklace of buckeyes she had strung
herself.
It had all the elements I loved about the color
brown:
it was a product of autumn,
and it was something I could wear to match my
chestnut brown hair.

Somebody Pinch Me

During the course of my junior year, I got three surreal surprises, the kind you usually wake up from with a sinking heart when you realize they were all a dream. But these surprises were real, and all three came to me by way of phone calls. The first one was from Mom on a brisk, early spring day. I walked up the three flights of stairs to my dorm room to the sound of my phone ringing. By the time I had gotten my door unlocked, I could hear my Mom's voice on my answering machine.

"Laurie, you're going to be very happy. Call me back."

Just as I got to the receiver, there was a click, and the answering machine beeped loudly, mocking me for having missed the call.

"Mom?" I said a minute later.

"Hi, honey, did you have a good day?"

"Yeah. What's the good news?"

"You're going to be singing for Joan Sutherland this summer!"

Though I always try to make a point of being courteous to my housemates, certain reactions are involuntary, like jumping back when you touch something burning hot. Such was the case for the loud scream that shot out of me after Mom's magic words, and disturbing the peace of the housemates doing homework in their rooms or knitting quietly in the second floor lounge did not enter my consciousness. My mom was talking about *the* Joan Sutherland, the singer renowned for the perfection of her bell-like high notes and the precision of her incredibly fast melismas, the vocal legend who some say sparked the rebirth of the Bel Canto era, and who took the opera world by storm from the '50s through the '80s. It was hard to believe that I would be in the same room with her, let alone have the chance to sing for her.

Several months earlier, I had gone through a circuit of auditions for summer music programs. In college and grad school, such programs are crucial résumé builders. Come January, the talk of the Oberlin conservatory was always about what auditions everyone was doing, and from March through May, conversations turned into what summer programs everyone got into and which ones we would end up choosing. I got some disappointing rejections, just like everyone else. This had been my third time auditioning for Tanglewood's program for college and graduate vocalists and instrumentalists, and I got my third rejection form letter in the mail, which had broken my heart. I had so much wanted to return to the place that had changed my life in high school.

I had also gotten some exciting acceptances, like the vocal program at Chautauqua that would allow singers to work with industry people, from conductors to stage directors of some of the best orchestras and opera companies in the United States, which I would participate in that summer, and a fellowship to the Aspen vocal chamber music program that selected six singers and instrumentalists to perform with one another, which I had done the summer after my sophomore year.

Back in January, I had auditioned for the Britten-Pears Young Artist Program in Aldeburgh, England. Most of the summer programs I had been to were anywhere from six to nine weeks long and consisted of diction and movement courses, as well as individual coachings and lessons in which we could work on repertoire. Many times, they would culminate in opera productions or several concerts. The Britten-Pears program, however, had many different master class courses that were about ten days long with various teaching artists who would work intensively with students on the repertoire for which they were known. Joan Sutherland was one such teaching artist, and she would be coming with her husband, conductor Richard Bonynge, to give master classes there this summer. I had been told, as early as high school, that my strong suit was my ability to sing fast, florid passages in impressive Rossini, Mozart, and Handel arias, and I had been encouraged by all my voice teachers to perform such arias in auditions. The auditions took place all over the world, and I chose the site at UCLA when I was home on winter break.

"How did it go?" Mom asked expectantly as my pianist, David Wilkinson, and I walked out of the large audition room.

"She sang the heck out of those pieces!" David said.

"I felt like it went well," I said.

Doing my best was all I could hope for. Hundreds of people were auditioning for this opportunity to sing for Dame Joan Sutherland, and I knew my chances were slim. As I stood in my dorm room, the sun coming through my window, the phone pressed to my ear, it occurred to me how random these things tend to be, how I could have my self-esteem compromised when getting my third rejection from a summer program, and in the same year, I could be one of twelve singers, selected from hundreds, to have this single opportunity to sing for and work with one of the greats. Such is the nature of this crazy field.

✤　✤　✤

Mom begged me to let her come.

"But you never come to summer programs with me," I argued. "And it'll be so embarrassing to be the only one with a mom there."

"Oh, Laurie, please. You got me into opera, and I've listened to Joan Sutherland recordings in the car so many times. I would just love to meet her."

After I returned home from Chautauqua, we were packing for England, and I soon discovered I was wrong. Mom was one of several mothers who sat in the class as observers.

Aldeburgh, a small town on the eastern shore of England, is most noted for being the place where the composer Benjamin Britten and his beloved partner, tenor Peter Pears, settled and eventually established a training center for young musicians and a world-famous music festival. As Mom and I walked into the small lecture-hall-like theater where the master classes were held, a chill went through us. Something about the cloudy grey light coming through the windows and the reverent quiet in the place made us aware of how many famous musicians had been in this room and the amount of history that had taken place here.

On that first morning, all twelve of us were asked to sing an aria of our choice in order for Mr. Bonynge and Dame Sutherland to get acquainted with our voices. Eleven beautiful voices sang well-executed renditions of Handel, Mozart, Donizetti, Bellini, and Rossini arias. As some richer voices the color of wine and some silvery lighter voices filled the reverberant room, I sat in disbelief that I too was in this class. When it was my turn to sing, I performed a victorious Handel aria, sung by the hero Ariodante after surviving a deadly storm. The aria featured several high notes sung in succession and many long, melismatic passages that would either create impressive, musical fireworks or the danger of breathlessness. It went well, and I was delighted to get an enthusiastic reception from the other singers.

"Thank you all for singing," Richard Bonynge said pleasantly. "We're both very much looking forward to working with you all."

"I'd like to say a few words," Dame Sutherland said in her grand and surprisingly deep voice that did not seem to match the crystalline high singing she was known for. "You all have nice voices, and mostly good technique. However, I am very disappointed to hear that what you lack, in general, is an emotional connection to your music and your character. I must tell you from my experience that technique is one thing that of course you must have under your belt, but all the musical fireworks in the world won't move an audience if you are not in character. You should all know better than to get up here without leaving yourselves backstage and totally transforming into Dorabella, or Rosina, or Juliet."

"She hates me, she totally hates me," I thought to myself, feeling as though all her words were directed at me. She couldn't have been talking about the eleven other performances, which had nearly moved me to tears.

We adjourned to the lounge for lunch, a traditional British meal of steak and kidney pie and sticky toffee pudding, a personal favorite of mine. My anxiety subsided and my mood lightened when my fellow singers joined me at the table where a mutual admiration society about each other's performances was held. For the first time, I was surrounded by singers from all over the world. Just a handful of us were from the States, and there were singers who came from Australia, Spain, Sweden, South Africa, Ireland, and of course England.

❋ ❋ ❋

I was surprised to find that Richard Bonynge did a majority of the teaching, and that Dame Joan didn't say much at all. It was true that he had been her husband, her coach, her collaborative pianist, and eventually her conductor for almost as long as she had been singing, and it was he who guided her into the repertoire that suited her best. He had an affinity for teaching singers, and we were the privileged twelve in that master class who got the benefit of the same ears that had made Joan Sutherland famous. He proceeded to take half an hour with each soprano, mezzo, tenor, baritone, and bass who sang, advising one to emphasize the word "bella" here, demonstrating how to get another vocal color there.

"Bel Canto singing is all about the line, singing beautiful legato phrases," he said. "Don't overinterpret. Let the composer's musical phrases guide your voice, and don't ever go against the current of the music."

Dame Joan would interject with sounds of agreement now and then. Once in a while, she would utter an opinion, at which point we would all fall silent.

"I don't sing anymore, but imagine it's kind of like this." She would hum the musical thought she wanted to hear, and just like that, we were all taken down memory lane with her into a performance at La Scala or the Met. Goose bumps and chills crept up and down my spine as she'd hum in a raspy voice, not even trying to recreate the vocal acrobatics she once was able to execute so perfectly, and yet, you could hear her voice as clear as day, as though this were some film about Dame Joan Sutherland's life, and we had just been taken into a flashback where a recording of a particularly magical moment of hers in live performance was playing. Then, within a split second, it would be over, and the master class would continue as if nothing had happened, even though everyone in the room had understood that we had witnessed something intimate and significant.

It was my turn on the chopping block the next day. My heart

beat fast, and the butterflies that had been accumulating in my stomach until that point had taken up all the room inside me.

"What are you going to sing for us?" Dame Joan asked, speaking to me directly for the first time.

"I'm going to sing 'Non Piu Mesta' from *La Cenerentola*," I said, trying to sound less nervous and more composed than I felt.

"Ah, quite a difficult aria," Dame Joan said.

My heart began to beat fast, and the pianist began to play the aria's victorious introduction. I stood there, in a state of terrified anticipation of the first notes that were about to come out of my mouth. They would either be shaky and poorly executed, setting me up for a performance I wasn't happy with in which I would be desperately fighting to get back on track, or they would be awesome, setting me up for a confident and controlled performance. As the introduction finished, I took my deep breath, preparing myself to take the leap of faith. The first notes came out rich, spinning delicately, like nimble and graceful ballet steps and turns, and I began to relax and enjoy myself. The fascinating thing about my psychology as a performer is that I could walk out of an audition for a summer program or competition having absolutely blown it in front of judges whose names I had never even heard before, yet I could get up there and absolutely nail it in front of someone I had idolized since I first started singing opera, like Joan Sutherland. When a performance goes as well as it did that day, I feel at home on stage, playing with the audience with comic timing when appropriate, letting my voice fly easily through fast passages and land gracefully on high notes. The sensation I feel at the end of such a performance is comparable to coming off of an exhilarating ski run or a favorite roller coaster.

"Brava!" said Richard and Joan in unison.

"Thank you," I breathed.

"Your coloratura is perfectly clean. I could hear every note clearly," Richard said. "Do you have Mediterranean blood in you? Your voice has a quality that has become quite rare as of late."

My heart stood still. The man who had been Joan Sutherland's vocal coach and conductor was calling my voice Italian, like Pavarotti's, Tebaldi's, and a host of many others who set the standard for excellent singing.

"Yes, it was very impressive," Dame Joan said. "You really have a sense of the character, the joy that Cinderella would feel at the end of the opera when uniting with her prince. Your energy is quite inspiring."

Richard proceeded to give me some suggestions about emphasizing a note here, getting a darker or lighter color there, but Dame Joan did not accuse me, or any of us for that matter, of giving flat performances again that week.

"Sometimes people like to come across as tough or strict at first, just to lay the ground rules," Mom said as we discussed the day of master classes over dinner in the hotel. "Then they relax a bit once their students know what's expected of them. Remember that from Oakwood?"

Each of us had three sessions with Dame Joan and Richard in which we sang different arias in the large lecture hall. Each time I went up, they said flattering things about my performance, and Richard proceeded to coach me to convey even more through the emphasis of certain notes and words. I perhaps learned better from listening to everybody else perform and receive feedback, as it was easier to be relaxed when it wasn't me in the hot seat.

There was only one instance where Dame Joan seemed agitated by a performance that was given in class. It is customary and stylistically expected for a singer to ornament and vary a melody the second time it is sung in baroque arias. One of the sopranos had given an impressive performance of a Handel aria Dame Joan was known for, and immediately after, she had let out a sigh of disapproval at the girl who stood before her.

"That was the most self-indulgent performance I have ever heard, girl," she said. "Those ornaments sounded nothing like baroque ornaments. Did you simply want an excuse for us to hear your exquisite high notes?"

"Actually," the soprano said in her proper British accent, completely calm and unperturbed. "I copied many of those exact ornaments from your recording, Dame Sutherland."

The entire audience fell silent as we tensely waited for either of our teachers to react.

"I do believe she's right," Richard said, sounding amused.

"I was in my twenties when we made that recording . . . who could remember?" Dame Joan said, and the room filled with laughter. "In any case my dear, those ornaments were hideous, so stop copying them from me, and start singing your own, please."

I was not the only one to cry on our last day with Richard and

Joan. We had all bonded through the intensity of concentrated musical work.

"You take care of that voice of yours," Dame Joan said. "And please keep in touch."

"I will," I said, fighting back tears.

❋ ❋ ❋

The second of the three surreal phone calls I received was from Richard Miller. It came one evening just before spring break as my girlfriend Olivia and I were studying in my dorm room.

"Hello Laurie," said Mr. Miller's unmistakable tenor voice. "Do you have a moment?"

"Yes, sir," I said, alarmed. Mr. Miller almost never called me at home. "Is something wrong?"

"Quite the contrary," he said, and now I could hear the big smile in his voice. "I took the liberty of sending a recording of a couple arias you performed in studio class recently in hopes that you might get a very exciting opportunity to sing for John Williams."

"John Williams?" I asked. "As in the composer who wrote the score for *E.T.* and *Indiana Jones*, the one who conducts the Boston Pops?"

"The very same," Mr. Miller said. "You see, the Oberlin Orchestra is giving a concert in the fall next year at the Getty Museum in LA, and John, who recently received an honorary degree from Oberlin, will be conducting. All of us on the voice faculty had a meeting and selected three students to be heard by John to make the decision of who would perform with him and the orchestra in concert. He chose you."

"Me?" I gasped. "Are you sure?"

"Of course I'm sure. Why do you sound so surprised? He requested that you sing Barber's *Knoxville: Summer of 1915*."

The text of this almost twenty-minute-long work is a prose poem by James Agee describing an evening from his childhood. As I listened to different recordings of Dawn Upshaw, Leontyne Price, and Kathleen Battle's renditions on headphones in the listening station at the library, I fell in love with the detailed description of early twentieth century Knoxville, and Barber's piercing, nostalgic music that somehow captured the fleeting simplicity of childhood. It's one of those pieces that almost anyone can relate to, about remembering details of the environment around you, of enjoying balmy summer weather, not comprehending but feeling comforted by the adult conversation around you, and knowing you're safe as long as your parents are near.

I studied the piece for half a year before meeting John. It's hard to say where my stereotype of conductors came from, but I had been expecting a surly man who would throw sparks if I did anything that didn't pay homage to the music. I went to the first rehearsal just two days before the concert, feeling terrified that I wouldn't be prepared for some obscure question he would ask me about the piece. Surprise and relief swept over me like a gentle, reassuring breeze when John took my hand and in a kind voice said, "Well hello there. You must be that lovely soprano I had the great pleasure of hearing. Richard Miller sent me a recording of yours."

"Hi, I'm Laurie," I said, my voice sounding small and shy.

"I'm delighted to meet you, and I'm thrilled we will be performing together. Oh, and before we begin, is there anything I should know? How I should cue you since you can't see me?"

"I can do a lot by ear," I said. "I can often hear when a conductor breathes in rhythm before a musical phrase."

A rehearsal pianist began to play, and we ran the piece without stopping.

"You know," he said after we finished. "This is one of my favorite pieces."

"Oh no, here it comes," I thought. "He's going to tell me how I just managed to butcher his favorite piece."

"And your performance just now reminded me why I love it so much," he continued.

"Really? You mean that?"

"Of course I do. Not only do you understand the piece, but you've internalized it, haven't you?"

"I guess I have. The music is so perfect."

"You can say that again."

"The music is so perfect," I repeated. He laughed.

" So, how was he?" Mom asked in the car on the way home from the rehearsal.

"Just like the kind of person you'd expect to write the music to Steven Spielberg movies," I said. "Really warm, like a favorite uncle."

The Oberlin Orchestra had been flown in to LA for the occasion. The instrumentalists were in high spirits, as though they were children on a field trip. It was strange to see the people I went to college with in my hometown. There was only one dress rehearsal with the orchestra, and then suddenly the evening of the concert had arrived. I shared a dressing room with a sophomore violinist who had been selected to play the suite from *Schindler's List* with the orchestra. She and her mother spoke to each other in Russian, and though I couldn't understand their dialogue, I could tell her mother was micromanaging the poor girl's preparation for her performance.

I heard the concert master's A, signaling the orchestra to begin tuning. The audience sounded large from the monitors backstage. I sat nervously listening to the orchestra play. The violinist scurried out of the room to take her place backstage before her entrance, and her mother rushed to claim her seat in the audience, leaving me alone. After the last, soulful notes of the *Schindler's List* Suite had ended, I heard the din of the audience. It was now intermission. I was next up. My heart beat uncomfortably fast.

"You ready?" John asked as I made my way to the wings.

"Yeah, and a bit nervous," I admitted.

"You're going to be great," he said, placing a hand on my shoulder.

Suddenly, I was feeling comforted by the fact that I would be going onstage to perform with him. It was though the man who was now guiding me onstage was Grandpa, about to take me sledding down the mountain in Lake Tahoe, and I was safe. Only good things could happen as long as he was there. Then came the audience's applause, the excitement, and the heightened awareness that I was standing there in the bright red strapless gown Mom and I had bought for the occasion.

The orchestra tuned again, and John took his first deep breath. The oboe, English horn, and clarinet began playing the first notes of the piece, and the strings followed. The sound of the orchestra rose and swelled around me, and there I was, in the center of this lush landscape of sound.

"It has become that time of evening," I sang. "When people sit on their porches, rocking gently and talking gently."

Together, we set the scene, John Williams, the orchestra, and I. The music continued to build in texture until the full orchestra had come in, making the fabric of the music rich and full as could be. It was easy to tell what John wanted, when he felt a crescendo, a place to slow down, a place to be more tender. It was all in the way he breathed, almost singing the phrases with me, how he audibly mouthed the words. I was near enough to him to sense his hands keeping time. I followed his strict rhythm through the passage of Agee's words describing the sounds of a streetcar as Barber's music emulated its industrial sound, and then we slowed into the quiet of lying on the grass with beloved family under the stars. Then I heard the impassioned deep breath, cuing the orchestra through the climactic moment, a child's plea to God to remember his loved ones in times of trouble. Then we slowed as the orchestra returned to the initial theme of the piece in a bittersweet ending.

It was a magical journey we all took on that stage, and we were welcomed back by the audience's enthusiastic applause.

John squeezed my hand as we bowed together. "Couldn't have gone any better," he said warmly. "Now when I think of my favorite piece, I will always hear it in your voice."

❋ ❋ ❋

The third phone call that came from out of the blue was from Brian. Calls from Brian weren't unusual occurrences, and in fact, they happened almost daily. The fact that it came in the middle of the workday, however, was highly uncharacteristic. I was back in LA on spring break with a monster of a cold. The phone rang just as I reluctantly extricated myself from a hot shower, which was temporarily relieving my stuffy head.

"Hello," I said.

"You sound awful. Are you okay?" Brian asked.

"I'm sick. What's up?"

"I just got a call here at my office from a Flicka von Stade. Do you know who that is?"

"Flicka von Stade?" I gasped. "She's only one of the most famous mezzos in the world!"

"Oh," Brian said sheepishly. "Then I guess I shouldn't have been as short with her as I was. I thought anyone calling my office looking for you must be some telemarketer or something. Guess she got my number off of your CD. Anyway, she asked me to have you call her back."

"Me? Call her back?"

"Before you call her, stop hyperventilating, okay? That might not make the best first impression."

My pianist David and I had done a recital at the Jewish Community Center that past October, which we recorded, and I used the CD for audition material. My parents had been handing it out to anyone who would listen. On the back of the CD, we had put Brian's work number as my contact so as not to give out any personal information. I had met Frederica von Stade, or Flicka as people called her, when I was in high school at a master class she gave in the LA area. I had not sung in the class, but I had talked with her at length afterwards. Mom recently saw her in a production at the Met while I was in school and waited backstage to hand her my most recent CD. I could not believe she had listened to it! And what could she possibly want to talk to me about?

"Hello," said the pleasant, lofty voice of an opera singer.

"Hi, Flicka," I hesitated. "This is Laurie Rubin."

"Hello, Laurie. Thank you so much for calling me back so quickly."

"Oh, no problem," I said while thinking, "*As if I'd wait to speak to Frederica von Stade.*"

"First of all, please thank your mother for letting me hear your CD. It's absolutely wonderful. What a voice!"

"Wow, thank you," I said, while thinking, "*Holy shit, Frederica von Stade loves my voice.*"

"I was wondering if it wouldn't be too much of an inconvenience for you to come in February to sing with me at a special event that is near and dear to my heart."

She broached the subject of singing with her as if she were asking me to help her with some burdensome task, like moving into a new home or babysitting a particularly difficult child.

"Of course I'd love to sing with you!" I said with unmasked enthusiasm. "When is it?"

"The event is on Monday, February 11th, and it's a benefit for an organization that researches ways of treating degenerative eye diseases. A good friend of mine has a daughter who is losing her sight rapidly, and she'd gotten very involved with this organization. They asked me to sing, but I really thought it would be fun to sing with you. A few duets, perhaps a solo aria each?"

A wave of exhilaration swept through me. Singing duets with Frederica von Stade!

"I don't think we'll need too much rehearsal time, maybe just two days. I would love to have you come spend the weekend with me. We have several guest rooms, so I would like to invite your mother. Oh, and if your pianist on the CD wants to play the event, we have plenty of room for him here, too."

I had forgotten my cold completely. The ache in my body had been replaced by a burst of energy that sent me running into Mom's office to tell her the news.

❂ ❂ ❂

I first met David when he was hired by Oakwood School as the pianist for the chorus. He had a mysterious quiet about him that made him hard to read. He almost never uttered a single word

254

during rehearsals. It wasn't until halfway through the year after a rehearsal when I playfully uttered a few operatic notes that David addressed me for the first time.

"You have a beautiful voice," he had said.

I found out soon after that he had studied piano at the Manhattan School of Music in New York, after which he spent seven years in Italy where he played for some of the most famous opera singers in the world. Then he returned to LA for a Master's at USC, and he was now playing for our high school chorus to make some extra money. He began to play auditions and recitals with me, eventually traveling with me to the White House for a disability awareness event, competitions in Italy, and a recital in Canada. Now he would be going with me to San Francisco to play for my duets with Frederica von Stade and stay in her house.

❀ ❀ ❀

David, Mom, and I flew to Oakland, where Flicka lived, and she and her husband greeted us at the airport.

"Oh Laurie, thank you for taking time out of your busy school year to come do this," she said, giving me a big hug as though we had known each other well for years. "And you must be David. I love your playing. I am so honored that you came out here to play this event."

She proceeded to give Mom the same reception, and then insisted on wheeling our bags for us to her large SUV in the parking lot.

Flicka's home was a bright, airy place that had a wonderful, lived-in feeling, with photos of her daughters on the walls and a living room furnished with comfortable couches and chairs. Mom and I occupied each of her daughter's previous bedrooms and David stayed in a guest room.

"Let me just fix us some sandwiches while you get settled," Flicka said.

After a brief lunch, we began to warm up in Flicka's living room.

"Are you ready?" she asked.

Flicka and I are both mezzos, and high mezzos at that, and just a few weeks before the event, Flicka decided it would be best if she sang the part of the lower voice in all the duets, relegating me to the high Bs of the famous "Flower Duet" from the opera *Lakme* about an Indian princess. The other duet from *Tales of Hoffmann* sat in the comfortable middle range for us.

I thought my twenty-two-year-old voice would be a tiny minnow next to her beautiful marlin. It poured out of her in a stream of effortless, golden notes, and miraculously, my voice moved in harmony with her, blending, matching her musical phrases. I learned in that one day some of the best vocal lessons could be achieved through singing with someone better than me. It forced me to rise to the challenge. Since my first time singing a duet in a recital with a friend I had made at the Spotlight Awards, I had discovered how almost sensual the feeling was. How you take on qualities of each other's voice, how you are attentive to each other's musical instincts. As I sang with Flicka and our voices moved up and down the phrases in harmony, I was taken over by emotion. Embarrassed, I turned away, hastily wiping away tears.

"This is un-fucking-believable," David said, his voice shaking. "I've never been this close to Frederica von Stade's voice."

"Okay, I'm expecting to wake up from this any time now," I said. "This is really happening, right?"

After rehearsing our two duets, Flicka had a sudden burst of inspiration.

"Have you heard the Rossini Cat duet? It's hysterical, and it makes fun of competitive, catty sopranos. I think the audience would love this."

The piece was easy to learn as it was set to the text of one word, "meow." Our rehearsal had turned into a jam session.

"Okay, how about you quote that *Traviata* aria here, and then I'll upstage you by showing off some coloratura from the *Barber of Seville*?" Flicka suggested.

"Ooooh, and wouldn't it be fun to end the duet by singing Vincero the way the tenors do when they end their concerts, trying to out-sing each other?" I said.

"Okay, I'm meowed out," Flicka said laughing. "Feel like some ice-cream?"

She drove us to a local shop where she addressed the girl behind the counter by name. Then, a group of three women whose daughters had evidently known Flicka's girls came up to say hello. One could see right away that Flicka had been an active member of her community, and that she was loved there not for her being a famous opera singer but for her contributions as a mother, a friend, and a person.

Monday morning began with a breakfast of pastries Flicka's husband had brought in for us from a local bakery. David, Mom, Flicka, and I sat at the kitchen table in our robes where we talked for over two hours, about how, like me, Flicka had been told for years that she was neither a soprano nor a mezzo, but something in between, about how she fainted in shock the first time she was able to utter a high C, and about repertoire she had done that would be good for me since we had similar voices. Then we moved to the piano for a last rehearsal before the event.

The benefit was a dinner in a hotel ballroom. The clatter of plates and the tinkle of forks could be heard as heart-wrenching videos about people losing their sight were played, followed by several speeches. Then, Flicka was introduced. She sang a lullaby that a composer friend had written for her.

"And now," she began. "It is my sincere pleasure to introduce Laurie Rubin. I've known Laurie since she was in high school, but when I met her, I had no idea that this tiny little thing would have such a big, mature, beautiful voice. I think you will fall in love with both her voice and her spirit as much as I did."

I proceeded to sing my aria from *Cinderella*, and our three duets followed. Before the Cat Duet, Flicka handed me a pair of sunglasses, the rims of which were covered in rhinestones she had glued on the night before.

"Now we look like Hollywood glamor queens," she laughed.

The audience roared with laughter as we performed the duet,

outdoing each other, showing off who could sing their high note the longest, and adding in our phrases from famous arias, playing dueling divas.

I ended our mini-concert with "I Could Have Danced All Night." During the repeat, it suddenly occurred to me to change the words.

"I could have sung all night," I sang. "I only know when she began to sing with me, I could have sung, sung, sung all night!"

Flicka and I exchanged tearful hugs of farewell. The weekend was all that music and friendship should be, fun-filled, spontaneous, full of laughter and harmony that touched us both. She made me promise to keep her updated with news on my career and to ask her for help or advice when I needed it.

Red

Red is the height of passion, anger, and intensity.
Red makes a statement.
I've always been told that red is striking on me,
against my fair skin and dark hair.
I relate to red, as I feel my personality is often
  conjuring up that color.
Red means deep feelings and emotions,
and it represents the fighter in me.
If people ask me what color my aura is, I would
  have to say red.
Red is the vivid color of the gown I wore on stage
  with John Williams,
singing Barber's Knoxville: Summer of 1915

Cinderella

The Oberlin conservatory was abuzz with speculation about the opera that had been chosen for the spring production. Since my voice type was suited to Rossini, who wrote florid, often fast, melismatic passages, I was hoping the rumor about *La Cenerentola* being chosen for my senior year was true.

La Cenerentola is Rossini's version of Cinderella, and it showcases an agile mezzo voice that can fly up and down the staff, creating impressive, ornate, musical fireworks while also being able to sustain long, lyrical phrases. I had been listening to my favorite mezzos' renditions of "Non Piu Mesta" ("No More Pain"), the aria that Cinderella concludes the opera with as she starts her life with her prince, addressing the family who had once rejected her. Cecilia Bartoli sang an impressive version at super speed in her famous tongue-in-cheek manner. Frederica von Stade performed a silky smooth version filled with warmth, her coloratura pouring out of her with admirable ease. Many more mezzos added their flavor to the piece in my collection of CDs, and I had been inspired many times over to make the piece my own.

"So, Laurie, what arias do you have on the fire?" Mr. Miller asked me one day, midway through my junior year.

"I've been working on "Dopo Notte" by Handel."

"Yes," he said, drawing out the word thoughtfully. "Have you ever considered singing 'Non Piu Mesta'"?

My heart leapt. "Really, you think I'm ready for that?"

"Well, of course," he laughed kindly. "Your voice is perfect for that aria, and you've certainly demonstrated your ability to sing coloratura very well."

The aria became my anthem. I took it with me everywhere, to the White House, where I sang in a concert organized for Disabilities Employment Week, to the local voice competitions where I won First and Second Place, and to my duet performance with Frederica von Stade, where I felt like I was dreaming because one of my favorite mezzos of all time was listening to me sing one of her signature pieces. The aria had found such a special place in my heart, and it conjured up a new dream inside of me, to someday sing the role of Cinderella in a fully staged production.

That dream became a very real possibility my senior year when Jonathan Field, our opera director, announced that Rossini's *La Cenerentola* would in fact be our spring opera.

I spent the entire semester preparing for the December audition. Each week that passed reminded me that I was one week closer, as Mr. Miller gave me vocal exercises to strengthen my agility and long, elaborate variations on scales to build my musculature.

The big day came all too soon. So much was riding on this one audition. If I did not get the role, I would be saying good-bye to my last hope of playing the lead in an Oberlin opera, and my dream of singing this particular role would be shattered. I had suspected in the past that I hadn't been cast in operas because it would have posed all manner of logistical challenges, and there just wasn't enough time to find a place for me in Mr. Field's staging concept. From having done staged opera scenes at Oberlin and some summer programs, I knew there must be a way, even with elaborate sets. If I could cross busy streets and walk around a college campus, surely I could learn my way around a stage.

Auditions were held in the large rehearsal room where we had opera class. I walked in to find Mr. Polivnic, the conductor of the Oberlin Orchestra, Mr. Field, Victoria Vaughan, the assistant director, and Alan Montgomery, the opera coach and pianist who would be playing for the audition. Though I knew all of these people very well, they now had a serious, almost emotionless, cold air that I knew all too well from judges at auditions. They spoke in low voices and clicked their pens as I entered.

"I am auditioning for the title role," I announced.

Alan began to play the first notes of "Non Piu Mesta," and my heart, which had been under control up to that moment, started threatening to jump out of my chest. Feeling out of breath, I began to sing.

"Laurie, calm down or you'll never get through this," I thought to myself, as I tried like mad to stay in character. I knew I could do this aria better. I could practically sing it backwards in my sleep if I wanted; I had been singing it so much the past year and a half.

"Thank you," Mr. Field said, his tone making no indication of whether or not he had liked my performance. "We would now like to hear 'Una Volta.'"

This much shorter aria is more wistful, and in a minor key, and the story she's telling in her song brings her comfort and hope.

"Okay Laurie, that's all we need," Mr. Field said after I had finished. "We will post the cast list up on the opera board by Friday morning."

Though the audition was on a Wednesday evening, and I only had a full day to wait for the outcome, each hour dragged out torturously. I had Italian first thing in the morning on Friday, in a building nowhere near the conservatory. It wasn't until 11:00AM that I made my way on the lightly snow covered paths that led to the conservatory. When I reached it, I heard excited voices coming from a crowd around the opera board. As I approached, a sea of arms enveloped me in a group hug and several people were shouting in my ear.

"Laurie you got it! You're singing Cenerentola."

My mouth opened in a scream I couldn't hear through the excited noise around me. My dream was about to come true. It wasn't just the role I wanted for my own artistic reasons. It was the chance to show people that a blind singer could carry such a big responsibility.

"Hey Laurie, I'm playing your stepfather," said the baritone, Kevin, excitedly.

"Oh yay," I cried. "You get to beat me up."

I made my way to the lounge to the pay phone, where a line had already formed to use it.

"I got into the opera!" shrieked enthusiastic singers to parents on the other end. "Oh, I better go . . . the girl playing Cenerentola is waiting to share the news."

❋ ❋ ❋

We had winter vacation to learn our roles. When we returned in January, we had a week's worth of coaching on the music with Alan in his studio.

"Make sure you flip the *r* in 'core,' not roll the *r*," he instructed. "And really emphasize *affanno*. Give it that nice darker color to show us the pain she's describing."

A week later, Mr. Field began staging.

"Okay, Laurie, here's what's going to happen. Cenerentola, as you know, is the stepdaughter of Don Magnifico. He and your two stepsisters, Clorinda and Tisbe, treat you like their maid and force you to wait on them, hand and foot, while doing all the housework. You being blind gives us a perfect reason to have them treat you differently. We're going to have you wear dark glasses, and the broom you use to sweep with will act as your cane, and means of getting around the stage."

I sat bewildered for a moment.

"Mr. Field," I said. "Not all blind people wear dark glasses. I'm afraid that's not a very accurate representation."

"Well, we want the audience to know. We need to give them something they'd expect so there's no question that you're a blind character. As I was saying, at the beginning of the opera, we'll have you sweeping while your sisters are primping and trying on their gowns and jewelry. You're going to sing 'Una Volta,' which is annoying your sisters, and they're going to tell you to shut up. Then, a beggar is going to come in and ask for a little bit of breakfast. Clorinda and Tisbe are repulsed and want to get rid of him. Cenerentola, you're going to be kind and offer him a tray of breakfast."

Mr. Field handed me a small metal tray with rolls and a coffee cup, empty for rehearsals.

"You don't know this now," Mr. Field continued. "But later, you discover it was a good move being kind to that beggar, because he is Allidoro, Prince Ramiro's tutor."

Mr. Field had us imagine the set and the stage that we would eventually be working on. He had me count steps to get from one place to another, a table where the kitchen would be, a bench where the fireplace would be, and so on. I oriented myself to set pieces, using others as reference points. The first few times, I would miss my mark, ending up just a hair to the right or left of my intended destination, but with repetition, I found where I needed to be.

Libby and Melanie, the sopranos who played my sisters, were told to be rough with me physically, and every time they had to push or shove me, they whispered to me, "I'm so sorry Laurie, it's so hard to be mean to you!"

"And it's hard to think of you two as mean girls who are victimizing me," I smiled back.

"Nice job, everybody," Mr. Field said, two hours later. "Laurie, I'd like to talk to you before you go." Mr. Field waited until everyone had cleared the room. "You know, Laurie, I hope you appreciate your role here," he said in a low voice.

"Oh I do," I assured him. "I can't tell you how much this means to me."

"Good, because I really would like to do the directing around here without being contradicted. If I want you to wear glasses, I hope I don't have to be told what is and what isn't politically correct."

I froze. I had not meant to cause any drama, nor did I mean to seem like the difficult diva, but it would be me on that stage, me going out there having to represent a stereotype I had been fighting my entire life, one which instilled such fear and negative reactions in other people.

"You're treading on thin ice here," he said, and then he excused me.

He was right; I was trying to keep a delicate balance. I knew that I had to be easier than the average singer so that people hiring me would realize that working with me wasn't as hard as they had thought. At the same time, I had to balance that with protecting my integrity.

One of the most rewarding aspects of being onstage was communicating my independence to audiences, not reinforcing the perceptions of weakness they had. I longed for a director to stop worrying about whether a character had to be blind or sighted. I was reminded of the time I had been called "not blind enough" for a TV character I auditioned for. I wondered if I would ever get the chance to perform in a way that would convey that there was no such thing as being "too blind," and that a character's personality and circumstance could transcend those categories. I said nothing more about the glasses, using a broom for a cane, or anything else, and tried to be the easygoing singer I had to be in my precarious position as a blind opera singer.

❋ ❋ ❋

After a men's chorus of courtiers comes to announce that the prince is looking for the most beautiful lady in the land to be his bride, Prince Ramiro, disguised as his servant Dandini, pays a visit to the house of Don Magnifico and his two daughters. He finds what is truly in the hearts of all the women who live there. Clorinda and Tisbe do not treat him well, thinking he's a servant, whereas Cenerentola is kind and charming to him, and, as often happens in opera, they fall in love over the span of a five-minute-long duet.

"Peter," Mr. Field said to the tenor playing the prince as we began to stage our duet, "just before you start singing your verse, I want you to remove Cenerentola's glasses. This is your chance to see the girl for who she really is, despite the status her family has bestowed upon her. Laurie, I want you to touch Peter's face."

I had to bite my tongue for fear of exclaiming about how a blind person would never, ever feel a new person's face, despite what they show on TV. It was one of my pet peeves for sure, but I cooperated, and decided not to risk losing the role or my reputation.

"Oh Laurie, it's so good to sing with you!" Peter said, hugging me after rehearsal.

"I feel the same way," I said.

Peter and I had bonded over a mutual love of baroque music. Though our friendship did not go beyond hanging out in the confines of the conservatory, we had been ecstatic to find out that we would be singing opposite each other. Our friendship created a magical synergy when we became our respective characters, and acting was easy with the mutual admiration and supportive energy we shared.

"Okay, Peter, take Laurie's arm, and bring her away from the fireplace she's been sweeping and more to the front. Sit her down, and sit across from her. Laurie, you are taken by how lovely he is, and he is one of the few people who has taken notice of you and shown you respect and kindness."

After the duet, Tisbe and Clorinda call "Cenerentola" incessantly, putting an end to the moment, and giving the prince a sense of how Cenerentola is treated.

I went offstage while Mr. Field blocked a comical scene between my stepsisters and father. We ended rehearsal that day on a light note.

So I was not prepared for what was to come the following day. In acting class, I had been told that you must give all of yourself, playing a character by digging inside yourself to find some of the most difficult emotions. The scene we would be staging was the one where Cenerentola begs her stepfather to let her go to the ball. Again and again, he fends her off, making fun of her, physically taunting and almost beating her. Mr. Field had Kevin take my broom, my only safety and means of getting around, and had him walk around the stage with it, doing a very nasty impression of his blind stepdaughter. He instructed Libby and Melanie to laugh at their father's performance.

The amazing thing about Cenerentola, aside from her kind heart, is her resilience. Many times in this scene, and presumably in her life, she has been beaten down, but she bounces back with still more hope for a better life. During the scene, just after Kevin, or Don Magnifico, beat me down or hurled insults at me, I would approach him, pleading my case, asking if I could please go to the ball. Again and again, he'd tease me, taunt me, growing more brutal and mean through the scene until Jason, playing the beggar, enters and tells Don Magnifico that his third daughter's presence is requested at the ball. And there it is, that glimmer of hope for Cenerentola, the thing that should surely force her father to allow her to go. But her last hope is shattered when Don Magnifico, in one last display of abuse, tells the beggar that his third daughter is dead.

"Laurie!" Mr. Field shouted over the music. "I need to see your hurt and shock at the blow Magnifico just struck by pronouncing you dead. Haven't you ever been hurt so badly that you just couldn't believe your ears?"

My heart was experiencing déjà vu. Yes, there had been another time when I had been hurt so badly that I wondered if I would ever come out of a place of darkness. It had been when I was in the eighth grade, and a close family friend who was eighteen at the time was my chaperone on a class camping trip. Out of a misguided sense of honesty she told me that I needed to face reality, and that I would never enjoy romance, have a real job, or a life independent of my parents, that my life was essentially worthless.

"Laurie, are you okay?" Libby and Melanie asked, rushing over to me.

"Oh, sorry," I said, snapping out of it. "I'm fine."

At this point, Mr. Field instructed me to dissolve into tears and crumple in a heap of my own rags by the fireplace. The beggar stays to comfort me while Don Magnifico and his daughters leave for the ball. For the first time in the opera, Cenerentola's sadness cannot be lifted by a kind word, and she tries to dismiss the beggar. Suddenly, the beggar reveals his true identity as the prince's tutor, and he assures her that her life will be blessed with wonderful things because of her pure heart.

Jason put his arms around me, forcing me into a standing position, and put my hands on an elaborate gown, which I would wear to the ball. As he sang his aria to me, he repeated a phrase, which also subtitles the opera, "Triomfa La Bonta," or "Good Will Always Win."

"Yes, Laurie," Mr. Field cried over the music. "That's wonderful; keep showing us the joy spreading all over your face at everything Allidoro is showing and telling you."

Before Jason could finish his aria, I found that I had gone too far when drawing from my emotions. The tears did not come slowly. A fit of sobs overwhelmed me, and poor Jason, who had released me to sing to the audience, now put his arm around me again to steady me.

"Alan, stop," Mr. Fields said, before Alan could finish playing the last notes of the aria. He rushed over to me, and for the first time, Mr. Field was hugging me, as were Libby, Melanie, and Kevin.

"That was amazing!" they were all saying.

"You own this character," Mr. Fields said. "You have truly become Cenerentola, and you understand who she is."

Cenerentola's light at the end of her tunnel was my light. Her joy was my joy because the prince saw beyond the stereotype of blindness that so many others could not see past. Now, I understood why Mr. Field wanted me to wear the dark glasses. They were the historical anachronism that the prince removed right away, and those glasses remained off throughout the rest of the opera.

❀ ❀ ❀

Opening night came, and Mom, Dad, Brian, and several family friends spent the weekend in Ohio just to see the performances. There were two casts, which we lovingly called the tall cast and the small cast. The tall cast, which literally had singers who towered over me, performed on opening night as well as the Saturday night performance. I was in the cast of people closer to my own height, which performed on Friday night and at the Sunday closing performance.

The energy was high in the dressing rooms. As we got into costume and had our elaborate nineteenth century hairdos done, people came backstage to wish us luck. Several of my closest friends bestowed chocolates, flowers, and other congratulatory gifts upon me.

"Hi Laur," Mom said. "I've got a surprise for you."

"What is it?" I asked. I heard her unfolding a letter.

"Dear Laurie, I'm sending you lots of love today. I'm so proud of you, and I know you're going to be a wonderful Cenerentola. I wish I could be with you tonight to celebrate in your success, and I am with you in spirit. Lots of love, Flicka."

My heart leapt and I felt a glow spreading through my insides.

"She sent you a beautiful bouquet of flowers," Mom said. Their fragrance seemed to fill the whole backstage with her positive energy. It was like the good omen I needed for a good performance, a letter from one Cenerentola to another.

Before we knew it, places had been called, and we were listening to the Oberlin Orchestra playing the familiar overture. There's nothing like the grand sounds of an orchestra, and there was nothing more wonderfully surreal for me than standing behind the curtain, knowing I was about to play a lead role, rather than marveling at the orchestra's first notes as a member of the audience. I stood there, my heart pounding, in a petticoat and thick layers of faded grey muslin, the maid's outfit that I wore for most of the opera. It was not only the singing I worried about. It was making sure that the techniques of squaring off with one set piece would in fact lead me straight to the one I'd have to reach in order to perform the next action, like picking up a breakfast tray for the beggar. This had all grown very easy in the opera room, but adapting the staging to a much larger set with multiple levels had proved daunting. Soon, I heard the last notes of the overture, and it was time for me to walk onstage alone with my broom and begin sweeping and singing.

My nerves and excitement electrified me, making me feel perfectly in character. As each scene came and went, I grew more confident, reassured that everything would go according to plan, just as we had rehearsed.

After Allidoro's aria, the dressers helped me change into my ball gown. Two bangles encrusted with rhinestones jingled lightly on my arm. It was time for me to make my debut. Jason escorted me out to the steps that led to the main stage on his arm, announcing me to the court. As he let go, and I took the first step down onto the stage on my own and without my broom for the very first time, a loud, unmistakable gasp from the audience filled the hall as they watched in terror. I fought off a fit of laughter that threatened my singing. I realized that a majority of the people watching the show had probably never seen someone blind handle steps by themselves, especially without the use of a cane or another person.

Intermission came and went, and suddenly it was time for me to sing "Non Piu Mesta," the piece that I had performed in concerts all over the country. Now, for the first time, I would be singing it in front of an audience in the context of the opera. The aria came alive as never before, and with the powerful musical force of the orchestra and the voices of the other characters, I was propelled into a new realm of excitement.

After I sang the final B Natural, my highest note in the entire opera, it was time for me to perform the last bit of staging given to me by Mr. Field. I took the broom, which had been specially rigged by the props department to break when I hit it against my knees, and cast the pieces aside in one last, powerful gesture. I then ran offstage without it until someone waiting in the wings caught me. For both Cenerentola and me, it was a dismissal of a stereotype that had bound us so unexpectedly together.

As Peter and I linked arms to take our bows, the audience hooted and cheered. I could feel that everyone, from cast member to audience member, sensed a momentous occasion, and I was now experiencing the power of becoming a character in an opera onstage. As I thought about all the close friends I had made at Oberlin in the audience, as well as my family, standing and applauding, I knew that performing in this opera represented more of a culmination of this chapter in my life than any graduation ceremony could ever be. It captured, in a nutshell, everything I felt my life represented. Perhaps Cenerentola and I were seen as the underdog, but when it came down to it, we both triumphed.

And Then There Was Yale

After doing extensive research on graduate programs, I decided that Yale Opera would be my top choice because it was small and the program focused on opera performance. Yale was also unique in that it was strictly designed to give everyone in the program a chance to perform lead roles in the main stage operas, with only sixteen students enrolled at a time to ensure everyone had equal opportunities.

It snowed the entire weekend I was at Yale for my audition. The skies were as intimidating as the audition process itself. Patricia Green, the director of the Yale Opera program, interviewed each applicant.

"You know, Laurie," she said in a businesslike tone as I sat in her studio during my interview, in which the two opera coaches and two other voice teachers sat silently taking notes, "this program is specifically focused on opera, nothing more, nothing less. With your, um, how shall I put it, sight impairment, why would you choose a school like this?"

"Well," I began, gathering my thoughts, "I realize that a career in concert work where I can just stand and sing with an orchestra behind me, and in chamber music where I'm collaborating with other musicians might be easier for me. I applied to Yale, however, because I feel that grad school is the time when I can be challenged in a nurturing environment, a place where I can push myself to learn the techniques that might come more easily to sighted people and which I couldn't learn anywhere else. It's also a chance for me to get opera experience under my belt so that the doors to at least a partial career in opera won't be closed to me, and I will have experience on my résumé to prove to opera companies that it is not impossible."

"I see," Patricia said seriously. "Thank you. We will take that into consideration."

❀　❀　❀

Even though I left Yale feeling good about my interview and my audition the next day, I was still nervous about my chances. I had heard one amazing voice after another echoing through the hall outside of the audition room, and knew that only two mezzos were graduating this year, leaving only two vacancies. I sat on pins and needles for weeks, hearing nothing. Then on the Wednesday I was back home for spring break, Mom called me excitedly into her room.

"You have to come hear this!" she said, calling the number for her voicemail and putting it on speaker.

"Hello, Laurie, this is Patricia Cross from Yale Opera calling. I hope you are well. I'm just calling to let you know that you have been accepted into our program. You will get your official information packet in the mail shortly. We look forward to having you."

"Yes!" I screamed. "I got into Yale!"

"I now have an Ivy Leaguer on my hands!" Mom said, giving me a hug.

❈ ❈ ❈

Yale, I soon found out, was a grand place with gothic buildings and old Ivy League traditions that students, professors, and trustees alike took very seriously. During orientation, I learned about a club named Mory's, just up the block from my dorm, which you could only enter if invited by a member (it is still a mystery to me how one becomes a member). Once inside, you could order mystery drinks, differentiated by color and taste. Nobody knew what was inside these concoctions, and you had to pass them around, drinking out of communal bowls which, in my opinion, were breeding grounds for mononucleosis and other unwanted illnesses. And then there were, of course, the secret societies, which groomed such luminaries as Bill Clinton and George Bush, and which nobody outside knew how to get into. Having just come from Oberlin, where anyone could join any club or student group, I quickly realized I was in for some major culture shock.

I lived in the Hall of Graduate Studies, a complex of gothic-style residences for graduate students in the College of Arts and Sciences and a handful of School of Music students. The central building, which held the dining hall, was flanked by two smaller residence halls, and in the center was a lovely, large courtyard with thick grass and benches to sit on. My room felt like a cozy bedroom and a quaint sitting room in one, with wood floors, an antique armchair, and a real, working fireplace.

The Hall, which we lovingly called HGS, was one of my favorite parts of Yale. I was neighbors with an applied physics major who had taken apart her bed, used the bedsprings as a rack for her pots and pans, and went to the dumpsters to find wood, which she made into shelves. In her spare time, she told me that she was rebuilding an old motorcycle engine. In the dining hall, I found myself sitting with economics, Russian Literature, history, comparative literature, and physics grad students, and soaked up their fascinating conversations about what they were studying like a sponge.

❖ ❖ ❖

"Good afternoon everyone," Patricia said in the same businesslike tone I had remembered from audition weekend. "This is your last day of orientation, and as you know, we're all here for a little tradition that you students like to call Death by Aria, where you will all get up and sing an aria for all the Yale Opera Faculty and for each other. Before we do that, I just want to give you a brief overview of what things will be like once classes begin. You will have movement class on Tuesdays and Thursdays where you will learn basic ballet techniques, as well as stage combat skills and gestures, all of these things very crucial to your success as a performer in opera on stage. Then, you will have diction class to continue refining your pronunciation of all the languages you sing in. This year will be focused on French and German, and next year will be focused on Italian and Russian. On Friday mornings, you will have acting class. Other than that, schedules are subject to adjustments as you will be coaching your opera scenes, which need to be memorized in two weeks and performed for the public next month. Do not make any plans for anything else until you receive your daily schedule, which we will email to you by 10:00PM for the following day. We cannot accommodate any projects that you may want to do on your own because we will have to make executive decisions about when more or less rehearsal is needed, especially once we cast the two operas this year. I expect you to learn your music quickly, and we will be forced to take your parts away from you if you have not learned them thoroughly by the specified date. Please do your part to make this a wonderful and productive year for all of us. Now, who would like to sing first?"

I listened with excitement to my new colleagues singing arias from *The Barber of Seville*, *Carmen*, *La Boheme*, *La Traviata*, and more. It was a wonderful feeling to know that as I sang my aria from *La Cenerentola* once again, I would soon be in operas with these singers. I would have a chance at another experience onstage like the one just the year before that had made me grow so much as a singer and actress.

When the last aria had finished, we all left Hendrie Hall, one of Yale's three music buildings, and headed home. Mom, who was staying at the Omni Hotel nearby, had not attended Death by Aria, and nobody else in Yale Opera lived in HGS, so I was prepared for my first walk on my newly learned route from Hendrie Hall back home by myself.

When I had first found out the good news about getting into Yale, Mom had worried over my safety in a city like New Haven, notorious for making the news more times than she would have liked for crimes and brutal murders. Though Yale had a definite campus, buildings were located across New Haven's main streets, which I would have to cross regularly. The city itself was a grid and was easy for me to navigate. As long as I knew which streets ran north and south, and which others ran east and west, I knew exactly where I was. Being a small woman going it alone made me nervous.

"I'm fine," I continued to say to myself as I walked. "Young women walk alone all the time here."

No sooner had I crossed College Street than I felt something or someone squeezing my behind. As I let out a squeal of shock, I heard laughter and the sound of a man hurrying away. My heart was jumping as I fumbled in my pocket for my cell phone. Before I could think of someone to dial, Mom put her hand on my shoulder.

"You just got your ass pinched," she said.

"Mom, where did you come from?" I asked.

"I knew you were getting out of class at five, so I just wanted to make sure you were okay getting back to HGS by yourself. You were doing great."

"What should I do now?" I asked, feeling frightened.

"There's nothing you can do," she said. "A middle-aged man on a bike decided you had a cute butt, that's all."

Though Mom seemed calm, I knew she was secretly reeling about her baby getting her first taste of city life in New Haven before classes had even started.

❀ ❀ ❀

I walked into movement class on my first day of school to a peculiarly somber group of singers.

"Hi, what's going on?" I asked cheerfully. I noticed the muffled sounds of an AM radio echoing in the otherwise silent room. Nobody answered for a while. As my cane noisily found an empty seat, I began to listen to the newscasters' indistinguishable frantic voices.

"The World Trade Center was hit!" sobbed Andrea, one of the new sopranos.

My mouth fell open, and I joined my classmates' silent vigil as more horrifying news seemed to reach the desks of the reporters who were announcing it to us as they were hearing it for the first time themselves. Brad, our movement teacher, had found a small TV, which he wheeled into the large room, and we sat there helplessly as the second tower was struck down.

Morning classes were canceled, and we all made our way to Naples, a restaurant located next to one of the music buildings. Several of us desperately tried to get a hold of our loved ones in New York.

"Thank God my best friend is okay," said a soprano named Tammy. "She works for Morgan-Stanley. If she hadn't left ten minutes late today, she would have been dead."

The phone lines were continuously busy. It was an hour before I managed to reach Mom, Dad, and Brian who were all safe on the Upper West Side. Because both of their kids were on the East Coast now, and Mom and Dad were tired of hotel bills, they had purchased a two-bedroom apartment shortly after I left for college. They had just helped me move in and were in New York when the towers fell. Brian, whose apartment in the Village was not far from the Twin Towers, walked over sixty blocks north to Mom and Dad's place. They were devastated but safe.

❅ ❅ ❅

Classes began in earnest the next day. Yale's president had announced several memorials that would be held around campus throughout the week. A large tower near HGS had a carillon, which students from the Yale Carillon Society would play at around 5:00 almost every afternoon, their beautiful, haunting melodies making me feel like I had gone back in time a century as I walked to and from class. Though the choir of bells was a near daily occurrence at Yale, its being so new to my ears made it sound as though it were a tribute to the lives that were lost and the seemingly indestructible towers that were now gone.

Black

Black is the sky when there is no light left.
Black or complete dark is not scary to me.
Unlike those who are sighted and can't find their
way through pitch black,
I have learned to entrust my orientation to my
other four senses,
and I can still make my way through pitch black
if I'm in a familiar place.

I often choose to sit in the dark.
I find the absence of light comforting at times,
intimate, almost romantic.

Black is the feel of a tuxedo or fancy dress,
sleek, serious, and formal.

Black is the color of my tall, handsome, majestic
guide dog, Mark,
a black lab/poodle cross whom I was matched
with in 2002.

Mark

It was the yellow Lab guide puppy in training we saw with its owner in a New York subway station that made me finally decide to get a guide dog. During Thanksgiving break, Mom and I were coming home from some Black Friday shopping. Mom never wasted an opportunity to pet any dog that was in our path and talk with its owner, and as we made our way down the subway platform to the front of the #2 train, Mom exclaimed, "Oh my gosh, look at that beautiful Lab puppy!"

It was wearing a bright yellow vest that said "guide dog puppy in training" and the woman holding the dog's leash was heading in our direction.

"Excuse me, Miss?" Mom called to her.

"Yes?" said the woman, who seemed used to being stopped to talk about her puppy.

"My daughter is blind, and many people have been telling her for years that she should get a guide dog. Is it okay to pet your dog?"

"Oh, how wonderful!" she said. "It is so good for us puppy

walkers to meet a blind person one of our dogs could potentially be helping. Let me just get her under control, and then you can pet her." I stepped forward as she said, "Gracie, sit," in a firm voice. The puppy obeyed, and the woman told me it was okay to pet Gracie.

"Gracie will be nine months old next week, and I've raised her since she was just eight weeks old," the woman told us.

"What do you teach the dog to do?" Mom asked.

"The Guide Dog Foundation where Gracie hails from asks volunteers like myself to housebreak puppies. We also take them into as many public places as possible to get them to behave around other people, and we expose them to many situations they would face every day with their new handlers."

"I couldn't imagine giving the puppy back to the school when they're ready for training," Mom said. "We have a yellow Lab who is almost nine years old, and we're extremely attached to her."

"It is one of the most painful things to give back a puppy when the time comes," the woman said. "But we have to look at the reward that makes all of that pain and sadness worth it. The first puppy I raised just got matched with his handler, and when I hear about the wonderful things he is doing to help his new person, I feel so good about having raised him."

❖ ❖ ❖

Everyone, from my loved ones to strangers who met me on the street, told me that I should get a guide dog. Nobody seemed to know exactly what it meant to have one, or what the dog would do to help a blind person, but they felt that a dog would somehow be the magical answer to something about my blindness that they felt needed to be fulfilled. Perhaps some people had read the human interest stories about guide dog/handler teams in the paper, like the one about the blind man who worked in the World Trade Center being led to safety by his guide dog just after the first plane crashed. Or perhaps, people just felt that having a big dog by my side would keep away strangers with bad intentions. Most people, I think, just liked dogs, and felt that I would really enjoy the company of one as I walked the streets.

I knew that I would want a guide dog some time in the future. I had fallen in love with Diva, who we got as a six-week-old pup, when I was fourteen years old. People would often guess that Diva was my guide dog since they often saw Labs guiding blind people, and I knew a dog as sweet and obedient as she was would be a pleasure to have by my side all the time.

However, even when I turned sixteen, the minimum age requirement for getting a guide dog, I didn't feel ready. As much as I loved Diva, I never had to take care of her when she was sick or hurt. She and our other two family dogs were like siblings who I could play and cuddle with any time I wanted, but I knew their well being was taken care of by Mom and Dad. Every year in college when the subject would inevitably come up again, I still put off applying for a guide dog.

✸ ✸ ✸

Mom told Brian and Dad about the puppy walker and the dog we had met in the subway station at dinner that night.

"Laurie, you've been dragging your heels about getting a dog for years. Why don't you just do it already?" Brian asked.

"I don't know," I said. "I'm not ready."

"You'll never be ready," Brian argued. "You have to bite the bullet and do it. You always talk about feeling so vulnerable with your cane."

"But what if I kill the dog by accident?" I asked. "I couldn't even keep my plants alive at Oberlin. The poor things had to be nursed back to health by Olivia."

"A dog is a lot different than a plant," Mom laughed. "Believe me, if our dogs were as difficult to care for as plants, or as fragile, they would be long gone by now."

"Say my dog gets sick. What do I do then?"

"Isn't it obvious?" Brian asked, turning to me suddenly with an incredulous look on his face. "You take it to the vet."

"I guess," I said, thinking of no other reason that I shouldn't get a dog.

"It is a lot of responsibility and time to take care of a dog, but I think it would be a labor of love for you," Mom said. "You know how close you feel to Diva."

❁ ❁ ❁

The following Monday, Mom urged me to call the Guide Dog Foundation. I obliged and asked for an application, which I filled out, sent back to the foundation, and promptly forgot about for two months. One day, late in January, I received an email from the foundation saying they were ready to schedule a phone interview with me.

On the following Tuesday afternoon, I rushed home after a voice lesson just in time for a phone call from a trainer named Kim who asked me a series of questions. How much time did I spend in urban settings, and how much time in rural ones? Did I have a consistent daily routine, or was my life subject to change at a moment's notice? Did I travel in areas with big crowds? How often would I be traveling on an airplane? Did I walk a lot, or did I mostly find myself in a car?

I told her that I planned to live in a city like New York for several years, to walk extensively, that I traveled a lot for my singing, and that life as a singer varied from day to day. The thorough interview went on for an hour, and Kim ended the call by saying she would visit me at Yale in person sometime in early spring.

"Man, you're a fast walker," Kim said as she watched me make my way from HGS to Hendrie Hall. "Do you always walk at that pace?"

"Yes, because I'm always running late," I laughed.

We spent an hour walking around campus as Kim surveyed the environment and scribbled notes furiously.

"I think I have all I need," Kim said as we returned to HGS. "I just want to warn you, it could be a while before you hear from us. Each dog's temperament and personality is so different, we don't always have a dog right away for everyone who applies. It can take us a while to find the perfect match for your walking speed, your lifestyle, etc."

"That's okay," I said. "When it's meant to be, I'm sure it will happen."

❋ ❋ ❋

Months went by with no word from the Guide Dog Foundation. My mind was occupied with finishing up my first year at Yale and getting ready for a two-week-long summer music program focused on the study of early music in England. It wasn't until after I returned home from England in late June that I got the phone call.

"Laurie," said a young friendly voice. "This is Stacy from Consumer Services at the Guide Dog Foundation calling."

"Oh, hi," I said.

"I'm very happy to tell you that we've found a dog for you. I know this is short notice, but would you happen to be available to come for our July/August class?"

The Guide Dog Foundation, located in Smithtown, a small, quiet town on the North Shore of Long Island, is a little more than an hour away from New York City. Mom drove me there and dropped me off for the twenty-five-day-long training program I would have with my new dog. The foundation provides dogs, training, room, and board at no cost to their students. People from all over the US and from other countries come to the foundation to get their guide dogs.

The building that housed many of the school's offices, the dining hall, and the residence hall was undergoing renovations, and trailers had been rented to temporarily take their place. Each trailer was its own apartment-sized unit with a front door that opened into a modest living room and a bedroom on either side of the main room. The trailer I was assigned to had the largest living room and was used to hold all of the evening lectures.

I shared a room with a girl my age named Taryn who was in graduate school for education at Harvard, and we teased each other about going to rival schools when we introduced ourselves. We shared our trailer with a woman in her sixties who occupied the second bedroom and who kept to herself.

❋ ❋ ❋

Before I had set foot on the foundation's campus, the reality that I would be sharing the next several years of my life with a guide dog hadn't hit me. Now, as I woke up in my trailer, I felt waves of nerves and excitement. The dog was becoming a reality, not just something vague that I kept pushing further into my future. Soon, my dog would have a breed, a sex, and a name, all of which I wouldn't find out about until the next day.

Our first day of class was spent being taken on walks with trainers who showed us the basic footwork and hand gestures that went with the commands "left," "right," straight," and "about," which meant an about-face.

"Don't forget that you want to advance your position and be

closer to your dog's head when you want it to turn left," said Sebastian, a young trainer who had just come to the foundation from England. "Your body will help communicate what you want from him. If you want him to turn right, you need to stay ever so slightly behind so he has room to move you around right."

"Now I'll show you how to give your dog a correction when he's not paying attention or is misbehaving," Sebastian said. He handed me one end of a training handle, which simulated the feel of the handle on my future dog's harness. "I want you to release all the pressure, and then give the handle a good snap." I did as I was told. "Much harder," Sebastian said. "You are not hurting the dog, you're just getting his attention, showing him you're his leader. Good, now I want you to let go of the handle, and give the leash around your wrist a good snap. This is a more severe correction for when the dog is riled up about something and needs an extra reminder of who the leader is."

❁ ❁ ❁

The first evening's lecture, given by a trainer named Mike who was on night duty, was designed to prepare us for meeting our new dogs.

"It's hard to say how your dog will react when you meet," he said. "Every dog is different. Some dogs will be excited to meet a new person, and will bound over to you when your trainer tells you to call the dog to you for the first time. Other dogs may balk at being left with a new person. Whatever happens, just be patient, and talk to and pet your dog calmly. You'll have twenty minutes alone with your dog for some initial bonding before your trainer will call you for your first walk."

The energy in the room was growing more intense as we all began to anticipate our first meetings with our dogs.

"You could get one of a number of different breeds or crosses. We have Labs, Goldens, Lab/Golden crosses, and now we're trying out Lab/Poodle crosses."

"Lab/Poodles?" Taryn asked. "What on earth would that combination look like?"

"Quite nice looking actually," Mike said. "They are super smart and alert, sharp as whips, but the Lab side tones the Poodle's highstrung side down."

❋ ❋ ❋

You could cut the tension with a knife the next day as we all sat in the lecture trailer silently, awaiting the announcement of our dogs' breeds and names. At long last, Krista, a young apprentice trainer, entered the living room, and we could hear her shifting papers.

"Are you guys ready to hear about your new dogs?" she asked.

"Yes, please!" we all said.

"Taryn, you're getting Lady, a female, black Lab/Poodle cross. Anthony, you're getting Gino, a male, yellow Lab/Golden cross. Ireanne, you're getting a male yellow Lab/Golden cross named Solo." She continued going down the list, until, at last, "Laurie, you're getting Mark, a male black Lab/Poodle cross."

I gasped. He was real! He was male! He was a cross between a Lab and a Poodle, and I was a nervous wreck.

After the announcement, we were told to go to the dining trailer for lunch and then to go back to our rooms where we would be introduced to our new partners. As I nibbled on the tuna sandwich and potato chips on my plate, I began to feel as though I were being set up on a blind date. Several thoughts and questions went through my head in rapid succession, "Will he like me? Will I like him? What if we don't click?"

And then my conscience would answer, "Laurie, he's a dog; of course he'll like you, and how could you not like him?"

❊   ❊   ❊

I was instructed to wait in the living room for Mark while Taryn would have time with Lady in our bedroom. After a few minutes, I heard a trainer say, "Forward," followed by the clicking of claws. Krista entered the living room and walked straight to Taryn, who I heard exclaim happily as Lady approached her.

"Sit," said Sebastian firmly just outside the door. Mark was here. The door to the trailer opened a second time, and Sebastian and a panting dog entered. "Laurie, this is Mark," he said, smiling.

"Hi, Mark!" I cooed happily. A skinny dog with thick, shaggy hair panted nervously in front of me. He was tall, his head reaching my mid-thigh when we were both standing.

"I'll leave you two alone," Sebastian said as he exited the trailer.

"I know you're confused," I told Mark. "It must be hard going from a puppy walker's home to a kennel, and then getting attached to a trainer, and now having to work with a total stranger."

Mark just panted in reply.

"Don't worry," I said. " I'm going to take care of you. You're going to be surrounded by people who love you. Mom and Brian and all my friends at school will adore you, and we're going to have a wonderful life together."

I marveled at Mark's long square face, the expressive hairy eyebrows, which, I was told later, made his face look human-like. Though he was thin, he had broad shoulders and a very noble, heroic appearance. Nobody could have asked for a more gorgeous blind date!

Minutes later, Sebastian was back to teach us some obedience exercises.

"Hold the leash in your left hand," he said. "Now take a step forward and turn your body slightly to your left while bringing Mark into a heel position along your left side. That's called the continental heel, and you will use it whenever you need to get your dog under control. Now tell Mark to sit."

"Sit," I said. Mark, who had suddenly gotten very excited and had begun wagging his tail and snorting, did not sit.

"Tell him again," Sebastian said, sounding stern. "You must get him to listen to you."

Mark obeyed the second time.

"Okay, you're going to make him go down, and then let go of the leash and start walking around him in a circle while telling him to stay."

I tried this a few times. On the first two tries, Mark would pop up as soon as I let go of the leash. On the third time, he stayed, wagging his tail, as if thinking this was all a game.

"Mark is a hard-headed dog," Sebastian said. "You're going to have to stay on him constantly and demand his attention. He's a great city dog, though. Doesn't let anything bother him. You should do obedience with Mark every day. Now let's try doing step refusal with him."

Step refusal tested Mark's ability to show me when we were approaching steps by stopping short of them. Without fail, Mark stopped when he had guided me to the steps down from the trailer.

"You will indicate to him that you're ready to go down by putting your left foot on the first step down. If he doesn't see your foot in that position, he should not move forward even if you tell him to. Try this out."

"Forward," I told him, both feet on the top step. He didn't budge.

"Good," Sebastian said approvingly. "That's called intelligent disobedience. That means he's not obeying a command you're giving him because you haven't shown him you recognize that there is a potential danger ahead. In this case, it's the danger of you falling down the steps. If he ever tries to go down before you're ready, you tell him firmly to watch it, and you re-approach."

❀ ❀ ❀

The strict, boot-camp-like schedule began at 6:00AM wake-up and ended with lights out at 10:00PM. We had regularly scheduled bathroom break times for the dogs, which required them to do their business on command in a designated spot. Meal times were at 7:30AM, 12:00PM, and 5:30PM. When it was time for our morning training at 8:00AM, we told our dogs, "Find the bus," and we were off to a variety of different places to give us a chance to work our dogs in every kind of environment the trainers could think of. We were taken to residential areas, which had the distractions of a dog barking behind a fence, a woman walking with a baby carriage, and flocks of birds above our heads.

"Leave it," I had to tell Mark many times, as every distraction seemed to be taking his mind off of his job.

We were taken to areas with busy streets and were told to trust our dogs as they stopped or slowed down to indicate cars that occasionally came too close for comfort. We went to malls and learned to navigate the busy aisles of department stores, between clothes racks, around shoppers, and around carts, which were often in inopportune places and forced our dogs to choose a different path.

"Okay, Laurie," Sebastian said as the escalator clunked rhythmically in front of us. "This is how you'll take Mark on escalators. You let go of the harness handle once he lines you up with the escalator, then you feel for the rail on the right side. As soon as your feet are in position on the ledge of the escalator, you tell Mark to go forward. Once you reach the end of the escalator, and you feel the steps growing level, you will pick Mark up by his collar so that his feet don't get caught. Dogs can get fatal wounds from escalators, so you must be very careful. Are you ready?"

I placed my feet on the stationary ledge of the escalator. As soon as I was in position, I called Mark forward, and we stepped onto the moving escalator. When I felt it level off, I lifted Mark just as he simultaneously decided to jump off, causing the goofy, furry beast to be at head level with me. Sebastian, along with the girls at the makeup counter, burst out laughing.

"Well, we did it," I said. "Albeit a bit clumsily."

"That was one of the funnier moments I've witnessed as a guide dog trainer," Sebastian said, trying to regain his composure.

❋ ❋ ❋

Working with Mark required me to take a leap of faith I hadn't anticipated. When I had walked with my cane, I was in control of where I was going, and when I was guided by a friend or a loved one, he or she would tell me what was in our path. I had to learn to interpret Mark's wordless communication from his movements through the harness handle.

"You must learn to follow and trust your dog," Sebastian had said as Mark weaved us around some construction on one of our walks in a more urban area. "Otherwise, you could get injured. Mark will keep you out of trouble, but you have to stay with him at all times and to not question his judgment."

"How do I know when he's sniffing, or when he's weaving because there's something he wants to get to?"

"That's something that will come as you get to know your dog. Some dogs will start to quicken their pace when they're going after something they shouldn't. Some dogs will have jerkier movements when they start sniffing. You will learn when Mark is all business and when he's walking with purpose."

❋ ❋ ❋

As I got to know Mark, I learned that his favorite time of day was first thing in the morning. As soon as I poured the food in his bowl, he would snort happily and do a little dance around the room. Then he would make a beeline for the front door when it was time for him to do his business. I also began to notice the way he loved to blow off steam at the end of the day by running around the room at intervals, and then freezing for a moment before running around again. He had a repertoire of different sounds, the most frequent of which was his loud yawns, which he would broadcast to the world around him. He had a beautiful deep bark and an ominous low growl. He would nudge me insistently, almost violently, for petting, which Sebastian told me not to allow him to do.

"He does not decide when you pet him. You do," he said. "Remember, you are always the boss, and he will feel better knowing he doesn't have to be in charge."

It did not take long for my heart to melt for Mark. Though I felt like I was just learning how to understand and communicate with him, I would forget at times that he was just a dog. Spending so much time with Mark made me realize how much I had underestimated what dogs are capable of.

❋ ❋ ❋

In the evenings, we were given lectures on how to brush our dogs' teeth, clean their ears, give them medicine, and, my favorite lecture, how to pick up after them. This lecture was given by a trainer named Barb, who had a deep voice and a cackling laugh.

"I'm warning you," she said. "The warm, wet washcloth I'm going to use to simulate poop feels pretty real."

She made us all take turns as she positioned our dogs in the pooping position, and placed the washcloth just so. Then, she showed us how to put a plastic bag over one hand like a glove, to gently feel the dog's arched back while in action, and to position ourselves near the present the dog left for us. Barb cackled away as we all shrieked upon making contact with the soggy washcloth with our gloved hands.

❋ ❋ ❋

"Okay everyone," Sebastian said as the bus parked in Flushing, Queens. We were approaching the last week of classes now, and our walks had reached a challenging peak. "As you know, Flushing is one of the most crowded cities you'll find. You will probably find it very challenging since it is very loud out there, there's lots of traffic, and there are vendors with carts selling food, flowers, and many other things. We brought you all the way here because we want you to get experience navigating congested areas like this, and to give your dogs the chance to make important decisions about how to get you from one block to the next. Then, we'll practice taking a ride on the subway. I know some of you aren't from New York or any big city, but we think it would be good for you to work the subway today because this is good practice for other means of public transportation you may find yourselves on one of these days.

"Okay, Mark, it's just you and me now," I said. "This is going to be our life, kiddo. I hope you like the city."

Sebastian stayed behind a bit and watched Mark's stellar performance, weaving me flawlessly and smoothly through the crowds, around vendors' booths, sharply pulling me left as a person who wasn't looking almost smacked right into us. It was like following the leader in a ballroom dance to the dissonant sounds of people shouting, car horns honking, and the subway's occasional deafening rumbling. Mark's city work was thrilling, like cruising the streets in a fast Ferrari or skiing my favorite run. I felt both terrified and safe as I held onto Mark for dear life as he zoomed this way and that.

"Looks like we found you the right match," Sebastian said. "This dog loves a challenge."

Mark treated the subways as if he was born to travel them and was always on the train side of the platform to protect me from falling into the tracks as we walked. When the train came zooming towards us, Mark automatically positioned us in front of where the open door would be.

"Right inside," I told Mark per Sebastian's instructions.

"Tell him to find you a seat," Sebastian said.

After a momentary sniffing distraction and a snap on the harness from me, Mark showed me the empty seat by the door. I had always found subway stations intimidating and scary with my cane. Mark's confidence made me feel better about the prospect of negotiating them than I had ever felt before.

* * *

The Guide Dog Foundation did not have a formal graduation ceremony the way some other guide dog schools did. Instead, they had an event for the puppy walkers to meet their dogs' new handlers and for the sponsors who had donated $6,000 to the foundation for the privilege of naming a dog. The gathering was held in the lecture trailer where tables and chairs were set up for each guide dog/handler team and their guests. Mark's sponsors did not come, but a couple in their seventies named Steve and Mary Trupp who had raised Mark were there. They were not allowed to be in the same room as Mark. The trainers worried that the dogs seeing the puppy walkers they had so recently been parted with would trigger them to be overexcited and stressed when they left again.

"We've raised nine dogs for the foundation," Mary said proudly.

"Yeah, and Mark was one of our favorites," Steve added, trying to keep his voice from sounding choked up.

Meeting Mark's puppy raisers made me feel as though I could glean something from the piece of Mark's life I had missed.

"He was a very quiet dog," Mary said. "He didn't chew much. He just loved to be petted."

"Is there anything I should know about him, things he likes or dislikes, any cute or funny stories?" I asked.

"Well, I can tell you this," Mary said. "We used to go to the foundation for class and socialization with the other puppies his age, and he always enjoyed it. But the last time I brought him back to the foundation for training, he did not wag his tail. I think he knew he wasn't coming back home. He actually climbed into my lap on the way there, even though he was way too big to be a lap dog."

My eyes filled with tears. "I'll take good care of Mark, I promise," I told the couple. "They told us that our dogs can see their puppy raisers in a few months, once the bond is stronger between us, so we would be happy to come visit you any time."

"I know he's in good hands," Mary said, grabbing my hand and giving it a firm little shake. "And we would love to have you for a visit."

Though Mary and Steve couldn't let Mark see them, they were allowed to watch through the window as I worked Mark in harness around the lecture trailer.

Before I climbed into bed that night, I put my arms around Mark, listening to his rhythmic breathing, nuzzling my cheek against his soft fur. I couldn't imagine how heartbreaking it must have been for Mary to cuddle with him for the last time after working hard to house-train him and taking him everywhere she went. I had only been around him for three weeks, and I was smitten.

"I'll never leave you," I said to him as he leaned into me for more petting. "We will do Mary and Steve proud, won't we?"

❀ ❀ ❀

Mark and I entered Sudler Hall for my second year at Yale and yet another Death by Aria.

"Find a seat," I said. Mark began snorting and wagging his tail as he noticed the room full of people. "Find a seat," I said more firmly. He began taking me to every person in the room, sniffing and saying "hello." I let go of the harness handle and gave him a sharp snap on his leash. Everyone gasped with horror.

"Find a seat!" I growled.

"There's one to your right, Laurie," somebody whispered. Though Mark had not done what I had asked, I did not feel like making a bigger scene to make him get it right. I sat down, feeling frustrated at Mark's antics the past few days. He had begun testing me the way the trainers warned us our dogs would once we got home, barking whenever people knocked on my dorm room door, taking his sweet time to do his business, and now he wouldn't find a seat.

"Down," I told him firmly. He obeyed for two seconds, and then got up again. "Down," I whispered as a first-year mezzo began singing her aria.

It took me half the recital to get Mark to behave. I knew we were causing a disturbance, and I felt all eyes in the room on me instead of on the current singer who was performing.

✹ ✹ ✹

Having Mark was like being taken on a constant emotional roller coaster, but he delighted me by committing my class routes to memory after having visited them only once or twice.

"Find Hendrie," I would say after I had crossed Elm Street, knowing we were just a building or two away. Miraculously, he would take me to the correct doorway I needed to enter.

"Find Leigh Hall," I would say. "Find Harkness." Though all these buildings were in the same general area, he knew exactly which one was which by name.

Yet, after one minute of impressing me to no end, he would lunge playfully after a skateboarder, almost making me lose my balance, or he would take us off course to sniff a plant. One after-noon, as I entered Leigh Hall, the School of Music building, I heard a group of girls giggling at him.

"What has he done?" I asked them. They went silent.

"Oh no, I don't want to get him into trouble," one of them said. "But he looks so funny with a bagel in his mouth."

"A bagel?" I exclaimed. "Where the heck did he find a bagel, and how come I didn't notice?"

Mark had learned how to grab things off the ground in a very subtle way, and I began checking his mouth on a regular basis.

✹ ✹ ✹

To add to the frustration, Yale had proven to be more like my middle school days in terms of my lack of connection with the other singers. I was shocked at their immediate discomfort around me, the fact I was never invited to social gatherings, which I was all too aware the other singers were all going to, and the unpleasantly familiar defensive responses when I wanted to be included. Mark was just another part of me my fellow singers did not wish to tolerate.

"You don't seem to have very good control of your dog," Liza, one of the sopranos, said to me as I sat down for diction class. "My dog Bubbles isn't even a guide dog, and all I have to do is look at her for her to go lie down."

"I've only had Mark for a few weeks," I said, annoyed at being judged on such little knowledge. "It takes a good year before a team like us is bonded."

Liza was not the only one who complained about Mark. My colleagues would get squeamish when I brought Mark into class after a rainy day. All the dry towels in the whole world would not get rid of that wet dog smell.

"How often do you bathe him?" asked Isabel, a fellow mezzo during one of our opera scene rehearsals, covering her nose.

"Once a month," I said.

"Yuck, Laurie, that's disgusting. Would you bathe yourself once a month?"

"No, I wouldn't, but that's because I'm not a dog. I was told over and over at the guide dog school that bathing a dog more than once a month could really dry out his skin."

"My parents bathe Bubbles once a week, and her skin is just fine," Liza said.

Fortunately, I had found a little group of friends shortly after starting at Yale the year before. Tina, a violist, and Ming, a clarinetist, were the people I spent most of my time with after class. They, and my other friends, had no complaints about Mark. In fact, people seemed to like my room as a hangout spot with Mark's energy in it. He became the School of Music's unofficial mascot.

❋ ❋ ❋

As Mark's testing phase began to subside, we found ourselves running into a few other issues.

"I'm sorry, he can't come in here," the occasional restaurant manager would say.

"You have to let us in," I would say. "It's against the law for you to refuse a guide dog." The argument would either go on for several minutes until I threatened to call the police, or they would realize their mistake and apologize profusely.

Passersby would sometimes get offended when I told them that I was sorry, but they could not pet my dog.

"Aren't you being cruel, not allowing your dog to socialize?" they would protest angrily.

"He might stop paying attention to traffic and get us both killed if he runs across the street to someone who will pet him in harness," I explained. "He gets plenty of love and plenty of free time."

And then there were the well-meaning people who were just trying to make conversation who said, "Oh, he must be your very best friend in the world," or "It must be nice to have a companion dog."

"If I wanted a companion dog," I would think to myself, "I would have gone to the pet store or a pound, not spent over three weeks working with a dog that had thousands of dollars and hundreds of hours of training put into him. And I also have plenty of human friends, thank you very much."

❈ ❈ ❈

At the end of the day when Mark and I would return to HGS, no matter how frustrating a day we had had, no matter what uneducated statements I had to endure, I never regretted my decision to get a guide dog for one minute. He became the four-legged extension of me. Walking with him made me feel what I imagined a sighted person would feel as they walked, enjoying their surroundings without worrying about every minuscule detail of their environment the way I did with a cane. Knowing that I was traveling independently yet never alone made me feel liberated. The frustrations that went along with having a new dog were a small price to pay, and besides, showing everyone how good a team we would become would educate those who didn't understand, and in so doing, Mark and I would make it easier for the next new team that would come along.

Jenny

"You have to meet my friend Jenny!" Ming told me after class one day, on one of his routine visits to my dorm room. "She's so nice. She's new in the clarinet studio this year, and she's in German class with me."

"When do I get to meet her?" I asked him, as I finished up my Italian homework.

"Well, can we study German in your room tomorrow night?"

Ming often made himself right at home in my room. After knocking and letting himself in, the first thing he would do was open my refrigerator, helping himself to whatever was inside. The second thing he would do, after pouring some chips and salsa into bowls, would be to take over the CD player, and no matter what I had playing at the time, he would replace it with one of his many CDs. Sometimes, he felt Brahms would create the perfect atmosphere for our late-night eating sessions, and for others, it would be Renaissance choral music or Argentinian music. Some might have been offended by the way Ming so casually took over someone's living quarters, but I liked it. It felt like having family come home after a day of work. And since Ming and I were inseparable while we weren't in class, the fact that he treated my room like his seemed natural.

"Yeah, sure, bring her over. Just make sure it's after seven, though, because I have an opera scene rehearsal until then."

❉ ❉ ❉

The hot summer weather had not let up yet, even though we were nearing the end of September. I was sweating like a pig, and my hair was in desperate need of a wash. It hung long and lank, and as I perspired on my way home from a relentless day of classes and rehearsals, it was plastered against my neck, making me feel itchy and unclean.

"Shit, I don't have time for a shower before Ming comes over," I thought, as Mark and I walked home from the music building. "Oh well, it's just Ming, anyway."

Mark began to walk even faster as he pulled me towards the familiar gate to HGS. His tail began to wag, and his whole demeanor told me he was just as happy to be home from a long day as I was.

Five minutes after I had gotten Mark some water and had him back on his bed chain, I heard Ming's muffled voice at my door. "Now you're about to meet my other half," followed by a knock.

"Hey, Laur!" Ming said. "This is Jenny."

"Hi there, so nice to meet you," I said.

"You, too," said a shy voice.

"Ming's told me all about you."

"Yeah, he's told me a lot about you too," Jenny said.

Mark began to bark, wrenching against his chain to say "hello" to Ming.

"No, Mark, quiet," I said firmly. "Sorry, Jenny, he won't hurt you; he's very friendly. He's my guide dog."

"He's so cute," Jenny said. "He looks like a puppet."

Ming put Anne Sofie Von Otter singing Brahms Lieder on my CD player before he and Jenny began practicing their German.

Jenny and I did not say much to each other that night. When she and Ming were not practicing German, they were talking about goings on in the clarinet studio. Even though what I needed was a break from work, I settled myself down on my bed and began to tackle my next Italian assignment.

✹ ✹ ✹

"You'll never guess what I just found out!" Ming said excitedly as we walked arm-in-arm to Leigh Hall. Autumn had set in, and mid-October had an unprecedented chill in the air, foreshadowing a freezing winter.

"What?" I asked eagerly, awaiting a juicy piece of gossip or interesting news.

"Jenny's gay!"

"She is?" I hadn't seen Jenny in several weeks, the last time being the night of the study session in my room. The news excited me. The Yale School of Music seemed almost entirely devoid of gay students after coming from the gay mecca that Oberlin was. I wasn't sure which felt worse, weirding people out once again as the only blind person in the School of Music or as the only lesbian.

"That's so neat!" I told Ming. "She's one of us! How come it took so long to find out?"

"The silly girl thought you and I were a couple," Ming said. "She's been so afraid to come out because she thought she'd be the only one. I asked her how she could have possibly thought I was straight."

"Well, you did introduce me to her as your other half," I laughed. "Anyway, how did it come up?"

"There's this new pianist named Ryo here, and he's gay too. He's been asking everyone he's becoming friends with if they're gay. The other night, when you were in Boston visiting Olivia, we were having drinks with Jenny, and it was her turn. When Ryo asked, she said yes, just like that, no hesitation. She has a girlfriend, too."

"Did you tell her about me?"

"I did, and she was super excited. She was starting to feel like the only lesbian here."

"Tell her that I'm going to buy her a drink some time! Tell her we can be the only lesbians here together."

❂ ❂ ❂

Ming wanted to celebrate his birthday at Bar. Most college towns have their quirks, and Bar was one of Yale's. They sold addictive pizza and hosted gay night on Tuesdays. Lucky enough for Ming, his birthday fell on a Tuesday this year.

Ming watched me primp in my closet and I held out a red tank top with safety pins lining the sleeves and gold chains hanging down the front. "Do you think I should wear this shirt?"

"Ooo, hot Momma," he laughed. "You gonna wear that short, leather skirt, too?"

"Yeah," I said. "Just got the outfit in London when I was on vacation there last summer. Been wanting an excuse to wear it."

"Well hurry up, let's go! I want to get there before the pizza runs out."

I was definitely underdressed. October had grown brutally windy, and I shivered under my shearling winter coat, which I had reluctantly pulled out earlier than I would have liked. Bar felt warm and inviting, and Ming and I claimed a large table near the back. Gay night and the '80s dance mixes had not kicked in yet, and macho country rock was still playing.

Minutes later, Jenny and an entourage of Ming's friends sat down around the big table. I was thrilled that Jenny had taken the seat right next to me.

"Hey Laurie, we met in your room about a month ago," Jenny said, her voice sounding much more friendly and less shy than the last time.

"Say no more, I know who you are," I said. "Welcome to our little family, the black sheep of the Yale Music School," I said, reaching out to pat her shoulder.

Jenny laughed, "So Ming told you, huh?"

"And he told you about me."

"So, how did you know?"

"Know what?"

"That you were gay."

"Oh," I said, thinking back. "It was when my first girlfriend took my hand. I mean, I had suspected since high school that something was different, and somehow I just knew that I needed to try being with a girl. When she took my hand, I don't even know how to describe what it felt like. It was as if everything in my life up to that point, even my own childhood, the feelings I had suppressed, just surfaced and made sense."

"I think I knew for sure when I held my first girlfriend's hand, too. It's probably something straight couples feel, but for some reason, I never felt that with a guy before. Do you have a girlfriend now?"

"Yes," I responded, referring to Olivia.

"How long have you two been together?"

"Four and a half years. Can you believe it? How about you?"

"About two and a half years," Jenny said. "Long distance relationships are hard, but it sounds like you two are doing just fine."

As we talked, I realized that having our gayness in common made us speed past the normal small talk into a potential fast friendship. Sharing the most intimate details of our sexuality was a therapy we both desperately needed, especially after a month of being around straight grad students with boyfriends, some even with husbands and kids. Though the group around us was in animated conversation, Jenny and I continued to talk to each other, as if we were the only two at the table.

❋ ❋ ❋

Jenny soon began joining the spontaneous and frequent gatherings in my room. Ming's music provided the soundtrack to our eating, drinking, and animated conversations. There was a true magic to the bond of this group of people who managed to find time for each other almost every night, whether for pizza at two in the morning, movie nights in someone's room, or Gay Night at Bar. Mark made his rounds, getting petted by all who adored him. Nothing could have been more perfect, or so I thought.

Jenny had taken to sitting next to me on my bed, and we engaged in conversations about everything. I began to notice something about the quality of her voice that one might find in someone's eyes. I could hear her winking at me through her laughter, and there was a silliness about her that reminded me of myself. We could be childlike together in a way that everyone else seemed to have outgrown. She brought me back to a place of self-abandonment I had not been to for many years.

❋ ❋ ❋

The Marriage of Figaro was announced as our main stage opera for the year, and one evening in the middle of November, the cast list was emailed to us with our schedule. I had hoped for the role of

Cherubino, a mezzo pants role portrayal of a young boy who is infatuated with the countess in a tangle of comical love stories. I had learned Cherubino's arias early on in my voice training, and the role seemed perfect for my voice. Just as I had done the year before, I began to move my cursor up and down the cast list, but the casting announcement read by my computer's monotonous, synthesized voice showed me that I, once again, was not in the opera.

By Cherubino's name, two names had been written, both of whom had played lead roles the year before. My heart plummeted. I sat in my desk chair, absently petting Mark, wondering how they could have rationalized doing this to me. This was the second year of my Master's, my very last chance at a role at Yale. Yet, they had found a way for me to be totally overlooked, the only singer in the whole program in this position. This was not the education I had bargained for, not the résumé builder I had planned. If professionals were going to give a blind opera singer a chance, they would need proof that I had experience. They would need to know that someone had taken the chance before them. As I sat there, hearing the November wind pound angrily against my window, my computer announced that all the reasons I had gone to Yale were for naught and that my two year plan had backfired.

The depression weighing heavily on my chest had turned to cold, hard anger when I woke up the next morning. Though I prided myself on never acting the role of the bitter diva, I was not going to simply let this roll off my back. They owed me the consideration of hearing me out, and I deserved to walk away from this situation feeling strong, not just settling on being the meek girl who would let them get away with what they perhaps expected me to be.

I arrived at studio class to the usual animated chatter that directly preceded an opera casting announcement. As usual, nobody acknowledged my presence or asked me to sit next to them, making me feel as invisible as I was on the cast list. Studio class was a place for us all to workshop our arias for each other, for Patricia, and for most of the Yale Opera faculty.

"Okay, let's begin everyone," Patricia said loudly.

"The long awaited casting announcement has been made, as you all know. Everyone on this faculty has entrusted each of you with a very important responsibility. It is absolutely imperative that you learn your role thoroughly before the sing-through, and that you utilize your coaching sessions so that your diction and understanding of your character is the best it can be by the time of staging. I know you all can handle this, and it is certainly the kind of practice you'll need for the expectations professional opera companies will have. Does anyone have any questions? Yes, Laurie."

"Patricia, I believe I noticed a mistake on the cast list last night," I said, keeping my voice airy and calm. I let the awkward moment of silence resonate before continuing.

"I noticed that I did not appear on the cast list. That must have been an oversight, right?" Silence again. "I mean, I know this program is meant to give everyone opera experience, and I knew that you wouldn't have chosen not to cast me two years in a row. That would be against everything this program stands for."

"Laurie," Patricia said, clearing her throat. "This must be very disappointing for you, but unfortunately, there has been no mistake. What you saw on the cast list is final."

I sat there in silence, awaiting Patricia's explanation. I could feel the eyes of everyone in the small recital hall on me. I knew that forcing everyone to confront this uncomfortable situation was causing resentment, but I didn't care. My name being the only one left off of the cast list was not going to be the elephant in the room that everyone refused to acknowledge.

"As you know, your situation poses some, um, difficult, how should I say it, limitations. It would be very dangerous up there on that stage for you, and it would be very hard for you to get around."

"Patricia, I travel this entire campus by myself every day," I said. "First, I used a cane, and now I use a dog. Around my dorm, the bathrooms, and around all the classrooms, I use no mobility aid at all. Do you mean to tell me that you don't think I can learn my way around a stage?"

"We are all amazed by how you get around, and everything you do. You have a room full of admirers here."

"I'm not asking for your compliments or your admiration," I said. "I'm just asking for the one thing I came to this program to get, and that is opera experience. I think you're not giving the stage directors you hired enough credit. If they are the imaginative, creative people that directors should be, we can figure out together how to make me being on stage in a full scale opera work."

"Laurie, our director has been involved in the decision-making process, and he feels that he doesn't have the time or resources to work with you."

"Why did you accept me? What made you feel that I was right for this program?"

"Because you have a beautiful voice," Patricia said. "And we felt that we could help you grow. Even if you are not in the opera, we did put you in opera scenes, and you got stage experience that way. Look how much you've improved. We're so proud of you. But we also must get on with studio class. It's not fair to keep everyone from singing their arias. Audition season is coming up."

Though I had kept my anger in check during my interrogation, it bubbled and boiled inside of me, and as each singer in that room got up to perform their aria, I felt that the value and emphasis on everyone else's career was perceived to be much more important than mine.

"We're all sorry that you didn't get a role," said Liza as we left the room after class. "But you always have to blame everything on your blindness."

"Yeah, and you wonder why none of us feel like hanging out with you," said Isabel. "Just suck it up already."

"I'm asking for special treatment? Is that what you think? Is being the only person left out of the opera and needing an explanation special treatment? Why don't you try to imagine how that feels, both of you!" I yelled.

Leave it to the wonderful loyalty of an intuitive dog to do exactly the right thing in a stressful situation. At that very moment, Mark, without waiting for a single command, took off at super speed, making a beeline for the door. Mark always seemed to know when I was late for class or when we had the time to stop and smell the roses. In this case, he knew that I needed to get out of that hall and leave my critics in the dust, to make the dramatic exit I would never have the chance to make in an opera at Yale.

❋ ❋ ❋

"Laur, I just heard about the opera. They're so stupid!" Ming said.

I had entrusted the task of getting home entirely to Mark, as I was too upset to think about where I was headed. Instead of heading to HGS, he had taken me to Leigh Hall, as if knowing that what I really needed were friends, not an empty room. Miraculously, Ming had been in the lobby.

"What happened?" asked Jenny, who seemed to emerge from a practice room at that moment.

"Those asses at Yale Opera did it again," Ming said angrily. "They didn't put Laurie in the opera."

"Oh my gosh, are you serious?" Jenny said, her tone like a salve on a throbbing wound. "Are you okay?"

"No, I'm not," I said, trying to keep myself from shaking. "But I will be."

Jenny put her hand on my shoulder, rubbing it shyly. Somehow, through my anger and hurt, I was able to feel comfort from her touch, and something inexplicably more than comfort, as if in that moment, she had become an even closer friend.

"Come on, Laur, let's get out of here," Ming said. "Let's go have dinner. Wanna go to Thai Taste?"

I recounted my conversation with Patricia. I told them about Liza and Isabel accusing me of demanding special treatment. Ming's getting worked up and Jenny's anger peeking out from her laid-back personality were making me smile again, and my heart felt lighter. Having them on my side was just what I needed.

"I'm going to beat them up for you. Which one is Liza? Isn't she the one that looks like Ms. Piggy?" Jenny said, making me laugh deeply.

"I never thought about that, but she kind of does," Ming joined in.

"And which one is Isabel?" Jenny asked.

"She's the tall one that everyone thinks is beautiful. I wouldn't try beating her up. She's bigger than you," I said.

"Oh, I can take her," Jenny said. "She probably spends a lot more time making sure not to break a nail than working out at the gym."

"You guys are the best. Did I ever tell you that?" I said, my stomach aching from the fits of laughter.

"What time is it?" Ming gasped suddenly. "I'm tutoring a student at 7:30." With that, he handed us a twenty and left.

"Hey, thanks for letting me vent," I said to Jenny. "I'm sorry I'm in such a crappy mood."

"Don't worry," she said warmly. "I'd be pissed off if it were me, too. And by the way, I think you have an amazing voice."

My heart did a little involuntary flip. "Really?"

"Yeah, I thought you were great in the opera scenes."

"Thanks, that really means a lot."

"So, what are you up to the rest of the night?" Jenny asked.

"Not much. I don't feel like doing any work."

"Me either."

"Wanna come hang out at HGS for a while? I'm sure Ming will come by as soon as he's done tutoring."

"Sure," Jenny said.

I took Jenny's arm and let Mark walk casually on my left side as I gently held his leash. It occurred to me that there was nothing too interesting or entertaining in my room, and I worried that two hours of hanging out without Ming would bore Jenny.

"I like your CDs," Jenny said, peering at the collection on my shelf.

"Oh cool, let me play you one of my favorite folk CDs. It's called Voices on the Verge, where these four awesome up-and-coming singers jam on each other's songs."

I felt myself moving rhythmically about the room and humming as Erin McKeown crooned "Four and Twenty Blackbirds" into my speakers. The music and Jenny sitting on my bed made me forget the events that had taken place over the previous twenty-four hours.

"If you like this kind of jazzy, folky stuff, you would like this CD by the group Hem, have you heard of them?" Jenny fumbled in her bag. "I actually have my CD wallet with me."

The two hours went by like minutes as Jenny and I shared our favorite musical moments, and I felt a happiness that reminded me of something I had felt at Tanglewood, where we all seemed to adore music for music's sake with a pure teenaged enthusiasm that gets lost when one's mind gets hung up on career and competition. It was that enthusiasm that made me want to be a singer in the first place, and being with Jenny made me realize how much of that I had been tucking away somewhere, like an old beloved stuffed animal. Music was something that should be enjoyed at that pure, visceral level, and I was happy that Jenny and I were on the same wavelength, enjoying it there together.

❋   ❋   ❋

The next few weeks turned into a series of final projects, tests, and wrapping up of the first semester. I did not see Jenny much, but I found myself thinking about her and wondering what she was up to. I knew I could have emailed or called, but something I couldn't pinpoint kept me from it.

"She's probably way too busy," I told myself.

Winter break came and went, and a few weeks later I managed to have some one-on-one time with her again.

"Jenny, Tina and I discovered a delicious dessert at Cosi the other night. It's their mud pie, and they serve it warm. Can I tempt you?"

"Yeah, that would be fun," she said, and a rush of excitement swept through me.

"Mmmm," we intoned together as we dug into the rich, warm, fudgy dessert.

"You're so right. This is as delicious as you said it was."

We ate the mud pie in silence, savoring each bite. The warmth of the ambrosia seemed to be loosening me up, making me feel tipsy as though I had just had a glass of wine. I was feeling adventurous and bold, with an urge in that moment to be honest with myself and Jenny. I was not prepared for the boldness that took over just after we had paid the check.

"You know something," I said, feeling lighthearted. "I would have such a huge crush on you if I weren't in a relationship."

I expected Jenny to laugh the comment off as any good friend might, but her response surprised me as much as my own sudden desire to be forward.

"Me too!" she said, her voice sounding surprised.

"You're just kidding, right?"

"Are you?" she asked.

"No, I'm not."

"Me neither."

I felt her eyes on me, and we both laughed as the coincidence of a reciprocated feeling dawned on us.

"It's a nice night. Do you want to go for a walk?" she asked.

The truth was that it was twenty degrees, but somehow, we found ourselves walking for blocks, past the music school, enjoying the weather as though it were a balmy summer evening with a light breeze. Neither of us shivered or felt any desire to return to the warmth of the school. I knew we were both in relationships, and that nothing more could develop than a close friendship, but it was exhilarating to know that Jenny and I felt the same way about each other. That was enough for me.

❋ ❋ ❋

Jenny and I found ourselves spending more time together than ever. We went to see movies, where she would tell me in a low voice what was happening on the screen, her lips gently brushing my ear. We went to our friends' recitals together, taking each other's hands when the music reached those moments we both loved. And we wrote emails to each other, which became something to look forward to every morning. What thoughts would appear in my inbox from her first thing in the morning before I took Mark out on his walk? Would we be seeing each other later that day?

Gradually, the emails became more and more personal, and Jenny revealed to me that things with her girlfriend had been strained for a while, and that she didn't know what to do. She became tortured by it until one day, I didn't get a message from her, and that day turned into two, three, and four days. The silence was creating a void that made me feel uneasy. Had I said anything to upset her?

Finally, on the fifth day, Ming and I decided to grab pizza at a place near HGS. No sooner had we ordered than Ryo and Jenny came in.

"Hey Jenny!" I said happily. "How's it going?"

"Not so good," she said, her voice trembling a bit.

"Oh no," I said, putting an arm around her as she sat beside me. "What is it?"

"Lisa broke up with me a few days ago."

My heart sank as Jenny's voice broke. "I'm so sorry." I felt my eyes burning with tears. "Why did she break up with you?"

"I was honest with her. I told her that I had feelings for someone else, and we were crying on the phone until four in the morning. I've really hurt her, and I wasn't ready to let her go."

Our pizza came, and my appetite disappeared as my stomach and heart seemed to tangle up in each other. This had all been my fault. I had opened my big mouth and had opened Pandora's box.

"Do you want to talk about this some more?" I asked. "You can come to my room after this."

"Okay," she said weakly.

She sat next to me on the bed, lost and silent.

"Jenny, you can't compromise your relationship because of me," I said. "This isn't fair to you. We just have an intense friendship, that's all. We can work through this."

"It's not just you," she said. "I think my feelings for you were just the last straw. Besides, I wouldn't expect you to leave Olivia for me."

Olivia, my wonderful Olivia, the girl who had been there during the times I was sick, the one who had never judged me for not understanding Virginia Woolf the way she did, and the one who always had an encouraging word for me, even when I didn't deserve it. Yet I had begun to have a shorter fuse with her since I left Oberlin, getting frustrated with her when we did not see eye to eye. Our lives seemed to be growing more separate, and yet, I knew she would never have thought to leave me.

❀ ❀ ❀

The emails from Jenny resumed the following morning, beginning with one thanking me for being there for her and reiterating that she did not expect me to leave Olivia for her, and that this unfortunate breakup had probably been coming for some time now.

I could not get Jenny out of my mind. Every time I was with her, it was as if I could see an entire future with her. I felt as though there was a part of myself in her, still left undiscovered. My singing had gotten better around her because she had inspired a rebirth of the rich enthusiasm for music I had forgotten. Olivia was getting her Master's at Tufts University, and I made the decision to go to Boston to spend the weekend with her in late February. I needed a reminder of how things were between us to help me decide what I needed to do.

Holding Olivia felt as wonderful as it did the first time we embraced, and yet I realized in that moment that it wasn't enough. She and I cried harder than we had ever cried that weekend, knowing that my decision was at the end of it. We had loved each other, shared so much together, had created so many memories over those last four and a half years, and yet I knew, perhaps from the beginning, that something basic had been missing between us, some common ground that the relationship truly needed.

❋ ❋ ❋

I did not call or email Jenny for the next several days. My heart was riddled with guilt for the two relationships that had gotten destroyed.

And then, a week later, an email with the subject line, "Warm mud pie" showed up in my inbox.

"Hi Laurie. It's really cold today, isn't it? I couldn't help thinking that what we both need is some of that Cosi mud pie tonight. What do you think? Should we go after my studio class tonight?"

Her words were just the thing I needed. Though I knew I deserved all the guilt that was eating me up inside, I also realized that life had felt like a heavy load of emotions to carry, and my heart needed some relief.

I couldn't help but feel as if Jenny had asked me formally on a first date. I put on makeup, something I rarely did, my jeans with the see-through lace on the sides of my legs, and a tight black sweater I had fallen in love with in London.

"You look nice," Jenny said, her voice taking on a breathless quality that became her.

The mud pie was exactly what we needed. It warmed our insides and opened us up to the conversations that were so easy between us, about our favorite TV shows from the '80s, or about the music we needed to play together in the future.

"I know it's late, but do you want to come back to my room?"

"I thought you'd never ask," she said in that enthusiastic, breathless whisper that had shot tingles through my entire body earlier that evening.

"I really missed you," I said, as we sat down on my bed.

"Me, too." She put her arm around me, and I pulled her into an embrace. In that moment, I could feel the magical snow that had recently sparkled over Yale causing a beautiful storm inside me, and at that same time, a current of electricity seemed to course through us, forcing us closer and closer together. I had never known tingles like this. Her body felt slight and delicate, but her arms were strong, firm, and tender. We began stroking each other gently, and suddenly, our lips met. From the moment I knew I was attracted to Jenny, I knew our kiss would feel just like this, like the best music, like an orchestra full of players who were in sync, creating a powerful force that could send shivers up and down anybody's spine. Our bodies fit together as if we had found the missing half of each other's soul, feeling something one can only experience once the soul's two halves have been reunited.

❊ ❊ ❊

The rest of my time at Yale was an exploration of a new kind of love. It was a series of long days of classes and preparations for the recital requirement to finish my degree and sleepless nights of endless conversations and loving each other in a way that epitomized everything poets write about.

Being with Jenny confirmed something I had been trying to explain to people for a long time when they would ask me how I can feel an attraction without being able to see.

"Attraction isn't about vision," I would say. "It's about an unmistakable vibe between two people. It's about your heart stopping for a second when that person touches you, when something completely ordinary can make you giggle, when the very presence of that person makes you speechless. Not even your eyes can do all of that for you."

The moment Jenny and I held each other for the first time, I knew that my instincts had been right on about her, and that neither of us had known these feelings for each other based on sight.

❋ ❋ ❋

Jenny had one more year to go at Yale after I graduated. We promised each other that we would visit each other often, and that if we were still together after a difficult one-year long distance relationship, we would move to New York together. These decisions perhaps seemed rash after a few months being together, but love does that to a person sometimes. Diving headfirst into a relationship with Jenny felt like the right thing to do. We knew that it would hurt too much to do the sensible thing, live in our own places, and take things slowly.

When I was sixteen, I had asked Mom the big question: "How do you know when you're in love?"

"Oh Laurie, that's something I just can't describe. There's no one magical answer. All I can say is that you just know," Mom had said.

Mom had been right. You just know, and it is unmistakable.

Blue

*Blue is a romantic walk when your heart swells
with that first kiss.*
*It can be the empty space you feel in between those
kisses.*
Blue is cosmic and ethereal, soothing and cool,
*like a breeze caressing the skin on a perfect, balmy
evening.*
Blue is the sky I painted years ago for a friend,
*always changing, limitless, and perfectly
untouchable.*

Back to Basics

Being thrust into the real world by one's respective academic institution is scary for any young person. Top it off with a disability in a society where a high percentage of the disabled are unemployed, and you get me, age twenty-four, with a Master of Music degree from Yale University, and a hand-me-down apartment from my parents in New York City, one of the most exciting but terrifying cities in the world.

After enduring one year of a long distance relationship in which Jenny finished her Master's while I auditioned and performed in LA, we decided to move to New York, jumping headfirst into starting a life together. Jenny and I were lucky in that we did not experience the normal growing pains of learning to live together. I learned early on about Jenny being a clean freak and her not wanting me to wear my shoes in the house after she had mopped the floor.

"Can you please wipe Mark's feet?" she would ask just after I had taken him to do his business.

Jenny learned that I am like the Princess and the Pea, and that if there's a single crumb of anything in our bed, I'll feel it, jump up in disgust, and start wiping the sheets like mad.

"Please don't eat in the bed," I would tell her.

We teased each other about our quirks, but we compromised easily and lived harmoniously. There were no disagreements about squeezing the toothpaste from the wrong part of the tube or leaving our belongings strewn about the apartment. We were both equally guilty of these things. It was how other people viewed us as a couple, which we never could have predicted, that caused annoyance and downright anger.

"They think I'm your Asian helper," Jenny would say in disbelief when our doormen would give her unsolicited reports on my activities. Jenny, who is fourth generation American, and who was born and raised in Hawaii, is of Japanese descent.

"You know, she took her dog out for a walk by herself," the doormen would say, shaking their heads, giving Jenny disapproving looks as though she had neglected her duties.

"But I've known these doormen since 1998 when my parents bought the apartment," I would say, my heart sinking. "Is that really what they've been thinking all along?"

It did not stop with the doormen. It trickled out into interactions with wait staff at restaurants who would ask Jenny what I wanted, the security officers at airports who referred to Jenny as my "helper," and the wealthy patrons of recital series that I performed in who would ask Jenny to get them glasses of water, mistaking her for a servant at post-concert receptions.

"It's partly because we're gay, you know," Jenny said. "People don't realize we're a couple because we're both women. Then you add the fact that you're blind, and I'm Asian."

The expectations my family placed on Jenny and the lack of expectations they placed on me also caught the two of us by surprise.

"No, Laurie, let Jenny and me carry that," Mom would say in a panicked voice as she noticed me lifting the heavy box containing the new Ikea coffee table.

From the time I was a little girl and we'd go on vacation with family friends, I was always ushered out of the way of large suit-cases, which everyone was moving from the van to our condo or hotel rooms. I had always known that vacation bonding started from the moment people worked together, even during the less desirable tasks of carrying heavy, awkward items.

"I want to help, too," I would say. "Please let me do something," I would plead.

"You know what would be very helpful?" someone would say. "If you could carry my purse for me, or this shopping bag," and I would be handed the lightest bag possible to indulge my desire to feel helpful or perhaps just to shut me up.

Apparently, the expectation that I should never have to lift a finger because carrying something heavy would be too dangerous for me had not gone away.

"What do people expect of me?" Jenny asked. "That I'm going to do every little thing for you? Do they really expect whomever you date to treat you like you're made of glass?"

"Whatever you do, don't you ever treat me like glass, and don't you ever stop letting me carry stuff," I said. "I refuse to be with someone who insists on mothering me. Besides, it's my eyes that don't work, not my arms and legs."

❊ ❊ ❊

After unpacking boxes and trying to make the place our own, the next step was to figure out how to survive financially. In addition to the impressed oohs and ahs our Yale degrees elicited from strangers, it also gave us some teaching experience. Every school of music student at Yale was required to have a certain number of teaching hours per semester. I had two undergrad voice students and two students in the school of music who took voice lessons from me as a secondary instrument, and Jenny taught secondary clarinet. After printing out several copies of our resumes and posters advertising our teaching services, we traveled from school to school, talking to anyone in the music department who would lend us an ear.

"You can leave these with us, but we have no openings for music teachers at this time," directors of elementary and high school music departments would say. "We'll put these on our bulletin boards, and hopefully some interested kids will tell their parents they want music lessons," others would say. After dropping off packets of information about our experience at several places, tacking posters up at every local coffee shop we knew of, sending cover letters and teaching résumés to every school in the five boroughs, and posting ads up on Craig's List, we found ourselves playing the waiting game.

We realized over time that with Juilliard, Manhattan School of Music, Mannes College of Music, and others in New York constantly turning out high quality musicians, there was a higher demand for students than for teachers. The six years of honing our musical craft and our time in New York trying as hard as we could to find ways of putting it to practical and financial use all seemed useless.

"What are we going to do now?" I asked at dinner one night. We had decided to treat ourselves to pizza at Big Nick's, a dive near our house with the old school New York waitresses whose bad sides you never want to get on.

"I knew this wouldn't be easy, but I thought we would have had at least some leads right now," Jenny said.

"I wake up each morning feeling optimistic. I get all excited about calling more schools on our list, and the most positive response I get is a receptionist who will at least transfer me to the voicemail of the music director," I said.

After weeks of receiving no responses from schools, and after I attended several disappointing auditions, we realized that we needed to do something different. Jenny got a temp job, and I began to think of other options. Temping didn't seem a viable solution for me. Every office had its own computer system, which would be a bitch to make compatible with my screen-reading software. And waiting tables seemed a logistical impossibility.

Since moving to New York, I felt as though I had no particular place in the world. I couldn't even be the homemaker with a hot meal waiting for Jenny when she returned from a day of work.

I had no cooking, cleaning, or any other basic skills to speak of. Before I did anything else, I realized I had to learn how to live as an independent human being, to take it upon myself to learn the things I should have learned as a child. I decided to make the best of my time, to make myself useful and valuable in my home before venturing out to find myself in the world. I would find a way to learn the things a Yale diploma couldn't get me, and that was by taking a crash course in cooking, cleaning, and other basic living skills 101.

❀ ❀ ❀

I received one of the best presents I was ever given during Chanukah and Christmas the year before Jenny and I moved to New York together. Mom and I decided to spend Chanukah that year in New York with Brian, who was hosting a party at his house. Jenny, who was still at Yale, was on winter break, and came to New York to join us, but her mood was a curious combination of giddiness and edginess. When I asked her about it, she'd change the subject.

The night before the party, I fell asleep while waiting for Jenny to join me. When I woke up several hours later, I discovered that it wasn't yet morning. I stretched, felt the empty bed next to me, smelled the unmistakable scent of magic marker, and heard the rasp of somebody drawing furiously.

"Jenny?" I said sleepily. "What are you doing?"

She giggled in reply from across the room, seated at my desk. "Go back to sleep," she said.

"What time is it?" I pressed the large, triangular button on my talking clock.

"It's 3:00AM," it said loudly.

"Shhhh, you'll wake your mom," Jenny whispered.

"What are you doing?" I asked, feeling irked that Jenny was doing some random art project in the wee hours of the night while I was trying to sleep, knowing full well she'd be grumpy and tired the morning of a busy day of holiday shopping.

"I can't tell you," Jenny said, trying to suppress another giggle. "Just go to sleep."

When it was time to exchange gifts the next evening at Brian's Chanukah party, Jenny handed me a large, flat, gift-wrapped box.

"What could this be?" I asked as I tore off the paper.

I opened the box, and pulled out a large object, unrecognizable at first. Two pieces of three-hole punched cardboard backed several pages of braille, all held together by rings. The top piece of cardboard was covered in bumps and lines, obviously made in puffy paint.

"Read the cover," Jenny urged. "It's in braille.

I began trying to decipher the large dots, which took up the top half of the cover. It read, "Il Ristorante di Laurimo."

"How did you do this?" I exclaimed.

"I looked up the braille alphabet on the Internet."

I gasped in disbelief. Nobody had done that for me before. Sure, I had received Hallmark cards that had raised pictures of balloons with brailled captions that simply read, "Balloon," on them. And Mom always wrote me braille cards because she had taken it upon herself to learn braille when I was little. But nobody else had gone out of their way to learn braille for the purpose of making it possible for me to read something they wrote. It was just like Jenny to understand the subtle importance of that, of me being able to take in her words without someone having to read them to me. It's a privilege most take for granted, and one I normally don't think about myself.

"Open it up," Jenny said.

Each braille page within contained its own surprise.

"Hi Laurie, this is the chicken and tomato egg I always make for you when you come to my house. Mmmm, writing it out is making me hungry!" wrote Ming, and a recipe followed.

"I hope you like your new cookbook," wrote Hannah. "Here's a rough recipe for my deviled eggs. We miss you at Yale this year, and maybe you'll make these for me when I come visit you in New York."

"Dear Laurie, here's a favorite recipe of Amy's and mine for brisket with cranberry sauce. Cook it and eat it in good health. Lots of love, your auntie Suzi."

The book was organized into three sections—appetizers, main courses, and desserts—and each page contained another recipe for one of my favorite dishes. The dishes I adored that nobody in my circle of friends or my family knew how to make, Jenny had found recipes for on the Internet. As I read the notes from my friends and family, my eyes filled with tears. I was speechless.

"Feel the cover again," Jenny said. "Can you guess what that is?"

She pointed out a raised drawing in puffy paint of a person.

"That's you, and that little creature next to you is Mark. See his curly hair? And that boxy thing is an oven."

Jenny had called all of our friends for weeks to retrieve all the recipes for the memory-filled dishes I had so loved. She had asked Mom for the recipes I had enjoyed since childhood and to procure some from my aunts and Grandma. Chocolate truffles, chicken with parmesan and heavy cream, Mom's mouthwatering kugel that I looked forward to on every Jewish holiday, and many more treats were revealed to me as I turned the pages. Mom had brailled them all out on the braille printer she had at home in her office. This was all the result of one of those intimate conversations we had in bed where I had confessed to Jenny that I didn't know how to cook, that I was afraid of fire, and that nobody trusted me around anything hot or sharp.

"But you could totally cook," she said.

"You think so?" I asked, half surprised, half delighted that she seemed so confident in my potential abilities.

"Oh yeah, you would just have to learn to do it by touch, by feeling the consistency change when you're stirring to know when the mixture is smooth, and by noticing the smells of something cooking in a pan to know when it has turned brown."

"I want to cook for you," I told her, putting my arm around her. "When we live together someday, I want to make romantic dinners for you."

"And you will," she said.

She had meant that, and the cookbook proved it. All the belief she had in me was inside of it, in those puffy painted brailled words and drawings she had made in meticulous detail. That book had changed my attitude about cooking from fear to an eagerness to learn how to do it well as soon as I could. It was that book among so many other things about being with Jenny that inspired me to be a better, more well-rounded person, not just a good singer, a good lover and confidant. Though it's not something one usually thinks about, being the kind of person who knows the basics of running a household is just as important to a relationship as the initial reasons that bring two people together. I never wanted the burden of housework or cooking to fall on Jenny, and in fact, loving her made me want to learn all the ways I could think of to take care of her and to be her equal partner.

❀   ❀   ❀

As a child, I had lived in fear of the kitchen. That room meant grave danger in the form of sharp utensils and hot appliances. If I happened to get too near the stove or oven when something was cooking, I would hear a shout of, "No Laurie! Get away from that. It's very dangerous in here right now!"

My picking up a knife would cause gasps, followed by fast footsteps and the ominous object being hastily taken away from me. Because I was too attached to my appendages to risk them being cut or burned off, I learned to give the kitchen a wide berth whenever I heard the sounds and smelled the aromas of cooking.

No meals in our house were devoted to lessons on how to cut meat or how to spread butter. Instead, Mom, Brian, and Dad continued to cut my food and put cream cheese on my bagels until I left for college. It would not have been an impossibility for me to learn by any stretch of the imagination, but Mom, feeling that I already had a lot to contend with in school, decided not to overwhelm me with the little things that she felt I could always learn later. My family adopted the motto, "Laurie, it's just easier," when they would do things for me that I expressed interest in learning how to do myself.

I grew afraid of pouring my own orange juice, water, or milk after a few times of getting more liquid on the floor than I managed to get in my glass. I didn't even know how to clean up the messes I made, and my guilt kept me from attempting to pour ever again.

I refused to make Jenny take care of me the way Mom and other family members had done. It was time for me to take control of my education, to fill in the pretty significant gaps.

❋   ❋   ❋

Brenda Garboos was a counselor at the New York State Commission for the Blind, a government agency that provides rehabilitation and vocational services. I came to her office one Monday in early October to discuss my need for a crash course in cooking with her.

"What can I do for you, Ms. Rubin?" she asked, not unkindly, but in a loud monotone that suggested she had been meeting with blind people with all manner of different needs and desires for years. The resolve in her tone told me that she had government regulations and limitations to work with when dealing with each of our cases, and I was prepared for this.

"Thank you for meeting with me," I said. "I'm here to see about getting some training in basic living skills, mainly cooking."

"Okay," said Brenda, beginning to scribble notes down on a piece of paper. She began asking me questions about how long I had lived in New York, had I been blind since birth, had I received services in the state of New York before. I answered easily and comfortably until she asked, "Ms. Rubin, are you employed?"

"No, not exactly."

"What do you mean, not exactly?"

"I'm an opera singer, so at the moment I'm freelancing and am self employed."

"I see. When was the last time you were paid to sing?" she asked, and I could feel her incredulous gaze upon me.

"Well, I just moved here last month," I explained.

"And have you been hired for any paid performances since that time?"

"No," I admitted sheepishly. "It usually takes a while to break into the scene here."

"As you probably know, music is a very difficult field to succeed in, and we usually tell our clients to consider some vocational counseling to help them find realistic ways of making an income. Have you been looking for work other than in performing?"

"Yes," I said. "I've been sending my teaching résumé to all the schools on the Upper West Side, and have been calling around to as many schools in the city as I can. Unfortunately, it doesn't seem like anybody is hiring, nor is there a great need for private voice instructors."

"When I open your case, I would like to put you in contact with a vocational counselor," Brenda said. "You might have to be open-minded to employment in some other field than music."

"That would be fine with me," I said, feeling my heart drop slowly into my stomach. I could sense that Brenda felt that I had been unreasonable for not seeking work as a switchboard operator or a customer service representative at any number of blindness organizations the way their other clients did.

"I will also connect you with a rehabilitation counselor who will come to your home and teach you the cooking skills you need," Brenda said after a deep sigh. "How are your mobility skills around New York?"

A wave of humiliation swept over me. The truth was that even though I had spent ample time in New York since 1998 when Mom and Dad bought our place, and I had lived here for an entire month, I did not feel the least bit comfortable. Crossing major avenues felt as terrifying as attempting to swim across an ocean, and I felt trapped in the small strip of neighborhood immediately surrounding our building. I still possessed my childhood fear of getting lost.

❋ ❋ ❋

After filling out the requisite government forms, Brenda opened my case. She referred me to the Jewish Guild for the Blind, a not-for-profit organization on the Upper West Side that offers many training programs for the blind. They are a partner of the Commission for the Blind, and Brenda was permitted to send me there for all the training I had asked for. It was there that I met Gertie Reigondeaux, a warm and immediately likable woman in her mid-forties who came to my house every Wednesday afternoon to show me all the ins and outs of the kitchen and all the safe techniques a blind person would need to employ when cooking.

"What do you think about starting with apple crisp?" she asked enthusiastically at our first lesson. "You told me you have a sweet tooth, and I have an easy recipe that is to die for."

Gertie unveiled an assortment of goodies from the Jewish Guild, including a small, manual timer with little raised lines and braille numbers to indicate the 5, 10, 15, and 20 minute markings. She then handed me a small, round aluminum disc.

"What is this for?" I asked.

"You put this in a pot of water, and it'll make a racket when the water starts to boil. Not that you'll need it. Boiling water is pretty loud as it is."

"This device has a cute name," she said, handing me an object that looked like a nine-volt battery with a clip on it. It's called a "Say When." It's a sensor that beeps to let you know when you've reached the brim of a mug when you're filling it with hot water. It'll keep you from having accidents or burning your fingers." She leaned in and whispered, "Most blind people hate this thing. Sometimes it beeps too much and becomes annoying because it's so sensitive."

The last gift from the Jewish Guild was a curious hybrid of a spatula and a pair of tongs. "This will make flipping meat much easier for you," she explained. "The fact that you can grip it will keep meat from taking a dive off your spatula."

And then the cooking commenced.

"Now keep your index finger just inside the rim of the cup," Gertie instructed. "Hold the box of sugar with your right hand, and keep your right thumb on the flap to make sure the box stays open as you pour."

I felt the cool, powdery sensation of the sugar touching my index finger, indicating that I had filled the measuring cup. Gertie showed me how to take a knife and to line up the flat part of it with its edge. As I scraped off the excess, I found that I was putting too much pressure on it and was not getting a nice, even, accurate half a cup. We tried it again, this time keeping my left index finger perfectly aligned with one edge of the cup while I scraped the excess with my right hand.

"It's like magic," I said, surveying my perfectly flat half a cup proudly. "What a neat little trick."

"This is something that many bakers use, not just blind ones," Gertie said.

She had me use a cookie sheet as my workspace, thus minimizing my need to clean up flyaway flower and sugar. She showed me how to pay attention to the consistency of my mixture as I stirred.

"See how it still feels kind of gritty? And you can tell that it's rough and hasn't yet mixed with the water and eggs."

As I continued to stir, Gertie proceeded to put tactile labels on the indistinguishable buttons on my microwave.

"Have you never used a microwave before?" Gertie asked in surprise.

"No," I said, embarrassed. "I'm ridiculously behind."

"You're not half as bad off as many of the people I work with," she assured me. "I just went to this grown woman's house last week. She still lives with her mother, and I had to argue with the mother for about twenty minutes before she let me take her daughter in the kitchen. When we eventually made it to the island to start cutting veggies, she gasped every time I handed her daughter a knife. I had to start from scratch with this girl, even to teach her how to hold a fork properly. I wouldn't be surprised if her mother feeds her."

"That's awful!" I said. "Being blind is nothing compared to the handicapping a parent can do. How is she ever supposed to entertain the prospect of living a normal life on her own?"

"Sadly, I don't think she ever will," Gertie said. "I asked her what she wanted to do for a living, and she said that her mother wouldn't let her even walk to the community college across the street to take classes."

The mixture was feeling nice and liquidy now, and Gertie pointed out the bits of flour that were stuck to the bottom and sides of the mixing bowl. "Just reach underneath it with your spoon and scrape and fold, scrape and fold until it gets mixed in."

Then it was time to melt a half a stick of butter in the microwave. Gertie had put large dots the size of my finger tips on each of the minute buttons so that I could count from left to right from the one to the zero. She had stuck larger dots on the start and popcorn buttons. It was so nice to become acquainted with my own microwave, to place the solid butter in a bowl, and to take it out thirty seconds later, all melted and bubbling from the heat.

The apple crisp required four apples, making this an excellent lesson in cutting and peeling. Gertie taught me to pick a certain point on the apple to start peeling from, and to use the peeler systematically until I had removed the skin in large sections. This was very quick and easy and certainly something I would have never thought to do. She took a corer from my utensils drawer and showed me how to plant it right in the center of the apple by the stem and press down. A perfectly clean core fell neatly out of the apple. Cutting proved a tad more daunting.

"Don't even think of slicing off your fingers while I'm here," Gertie laughed. "Keep your fingers curved, and use them as a way of lining up the knife with the section you want to cut off."

She showed me how to hold the apple together, even once it had been sliced, and then to turn it around so that I could cut several slices at once. "This is a great technique for onions as well," she said. "That way, all the pieces don't get separated and make the cutting process more tedious."

She handed me potholders after we had gotten the batter, apples and all, into the pan. "Don't worry, you won't hurt yourself so long as you've got these babies on. Now, just pull the handle and open the oven."

I hadn't been expecting the immense heat that shot out of the oven when I opened the door. I clumsily gripped the oily pan with my oven-mitt-clad hands, which was as difficult as holding ski poles with gloves for the first time. I gingerly felt for the center of the oven rack and closed the door.

After forty minutes, the bell on my timer made a loud "ding," and it was time to check on it. I donned the large oven mitts again, and Gertie showed me how to take a fork and scrape the surface.

"Wait until it cools a second, and then feel the fork. Does it have any residue on it?" It did. "Then it's not quite done yet. Also, did you notice that it wasn't crispy when you scraped it?"

In five minutes, I checked again. This time, my fork came out clean, and there was an unmistakable and scrumptious scraping sound when my fork made contact.

"You did it!" Gertie said. "You made your very first apple crisp by yourself. How does it feel?"

"Pretty darn awesome," I said, sighing deeply and happily as our nostrils filled with the cinnamony smell of apple crisp.

Jenny and I celebrated my newfound skills that night by eating the delicious dessert.

"Wow, it's really good," Jenny said. "See, I told you you could do it."

❋ ❋ ❋

The following Wednesday, Gertie taught me how to make scrambled eggs. It was fun to feel the eggs solidify under my spatula as I stirred them on the stove. When they were firm and almost bouncy feeling, I could tell they were well done, just how I liked them. The following week, I made pasta, and Gertie advised me to use what she called, "the cold method," which meant that I put the pasta in the water before I set it to boil. This made things much less precarious and eliminated the possibility of me dropping pasta onto a hot burner. It was that week that I learned an interesting trick with oil.

"Oil is hard to feel at room temperature," Gertie said as I spilled a copious amount of olive oil when overflowing my measuring cup. "The best way to handle this is to put the bottle of oil in the freezer for about ten minutes before you use it. That way you'll feel it when it reaches your finger and the top of the measuring cup."

My recent cooking experiences had taught me that the best and most precise techniques are not executed with the use of sight and that cooking is actually an olfactory and tactile art. Everything from proper cutting to safety around the stove and the oven could easily be managed without being able to see, but I knew that my parents and everybody else was so used to attributing all their functionality to their dependence on their sight. If only I had known in childhood what I know now, all the fine motor skills used for things like pouring, cutting, and stirring would be so much easier for me, and I wouldn't have to give them a second thought. To this day, those things that come naturally to most take extra effort on my part because of my inexperience, not my lack of sight.

❂ ❂ ❂

Shortly after I began working with Gertie, my orientation and mobility training began. Carol Mogue, also an instructor from the Jewish Guild, met me downstairs of my building at 9:30 on Tuesday mornings. She too had interesting tips that made getting around New York seem much easier. Many people tell me how they could never imagine getting around New York without sight, but to tell you the truth, New York is one of the most blind-friendly cities in existence. Most of Manhattan is a grid system with numbered avenues and streets, so if you lose count and forget where you are, you can just ask, and someone will say, "You're at the corner of 10th Avenue and 45th Street." Even if you've never been on that block in your life, you will know where you are in the grand scheme of things, and it'll be easy to get back on track.

Carol also made the subways seem easier. It was she who taught me that the train doors will open on the right side at express stops, and on the left side at local stops. That way, I would always know which door to head towards before the train had reached my stop. She also taught me how to find bus stops, which were mostly off-set from the corners. Mark began to recognize them very quickly and would take me to them when I told him, "Find the bus stop." I realized that I had soon learned more about traveling around New York than the average sighted person. I was amused to find that most people didn't know their cardinal directions, and that when in a rush, they had to look around frantically for building numbers while Carol had taught me that the odd numbered addresses were on the north and west sides of streets, whereas the even numbered addresses were on the south and east sides of streets. It was the little rhyme and reason to the way New York City was laid out that made me feel at home there at last, and after several weeks of learning from Carol, I knew it was time for me to go it alone and continue to discover New York without help.

The LR Look

I had resisted Mom's attempts to get me to watch *Sex and the City*. It sounded like everything that went against my Oberlin hippie principles. My college friends and I were all about loving ourselves with our unshaven legs, our hair that we let grow wild, our loose-fitting broom skirts, and our convictions about freeing our breasts from the constraints of the bras forced upon us by society. We viewed makeup as a mask that women were brainwashed into wearing to make them feel beautiful, and designer clothes were an ostentatious display of status and money. But when Mom and I found ourselves in a hotel room in Erie, Pennsylvania, on the way to my Chautauqua summer program, close to nothing except for a Wal-Mart that closed at 6:00PM, Mom could only think of one way to spend our evening.

"I have the first two seasons of *Sex and the City* with me," Mom said. "We can watch the DVDs on my computer."

I groaned.

"Come on, Laurie. Just give it a chance. It's really a good show."

Within minutes, I found myself addicted, and it was I who ended up begging for more.

As I lay in bed that night, I found my mind's eye staring at the images Mom had described to me, Carrie in the multicolored dress with the baby blue boa and red coat when on her date with the French architect, or in the red top, plaid scarf, and brown blazer on a day of shopping for Manolos and lunch with the girls, or in her turquoise top with the red apple necklace when at her desk, earnestly typing her day's worth of revelations and research about sex, men, and being single in New York. They made a permanent imprint on my brain even though I had always thought of fashion as something that the popular girls in high school dabbled in, something I never wanted to touch with a ten-foot pole. Nothing put me in a more foul mood than days of shopping in which I inevitably played the role of Barbie doll as my mom and enthusiastic salesgirls dressed me up.

So what was it about those four New York City women who went to glamorous parties dressed to the nines that had such a profound effect on me? Against my will, I found myself wanting to experience beauty just like them. I wanted to know how to make visual statements about myself, giving off in an instant the same impression as a firm handshake, a flirtatious smile, or that perfect one-liner that makes everyone laugh and think you're cool.

❈ ❈ ❈

I've heard that when a baby starts talking, when she discovers to her delight that words will get her what she wants a lot quicker than baby babble and grunts, there's no turning back, and she will never stop. This is how I was when I started to use clothes to communicate who I am. I also started knowing my specific tastes very quickly. This baffled the salesgirls who were used to me being a passive and grumpy shopper.

"What do you mean it's not quite your style?" they'd ask, bewildered.

"I don't know, I think this sweater is a little too Park Avenue for me," I'd reply, trying not to be insulting while attempting to get my style across to them. "I'm thinking a little more bold, a little more textured, like something someone might stitch together in their loft in Soho with random recycled materials lying around, which then becomes the next hip thing."

Sometimes this would work. Other times, I'd get a noise, which I imagined would be accompanied by blank looks. I took an evil pleasure in observing people process the idea that a blind person could have an opinion about something visual.

And how exactly does a blind person know what's in? Fashion is not always about looking. It's about listening and feeling. When you watch *The Today Show* or *Oprah* and they have stylists on the shows preaching about the latest trends, they describe in great detail what the average Joe and Jane should be keeping in mind when putting together an outfit. You might tie a scarf as a belt over a sweater to dress it up, wear a rich brown top and accent it with a long turquoise necklace, or wear leggings with knee-high boots with a long tank top and a thick belt. You can feel how a skirt billows and flows as it makes that gentle feminine swishing sound, how a tight, low-cut top hugs your waist sensuously and reveals that perfect amount of smooth bare skin, or how the wide flares at the bottom of a pair of jeans flatter you more than the others. None of this requires a mirror if you've had a pair of eyes or two helping you out before making a purchase, and who doesn't defer to pair of objective eyes?

Color is another kettle of fish, and a tricky one at that. How do you confuse a blind person? Give her an object that one person calls dark blue and another person calls plum. I've had many of those "huh?" moments. I'm told blue and brown go nicely together, so I'll put on what I understand is a blue dress with a pair of brown shoes. But Jenny will sometimes look me up and down, and I can just feel the "hmm" in her demeanor. Something isn't right.

"What's wrong with what I'm wearing?" I'll sigh, heart sinking.

"You're wearing brown shoes with a purple dress."

"The salesgirl swore up and down the dress was blue."

"I don't know what sane person could call that blue. Maybe she was smoking something."

"Frankly, I'm a little disappointed. I had everything banking on this being a midnight blue. It made the dress sound ethereal to me."

"It's still ethereal," Jenny assures me. "Why can't purple be ethereal?"

We have those conversations a lot. So I've learned that even with perfect sight, one person's midnight blue is another's plum. Anyway, I decided to go with the black shoes that particular day. I always defer to the nearest sighted person before I leave the house.

After I've verified that I've done a good job making the perfect match, I know from then on I can wear those same pieces together again. When someone sighted isn't around, I go with those safe options. If I'm up for something revolutionary and new, I try a different combination and get it approved before going on my merry way. I do know that red absolutely cannot go with purple, that it's probably not a great idea to wear red and green, unless you want to look like a Christmas tree, and that you probably wouldn't want to be caught dead in orange and purple. I also know that people enjoy a nice combo of pink and green, sometimes even purple and green, camel and turquoise, and silver with black. I've made it my business to pick up on those otherwise forgettable tidbits of conversation. It's all material for my self-taught color theory course.

❋ ❋ ❋

Before I fell in love with fashion, jewelry and chocolate had always been my two vices. I have never been able to resist going into a chocolate store or a jewelry shop. So when a good friend of my mom showed me some gorgeous bracelets she was wearing and informed me she had made them herself, I was intrigued.

"You know, Laurie," she had said. "Jewelry is something you could make."

"You think so?" I asked enthusiastically.

"Oh, absolutely. I do it by touch most of the time anyway."

The next day, I made a beeline for the Jewish Community Center just a few blocks from where I lived, as they had an entire floor dedicated to a variety of different craft-making studios. Melissa, one of the jewelry-making instructors, agreed to take me on as a private student, showing me many of the beading and wire wrapping techniques hands-on. This new skill turned my vice into the very adventure I needed while still feeling lost in New York City in my second year living there, wondering just exactly what my purpose in life was supposed to be.

Stone USA was a bead shop in Midtown on the tenth floor of a dingy office building. Suite 1011 was at the end of the hall, and when I knocked on the locked door, I was greeted by a very friendly Indian man.

"Oh, so you're Laurie, Melissa's latest student!" he said warmly. "Come on in, come on in! Melissa always sends her students to us."

The room was stuffed to the gills with beads, and both sides of my body brushed against walls covered with stones of all shapes and sizes. My heart began to beat fast with wonder and excitement.

"You just start touching what's around you, and tell me if you have any questions. My name is Sam."

As my fingers trailed the bead-clad walls, I heard the music of the many strands hitting each other. The stick pearls had an almost metallic, very present sound, like the gentle clinking of tiny wind chimes. The large stones made the sound of building blocks when they collapse into a giant heap. The small beads sounded like jellybeans being poured out of a bag, and the tiniest beads sounded like large grains of sand when you walk on a beach. There were nuggets of turquoise in every shade of blue and green with varying amounts of brown veins in them. There was faceted quartz in every color, shape, and size. Sam showed me creamy smooth amber, garnets that felt like grape clusters, and a particularly large and irregularly shaped lemon topaz in a translucent yellow that could be used for a very bold necklace centerpiece. If Melissa's bead drawers made me feel like a kid in a candy store, Sam's endless walls of beads put me in the center of a massive candy factory.

After purchasing what felt like twenty pounds of beads in every shape and texture imaginable, Sam asked, "How do you do it?"

"You mean, how do I design jewelry?"

"Yeah," Sam said.

"I don't know. I mean, I can almost imagine what the colors look like, but I don't know how to explain it. Sometimes I feel as if I must be remembering them from a past life. I can tell you that colors do resonate for me in certain ways because of how my other senses have associated with them. Cinnamon just smells brownish red to me, and crystals feel translucent and sparkly with their smooth surfaces and very precise edges."

"Apples are red, but they look very different from cinnamon," he pointed out.

"Yes!" I said enthusiastically. "I usually know the category of stone if it's more like an apple or cinnamon."

"When I describe stones to you, should I help make those distinctions?"

"Sure," I said, delighted.

"And how do you know what styles people like when you're making jewelry for them?"

"I can usually tell by the kinds of things they say, the way they mention things they like in passing, the sound of their voices, how large or small they are when I hug them. Colors and styles are like perfume. When someone walks by, the perfume they wear or the shampoo they use becomes a part of their aura in a subtle but striking way."

"That's true. Those are things you don't realize you notice."

"And the sound of the jewelry clinking gently as a lady moves her head is very becoming too, kind of like music in harmony with her voice," I added.

"Do you ever get it wrong when you predict people's styles?"

"Not really," I said. "Their voices, their stature, and their personalities tell me a lot, and when I'm unsure about something, I ask. Everyone has such unique qualities that I can go to town with my inspiration, and they seem to appreciate what I make for them. Either that, or they're just being nice," I smiled.

❁ ❁ ❁

When making jewelry, I found myself creating unusual color combinations just the way I had done with clothes. My signature look started to voice itself in my chunky double-stranded necklaces with mixtures of pearls, turquoise, and vintage glass beads, or long dangly earrings in differently shaped Swarovski crystals.

I began experimenting with the juxtaposition of modern chains with earthy gemstones or sparkly, diamond-cut crystals with stones in their natural shapes. Even though my descriptions of what I was about to make got a few shrugs from friends who had the patience to hear my enthusiastic jewelry brainstorms, the pieces in their finished state seemed to work as I had imagined they would. I realized as I sat there stringing beads that our own individual styles don't necessarily come from one's visual experience. We are born with certain likes and dislikes of color combinations and styles, just the way we are born with a liking of various foods. Though I had never used my eyes to see, a visual part of me that I had found in my New York soul-searching time had finally made an appearance. I decided to not only make jewelry for friends and family but to sell it in local boutiques. I called my jewelry line The LR Look, as I know the eccentricity, the boldness, and the unlikely pairing of stones and metals in different shapes and textures represented all the unique parts of myself that had accumulated into the woman that I am.

Colors of Sound

When starting a music career, being lucky enough to meet the right people who believe in you can make all the difference. It is those people who can turn a distressing musical famine into an exciting feast. The summer before I moved to New York, I met two such people at a summer music program of master classes in Los Angeles called Songfest.

Songfest was new to the summer music program scene. Though it hadn't developed a name for itself like Tanglewood or the Aspen Music Festival, it attracted teachers just as renowned in the field. Graham Johnson, who was known for his collaboration with famous singers all over the world and for his encyclopedic knowledge about German and French art song, has been giving master classes there since the summer I went to study with him. The composer John Harbison, whose music I had heard at Oberlin and on classical radio stations, was another teacher at Songfest that summer. Both had a true gift for teaching, Graham giving lessons in music history as a context for our musical interpretations and John being very specific about the color and sound of each note creating the right musical effect. I had no idea that just as I was about to give up in New York, both of them would come back into my life and change its course dramatically.

❋ ❋ ❋

I returned home one afternoon after a particularly uninspiring class on resume writing and interview skills to find that Scooby, our chocolate Toy Poodle puppy I had gotten Jenny for Valentine's Day, had peed all over his crate, soiling himself completely. The last thing I wanted to do after my tiring day was to bleach the crate clean and to give a Toy Poodle yet another bath, which would require an extra hour of brushing and drying his hair in order to avoid it getting matted. Just as I put him into our bathtub, the phone rang.

"Aaaaaaarrrrrrgh," I shouted. It was my pianist from LA, David. As Scooby squirmed and whined in the tub, David told me that Graham Johnson had invited both him and me to London to come study with him at his home. He had taken a liking to David and his playing and had enjoyed my singing the previous summer, and he wanted to work with us for an extended period of time. So maybe I wouldn't be spending the rest of my life going back and forth from the Jewish Guild for the Blind and cleaning up after a puppy. Graham's invitation helped remind me of my value in the world and came at just the right time for my wavering self-esteem.

❀ ❀ ❀

Working with Graham the following summer was like going back a century to the living rooms of Schubert, Schumann, and Brahms. It was as though Graham himself had been a close friend of theirs, knowing the ins and outs of their relationships.

"Robert Schumann was a very sick man, you see," Graham would say in an earnest voice and refined British accent. "Clara really had to remain the strong one, to wear the pants as it were. You can really hear that quality in her music, even when she sets a very tender poem."

He mentioned events that took place in their living rooms, specific things somebody in attendance would say about Schumann's music, or he would recount certain arguments or revelations that led to the conception of one piece or another. And in the middle of a phrase of music David and I were playing, Graham would stop us and say, "I think that color is just a bit too wooden. Let me show you, David, what I think might work better here."

He proceeded to play the same notes, but with a lighter, smoother quality, as though the piano keys were playing the notes of a magical music box.

"And let's see if that changes the way you sing it," he would say. "Oh yes, that's better. You see he's creating the picture of a fantastical place, one that does not exist in reality, so you really have to get that across in your voice."

At the end of our third session, Graham asked, "Would you like to stay for a glass of wine?"

It was easy to see why Graham had the extensive knowledge that permeated his teaching and his playing. His walls were covered in bookshelves, displaying original manuscripts with scribbled notes the composers had made. As we sipped our wine, he played recordings of songs he felt David and I should perform.

As David and I walked back to the Tube, London's subway, we would recount the events of the day. It was hard to believe that the man who had made the famous recordings of German Lieder and French chansons that I had heard years ago in my repertoire class at Oberlin was asking us to stay for wine and peruse his collection of books.

❋ ❋ ❋

"Laurie," Graham said thoughtfully just after we had finished some intense work on the song Robert Schumann had written as a wedding present for his wife, Clara, "I have taken the liberty of speaking to a friend of mine about you. This man has a large foundation that supports young singers. I asked him if he would be interested in supporting a project I think would be very beneficial for you."

"A project?" I asked.

"How would you like to make a recording?"

"With you?" I stammered.

"With me and David," Graham said, his voice growing brighter with a smile. "I think it would be good to have a recording that represents you as a well-rounded artist. I would love to play some German and French repertoire with you, and David, would you be willing to play some American songs with her, some Copland and Rorem, perhaps?"

"Are you kidding? I'd love to," said David, expressing more candid enthusiasm than was characteristic of him.

❊ ❊ ❊

London was beginning to feel like a regular stomping ground for us now. We returned there the following December to record and the Christmas season was in full swing. The windows of Harrod's were filled with holiday decorations, and I could see bright, festive lights in all the windows. The perfume of a Christmas tree filled Graham's house during our rehearsals before the recording.

We had decided on over seventy minutes of music for the recording, everything from Mozart to Brahms, Bizet to Hahn, and Copland to Harbison. If there's any harrowing musical experience, it's having to get several takes of thirty songs in the space of three days. Graham had hired French and German diction coaches to hang out in the studio for the duration of the recording and to listen for any imperfection in my pronunciation.

"I always have them come to recording sessions with every singer I work with," Graham said.

Between having my pronunciation of the French and German languages polished and Graham's musical coaching, my recording session doubled as a three-day-long immersion course in art song.

Adrenaline can make you accomplish some pretty challenging feats. Though we had the great fortune of recording in a church with perfect acoustics and a wonderful piano, we had to capture all the feeling, electricity, and beautiful moments that come more naturally in a live performance. The perfect climax that sends shivers down the listener's spine is a challenge to recreate in the recording studio. One is also concerned with every note being perfectly placed. Thinking about all of this could give someone an ulcer, but in the end I obtained a recording I was happy with, and a better understanding of how my best singing could be accomplished.

❋ ❋ ❋

Just a month after I returned from London, I received a message from my other Songfest teacher. This time, it came via a call from Carnegie Hall. John Harbison would be leading a workshop with his colleague, soprano Dawn Upshaw, in which four singers and four composers could participate. Each composer would have to write a piece, showcasing the vocal range and abilities of the singer she or he was matched with.

"Oh my gosh, Mo, how are you going to sing this?" Jenny asked in bewilderment, looking at the score my composer, Keeril Makan, had written for me. Our contact information had been passed to each other by Carnegie Hall, and we had four months to talk amongst ourselves, to share recordings of each other's previous work, and for the composers to write their pieces.

"Scream on a high G?" I exclaimed. "Are you serious? It actually says that? No wonder singers and voice teachers don't like touching new music with a ten-foot pole. It ruins your instrument."

When I flew to LA for Passover, just a month before the workshop, I asked David to help me learn the piece. Since I would be the first one singing it, there were no recordings of it I could use for reference.

"Okay, this is really complicated. There's one measure of 3/4 followed by several measures of 9/8," David said. "Let me try to sing it for you and count." He began singing the words, counting the beats on each one. "Damn it, sorry, let me do that again."

All kinds of instructions were written in. I had to inhale while singing at several intervals through the third movement. Then I had to sing an entire movement of fast minimalism with absolutely no time to breathe for several measures. The cellist was instructed to play one movement with chopsticks, but not just any chopsticks; they had to be plastic to produce the perfect color.

I had no idea what possible interpretation I could come up with to make sense of the score. There were random fragments of words like, "add bananas to a bowl of fruit" interspersed with military language and war propaganda. Now, I would be faced with the task of singing it in front of Dawn Upshaw and John Harbison, who were well versed in new music performance.

My fears turned into excitement the day before the workshop began. Rehearsals were scheduled for us to read through each of our pieces with the instrumentalists that had been hired by Carnegie Hall for the occasion. Keeril, a man in his early thirties, shook my hand and introduced himself. We stood in the large rehearsal room, chatting over the din of strings and winds warming up.

It turned out that the piece was a convoluted set of texts related to the war on Afghanistan following 9-11. When the instrumentalists began to play, the piece suddenly made sense and came to life. The clarinet, cello, violin, percussion, and my voice were to create the chaotic world a place becomes during war, emulating air raid siren-like sounds, bombs, and the emotionless recitation of propaganda. This was my first time singing a score in which the music was more of a painting of sounds to powerfully illustrate a current political situation.

Our next rehearsal was in front of the other three composers and singers. Though I was singing texts, I began to think of my voice as another instrument, creating the effects through slurred and bent pitches, some devoid of vibrato in order to create an otherworldly effect, some more full and radiant to bring back the poignant, human-like quality.

"But how do I scream on a high G?" I asked Dawn Upshaw, who seemed down-to-earth and savvy about vocal techniques for new music.

"You have to think of a scream as more of a sung sound, not so much of a shout. The scream is more in the emotion and volume of the pitch. Don't ever make it sound like a shout. You'll kill your voice."

"Like this?" I asked, attempting the note.

"Support it more. Use your air. Yes, like that."

"Just so you know, Keeril, this is not a piece for the mezzo range," John Harbison said. "You have her sitting around high C for a good part of the first movement, and there are several B-flats and As throughout."

"I know," Keeril said. "But I had the feeling she could handle it from all the recordings I heard and from her description of her range."

"Laurie's range is highly unusual," John said.

"Yeah, they sound like effortless, soprano notes for you, Laurie," Dawn said. "And yet you have the wonderful richness of a mezzo."

Hearing these candid compliments from John and Dawn and then hearing the enthusiastic sounds of agreement from the others in the room replenished my belief in my singing abilities, and the workshop was making me discover an intuition for a kind of music I would have never thought to sing. There was something powerful and freeing about singing music that demands a different level of risk-taking than everything I had been used to. It was as though a caged bird inside of me had been released, and something eccentric, some pent-up emotion was given permission to express itself as I let out angst-filled utterances and forced the audience into the disturbing discomfort of war propaganda. Keeril's music was enabling me to make the kind of statement I realized I had always wanted to make as an artist, and somehow, my whole personality seemed to gel with it. I was beginning to know the thrill of brainstorming and creating the first interpretation of a piece with its living composer present.

"What kind of voice did you have in mind for this spoken part?" I asked.

"Not quite sure," Keeril said. "What are you thinking?"

"Something like this," I said, speaking the line of propaganda in an eerie, cartoon-like voice.

"Ooooh, yeah, that's really effective," Keeril said, sounding satisfied and impressed.

Another advantage of singing a piece for the composer is that you hear, directly from the horse's mouth, what kind of interpretation s/he had in mind when writing the piece. This is something I will never have the benefit of when singing Mozart, Rossini, or most of the composers in my repertoire. The whole collaboration left me wanting more, and that is exactly what I got once the workshop had ended.

Keeril and I got a lot of mileage out of "Target." Singing it in the workshop got me my first review in the *New York Times* in which Anthony Tomassini, chief classical music critic, wrote that I possess "compelling artistry," "communicative power," and that my voice displays "earthy, rich, and poignant qualities." In 2006, two years after the workshop had passed, we performed "Target" in an Election Day concert with a new music ensemble in LA, landing me my first review in the *LA Times,* where critic Joseph Woodard wrote, "Rubin's voice is a compelling force at the center of the music, and she gives a charismatic performance." Two months later, I received a phone call from the Chamber Music Society of Lincoln Center, asking me to perform the work in their series, one of the most high profile gigs in town.

The workshop had caused me to stumble upon a career path that began to guide me forward. I started receiving calls from many other composers who attended the workshop's culminating concert where I premiered "Target," asking me to perform their work. It was one of those phone calls that led to a milestone I had been trying to reach since my school days had ended: my first opera gig in New York City.

❈ ❈ ❈

The Rat Land is an opera that depicts a dysfunctional family in the Midwest. The protagonist is Karen, a fourteen-year-old girl who is molested, abused, and terrorized by her father, neglected by her mother, and is the middle child with a gay older brother and an autistic younger brother. Gordon Beeferman, the composer, asked me to play the role of Karen in a fully staged performance of the prologue and first scene of the opera at the Improvised and Otherwise Festival in Brooklyn. The prologue begins with a dream-like suggestion of Karen being molested by her father, followed by an ominous fade to black. We then move into the first scene where you see the chaos and discord of her family. There is a dinner scene in which her father, Theodore, gets more and more agitated until he accuses his wife of being a terrible cook, a bitch, and a sow, throwing the dinner steak at her. Karen retreats to her room where she takes out her pet rats, creating a fantasy world in which they are her protectors, sent by her true mother and father, who are King and Queen of another planet she hopes to return to. Throughout the opera, family life becomes more disturbed, forcing Karen into a psychotic break, after which she has trouble distinguishing between reality and her fantasy world.

"Laurie, hold out the rats so we can see them," said Beth Greenberg, an opera director from New York City Opera who Gordon had hired. Beth was nervous about my abilities on stage.

"You need to walk a straight line to that table to put the rats down," Beth sighed, after my fourth time veering just slightly to the right, thus missing my target.

"Beth, it's really hard for me to know where straight is," I explained. "People usually find straight by using a visual reference point."

"Well, how are we going to get you there?" she asked, sounding worried and stressed.

I was beginning to feel discouraged. Perhaps I was learning the hard way why opera wasn't for me, and that all the teachers who had warned me about this were right.

"Would it be possible for my room on the set to have a rug?" I asked. "That way, I could follow the line of the rug with my foot, and it will lead me straight to the table with the rats' cage."

"Brilliant!" Beth said, giving me a hug of relief. "Thank you for helping me help you, Laurie."

I realized that is what it's all about. Opera has to be a collaborative effort. There are work-arounds, just as there are for other things for me in life, like using landmarks to help me get from point a to point b and adaptive technology so that I can read email.

Beth also showed frustration in my lack of facial expressions to show enthusiasm, fear, longing, or sadness.

"Laurie, you're not giving us enough. We have no idea how you're feeling here. It can't just all be in your voice."

I tried and tried again, but my face could not replicate the kinds of expressions she was used to seeing.

The Improvised and Otherwise Festival took place at a black box theater in Brooklyn. The librettist for *The Rat Land* had put together some simple costumes, and we assembled a makeshift set and procured some basic props. Nervous doesn't even begin to describe my state of mind backstage. I had only rehearsed on the Brick Theater stage twice, one time being a quick run-through the day of the performance. From Beth's reaction, my acting still wasn't up to par in our final dress. The only thing to do in a situation like this is to go into survival mode, to wing it, and to improvise.

There were no scary moments during the performance in which I found myself disoriented. The rug worked like a charm, and I found my way around the small stage, from the dinner table to my room and then to the area where the Rat Gods' cage was placed. One thing a blind opera singer has to remember is to place his or her props in exactly the same place all the time, so that they will be there consistently when one reaches for them. Being the disorganized person that I am in real life, misplacing my phone, my purse, and my dog's leash all the time, this skill was hard for me to remember. Failing to consistently place my props would lead me to feeling around, moving to my next destination too late for the music and throwing the whole scene off course. Thankfully, during the performance I always remembered where I placed the plastic toy rats, which I had to use several times in the scene. The most pleasant surprise of the evening was the audience's response to my lines. They laughed heartily at the humorous passages Beth had been trying so hard to get me to convey and they gasped in more frightening moments.

"Laurie, you stage animal!" Beth said, hugging me tightly as the audience still applauded. "Why didn't you tell me that you suddenly come to life onstage? Would have saved me a few grey hairs if I had known that in rehearsal."

The performance transformed Beth from the concerned stage director to my most loyal advocate. She also became a champion of Gordon's opera, introducing him to the director of a new music festival at New York City Opera, in which excerpts from new operas are showcased.

In 2007, *The Rat Land* was accepted, and just two months before the festival, I received an email from the dramaturg at New York City Opera, asking me to sing the role of Karen in the festival.

❋ ❋ ❋

Shortly after that performance, I received my second opportunity to perform a lead in an opera. Ted Huffman, a guy who had gone to Chautauqua the same summer I was there, had started a music festival in Greenwich, Connecticut, that was growing successful and well known. Now in its fourth year, the Greenwich Music Festival was about to put on its first, fully staged opera. Ted had sent an email to my website, asking me to contact him.

"I have a role in mind for you," the email read.

It was hard to believe that Ted had thought of me, of all people, for a specific role. I knew he was close friends with many successful mezzos. During our summer in Chautauqua, we hadn't spoken much, but Ted had always struck me as one of those quiet, soft-spoken people who took to spending his time thoughtfully observing those around him. When I called him, I found out that the role he had in mind for me was that of Penelope in *The Return of Ulysses*, the suffering wife who remains faithful to Ulysses even after everyone around her is certain he would never return. At the end of the opera, she is rewarded by a tender reunion.

Ted seemed to have an intuition for directing me successfully on stage. He had me line up with the back wall of the stage, which I trailed, turning left with it, until I reached the place downstage where I began my aria. He kept me active as I sang, always showing me furniture to line up with in order for me to square off and find my next destination.

Ted always seemed to know how to get the best acting out of me, finding poses to portray Penelope's vulnerability and sadness that I could relate to and letting me express myself from an organic standpoint, rather than having me try to emulate things sighted people do.

Performances took place in the basement of a church, a black box space. The minimalist set came alive with dramatic lighting and a small chamber orchestra with authentic early instruments. It was a real, professional opera with singers who performed in companies all over the country, and Ted had been that someone who gave me the chance to do the one thing so many directors and competition judges felt I could not realistically expect to do in my career. So, after a long, painful waiting period in New York, I was beginning to find my people, the ones who were showing me my value in this crazy career. These were the people who felt that it was not the ability to see that made me worthy of getting hired, it was my ability to sing, and I would never let anyone reduce me to some charity case, some girl with a pretty voice looking for ways to fill her time. Everyone in the world wants to feel needed and to understand her purpose. Mine is to be an artist, an educator, a responsible tax-paying citizen who is paid her worth, and to be a contributing member to society who just so happens to be blind.

What Do You See?

When I walk the streets of New York in my sweats on the way to the gym, or in funky jeans with my face all made-up on the way to dinner with friends, or in concert black on the way to a performance, I often amuse myself with thoughts about what people around me see as I pass.

Do they see me as another confident New Yorker who happens to be blind? Do they pity me? Do they think I'm in need of help? Or do they not even know I'm blind at all and see only a woman walking a black shaggy dog? Three decades of experience tell me that the vast array of first impressions and thoughts that are going through each individual's mind are as diverse as the people themselves.

As my guide dog Mark and I wend our way through the crowds, I take in my surroundings, just as my sighted counterparts do. I smell the chestnuts as they sizzle at vendors' booths on almost every block of Manhattan. I hear bits of phone conversations and people laughing with their friends. I feel the vibration of the subway trains as they pass underneath my feet. I am deeply affected by the sun happy when it's out, depressed a bit when the clouds have covered it.

Do you dream in color?

No, not exactly, because I've never seen colors.

Do you dream?

Yes. I do.

I dream I've won the lottery, or that it's finals week and I realize with horror that I forgot to attend all the classes. I dream loud, scary noises; I dream my worst fears of drowning, of being alone, of dying. I dream the smell of spring, the taste of chocolate cake, the feel of velvet. My dreams are like those of anybody else, as vivid or as vague, as realistic or as random as the range of dreams can be.

❋ ❋ ❋

I will always remember that day I lost my glass slipper in the elevator at Merkin Hall just before singing in a concert. Afterwards, Katja, the director's ten-year-old daughter, came up to me and wanted to ask me a question. I could feel that she saw something in me that just made her think a little bit deeper. Maybe she didn't see my blindness as a flaw. My flaw that day was my missing shoe.

She asked me just one simple thing: "Do you dream in color?"

Now I have the answer to the question that Katja and so many others have asked. It is not the dreams at night that are important. It's the daydreams I have that guide me towards my desires and my purpose in life. Sure, I dream in color all the time.

386

Do You Dream in Color?

"Do you dream in color?" she asks.
watching me apply my makeup.
Her question gives me pause
as I fumble in my bag
for that perfect shade of silvery purple
that matches the dress I'm about to wear,
the one that fades from a dark plumb to white.
"I dream
what I experience," I say simply.
"I dream
the smell of flowers,
or the taste of chocolate,
or about an argument my subconscious devised between my mom
and me,
the kind where you wake up just before you say the perfect thing.
Do I dream in color
or black and white?
I'm not sure
as my eyes have only seen dark and light."
"Do you dream in color?" he asks,
watching me choose from his wall covered with strands of beads.
There are perfectly smooth round pearls in a midnight blue.
There are raw nuggets of turquoise
whose veins of brown running through each stone
can be detected by my fingers as I feel the beautiful imperfections.
Then my fingers find the stick pearls in an iridescent bronze and
green.

"That's it!" I cry.
"That's the necklace!"
I seize the beads, and envision how they will fit a woman's neck.
"How do you know?" he asks.
He really desires to know.
"Because I just dreamed it!" I say,
not knowing how my world of color differs from his.

"Do you dream in color?" asks the little girl,
holding the program she wants me to sign.
I sense her hands in front of my face
and take the glossy book from her.
"I don't know," I tell her.
"Why don't you explain colors to me,
and I'll tell you if I dream them."
"Well," she begins.
"Blue
is like the ocean in the morning when the sun is out.
Green
is like the trees when it's spring.
Yellow,
yellow,
yellow
is the color of my hair.
Pink
is the color of cotton candy.
White
is the color of marshmallows.
Red
is the color of fire engines,

and rubies,
and blood."
"Well then,
I guess I do dream in color
because I dream of all those things.
Just last night, I dreamed I was in a swimming pool
full of pillows the texture of marshmallows,
and once I had a dream
that I was sitting by the ocean,
and the sun was out,
and the waves were making a rhythmic music."
She seemed satisfied as she watched me print my initials.
I wish that I could have written,
"To the girl who gave the colors of my dreams
their proper names."

"The question is,
'Do you have realistic dreams?'"
he asks me.
I answer,
"I hate to answer your question with another question.
Shouldn't you be asking me
if I dream in color?"
I sense his unease.
It was hard for him
to do what he felt he must do,
to tell the girl who is more than admirable for getting out of bed in
the morning,
endearing to have dreams of singing on stage,
to tell this girl

that she must be
"REALISTIC."
"Dream in color?"
He is confused.
"Yes!" I say.
"I dream
of the red gown that I'll wear on stage,
that is striking against my fair skin and dark brown hair.
I dream
of my lover's black hair.
I dream
in all the colors of the rainbow.
You didn't ask me if I dream in color
because you don't believe I can.
You imagine my world
a dark place.
You are afraid to know
that I walk the streets of New York with purpose.
That I come home to a family I have cultivated,
that my life is full of dreams,
and my dreams are full of colors,
and my dreams are real,
because they come true every day."
He says,
"I see."
I ask,
"May I ask you a question?
'Do you dream in color?'"

About the Author

Blind since birth, mezzo-soprano Laurie Rubin received high praise from *New York Times* chief classical music critic Anthony Tommasini, who wrote that she possesses "compelling artistry," "communicative power," and that her voice displays "earthy, rich and poignant qualities." Career highlights include her United Kingdom solo recital debut performance at Wigmore Hall in London, as well as her solo recital debut at Weill Recital Hall at Carnegie Hall. Ms. Rubin has performed concerts of new music with the Chamber Music Society of Lincoln Center and has performed numerous roles, including the lead role of Karen in *The Rat Land* by Gordon Beeferman with New York City Opera, Penelope in Monteverdi's *The Return of Ulysses*, and the title role in Rossini's *La Cenerentola*. She has recorded a CD of art songs with renowned collaborative pianists Graham Johnson and David Wilkinson on the Opera Omnia label. In 2012, Bridge Records released her CD, also titled *Do You Dream in Color?*, which sets her moving poem to music by Bruce Adolphe. She is cofounder and associate artistic director of Ohana Arts, a performing arts school and festival in Hawaii. She also designs her own line of handmade jewelry, The LR Look.

About Seven Stories Press

Seven Stories Press is an independent book publisher based in New York City. We publish works of the imagination by such writers as Nelson Algren, Russell Banks, Octavia E. Butler, Ani DiFranco, Assia Djebar, Ariel Dorfman, Coco Fusco, Barry Gifford, Hwang Sok-yong, Lee Stringer, and Kurt Vonnegut, to name a few, together with political titles by voices of conscience, including the Boston Women's Health Collective, Noam Chomsky, Angela Y. Davis, Human Rights Watch, Derrick Jensen, Ralph Nader, Loretta Napoleoni, Gary Null, Project Censored, Barbara Seaman, Alice Walker, Gary Webb, and Howard Zinn, among many others. Seven Stories Press believes publishers have a special responsibility to defend free speech and human rights, and to celebrate the gifts of the human imagination, wherever we can. For additional information, visit www.sevenstories.com.